In *Undivided Love*, Janet Gear has m̶ in which we honour and value our collective beliefs and traditions as an asset and a credit to our communities of faith. Confronting the idea that our tradition is bereft of a "theology," she presents to us a stunning rubric that creatively captures the varied ways in which we know, believe, and speak about the divine.

Rev. Dr. Carmen Lansdowne
Kwisa'lakw, member of the Haíɫzaqv (Heiltsuk) First Nation,
Executive Director of First United Church Community Ministry Society and
First United Church Social Housing Society

Finally, a book that truly recognizes how my faith is expressed. As a racialized immigrant who still endeavours to claim the United Church of Canada as his spiritual home, I can now confidently say that I belong. Throughout *Undivided Love*, I felt seen, heard, and respected. Gear's wonderful hospitality permeates her book.

Rev. Min-Goo Kang
Congregational Minister at Fort Garry United Church, Winnipeg

Janet Gear has listened with respectful attention and an open heart. She has created a new, vivid, and appreciative way of understanding how different individuals and congregations inhabit their Christian identity. This accessible book is a great resource for helping church leaders and members grow in understanding both of themselves and of others who share God's vision in different ways.

Rev'd Dr. Ellen Clark King
author, *The Path to Your Door: Approaches to Christian Spirituality*
and Dean, Kings College London

Filled with examples, stories and analysis, *Undivided Love* explores five different theologies found in mainline denominations—all life-giving, all needing one another. This book will not only illuminate your personal faith journey, but also provides a useful framework for understanding communities of faith, discovering how, in our differences, we can find a deeper life-giving unity.

Very Rev. Dr. Gary J Paterson
41st Moderator United Church of Canada

Warm, wise and intellectually stimulating, *Undivided Love* makes visible the hidden theological architectures of the living faith in the United Church.

Rev. Molly Baskette
author *How To Begin When Your World is Ending*
Minister at First Congregation Church of Berkeley, United Church of Christ

Janet Gear's understanding of the dilemmas of leadership, coupled with her unwillingness to indulge in sentimentality, make this book insightful, practical and encouraging. *Undivided Love* opens the mind and widens the heart. Perhaps most importantly it is wise and engenders respect.

Very Rev. Peter Short
author, *Outside Eden: Essays of Encouragement*
38th Moderator United Church of Canada

Janet Gear's *Undivided Love* is beautiful and bold, inclusive and illustrative. It is a compelling read for anyone who seeks to practice a love for self, God, neighbour, and world undeterred by divisions and unalarmed by differences of theology.

Rev. Dr. HyeRan Kim-Cragg
author, *Postcolonial Preaching* and
Professor of Preaching, Emmanuel College of Victoria University, Toronto

Often we think we are alone in how we see the world. Often we can't understand people who see things differently. *Undivided Love* helps us see, accept and celebrate difference on the spiritual journey. It helps us feel at home and inspired to be ourselves in the world.

Rev. Dr. John Pentland
author of *Fishing Tips: How Curiosity Transformed a Community of Faith*
Minister at Hillhurst United Church, Calgary

We need each other, to learn from one another, to continue to evolve and grow and enlarge ourselves and heal the world. Undivided Love validated my own journey through various forms of Christianity. Having exposure to these forms and teachers creates a world where we each can learn, explore, grow and change, guided by the Spirit to continue the pursuit of truth. This book is a blessing for all Christian seekers and believers in whatever form we fall.

Rev. Ward Bauman
author, *The Anglican Rosary: Meditating with the Mystics* and co-author with Cynthia Bourgeault and Lynn C. Bauman, *The Luminous Gospels: Thomas, Mary Magdalene, and Philip*

Helps us delve deeper into the richness of our diversity.

Rev. Brenda Fawkes
Office of Vocation Minister for Pacific Mountain Region, UCC

A must read and resource for anyone seeking a more sophisticated and unromantic understanding of diversity and its irrevocable gifts for community well-being. By providing non-binary, non-judgmental ways to make sense and strength of difference, Gear reframes much of the confusion and conflict that challenges the contemporary Church. Her analysis and pastoral encouragements offer fresh attitudes, insights and practices to help us journey together more cooperatively. *Undivided Love* is a thoughtful, hopeful and helpful book.

Rev. Jim Ball
Guelph Ontario

Helpful beyond the UCC and Canada, the framework for learning to read a congregation in order to lead the congregation would work well in a UK setting. *Undivided Love* opens conversations that create understanding and respect for difference. Valuable in any united church.

Rev'd Dr. Simon Walkling
Moderator of the United Reformed Church National Synod of Wales

 FriesenPress

One Printers Way
Altona, MB R0G 0B0
Canada

www.friesenpress.com

Copyright © 2022 by Janet Gear
First Edition — 2022

All rights reserved.

No part of this publication may be reproduced in any form, or by any means, electronic or mechanical, including photocopying, recording, or any information browsing, storage, or retrieval system, without permission in writing from FriesenPress.

Copies of charts and other teaching material can be requested from the author at TheologicalBanquet@united-church.ca or through leadershift.pacificmountain@united-church.ca

Cover image by Neil Thorogood, *Seascape*

ISBN
978-1-03-914013-4 (Hardcover)
978-1-03-914012-7 (Paperback)
978-1-03-914014-1 (eBook)

1. RELIGION, CHRISTIAN CHURCH, LEADERSHIP

Distributed to the trade by The Ingram Book Company

For congregations and communities of living faith
and those who lead them

Table of Contents

Preface	1
The Project	9
The Learning	10
The Invitation	12
Chapter One The Sound of God's Name	17
The Language Faith Speaks	17
The Sound of God's Name	19
Underground	22
Seeing the Believing	28
One and Not the Same	32
Table Settings	34
The Evangelical Banquet Table	
Chapter Two Meeting Evangelical Lived Faith	41
Who are the Evangelicals?	43
What's in a Name?	47
Flashback	48
One Line Credo	49
Distinctive Features: Intimacy and Atonement	50
Credo Unpacked	51
Gifts	53
Dangers and Shadows	54
Antidote	55
Chapter Three Living Evangelical Faith	59
Congregational Snapshot	59
Sacraments	62
Trends and Sources: What Else is Going on?	63

The Ecclesial Banquet Table

Chapter Four Meeting Ecclesial Lived Faith — 71
- Who are the Ecclesials? — 73
- What's in a Name? — 79
- Flashback — 80
- One Line Credo — 82
- Distinctive Features: Identity and Community — 82
- Credo Unpacked — 84
- Gifts — 87
- Dangers and Shadows — 88
- Antidote — 91

Chapter Five Living Ecclesial Faith — 95
- Congregational Snapshot — 95
- Sacraments — 96
- Trends and Sources: What Else is Going on? — 98

The Missional Banquet Table

Chapter Six Meeting Missional Lived Faith — 111
- What's in a Name? — 117
- Flashback — 118
- One Line Credo — 119
- Distinctive Features: Concrete Action — 120
- Credo Unpacked — 121
- Dangers and Shadows — 125
- Antidote — 126

Chapter Seven Living Missional Faith — 129
- Congregational Snapshot — 129
- Community Ministries — 129
- Sacraments — 134
- Trends and Sources: What Else is Going on? — 134

The Ecumenical Banquet Table

Chapter Eight Meeting Ecumenical Lived Faith — 143
- Who are the Ecumenicals? — 145

What's in a Name?	148
Flashback	149
One Line Credo	151
Distinctive Features: Expertise and Hope	152
Credo Unpacked	154
Gifts	156
Dangers and Shadows	157
Chapter Nine Living Ecumenical Lived Faith	161
Congregational Snapshot	161
Sacraments	163
Trends and Sources: What Else is Going on?	165

The Spiritual Banquet Table

Chapter Ten Meeting Spiritual Lived Faith	175
Who are the Spirituals?	177
What's in a Name?	182
Flashback	184
Distinctive Features: Discipline	185
Credo Unpacked	187
Gifts	188
Dangers and Shadows	189
Antidote	190
Chapter Eleven Living Spiritual Faith	193
Congregational Snapshot	193
Sacraments	196
Trends and Sources: What Else is Going on?	196
Chapter Twelve Read to Lead	207
Gifts of God for the People of God	207
Leading in the Context of Theological Diversity	209
Pastoral and Strategic Leadership — Case Studies of Interruption and Disruption	219
Strategically Pastoral Leadership – Thinking about Adaptive Challenges	229
Summary	232

Chapter Thirteen The Theological Banquet	235
The Flesh of our Words	235
A Word to Leaders	239
Love in Translation	247
Posing for Perspective	248
A "We" Made-of-difference	249
A Yet More Courageous Love	251
Acknowledgements	255
About the Author	257
Works Cited	259

List of Figures

Figure 1: Tracks	22
Figure 2: Colour wheel	24
Figure 3: Distinct roots	25
Figure 4: Colour spectrum cone	33
Figure 5: Evangelical symbol	50
Figure 6: Ecclesial symbol	82
Figure 7: Missional symbol	120
Figure 8: Ecumenical symbol	152
Figure 9: Spiritual symbol	185
Figure 10: Dancer: This is my prayer	200
Figure 11: Minister's lived faith depicted. Used with permission	211
Figure 12: BC Conference 2017 (Doug Goodwin photo credit)	240
Figure 13: BC Conference 2017 (Doug Goodwin photo credit)	242

List of Tables

Table 1: Theo-logic	27
Table 2: Names for lived faith	29
Table 3: Evangelical	66
Table 4: Ecclesial	107
Table 5: Missional	138
Table 6: Ecumenical	171
Table 7: Spiritual	205
Table 8: Activities as artefacts	213

Preface

THOUGH HUNDREDS OF PEOPLE OVER THE PAST SEVEN YEARS HAVE BEEN engaged in the workshops that shaped the material shared here, at no time was a formal or comprehensive study of lived faith or operative theologies attempted. Rather, I was simply doing what educators do by reflecting on practice alongside the practitioners themselves. Insofar as anything I was doing could be considered a research method, it was by way of gathering, mirroring back, and listening. This practical theologian's description of pastoral ethnography is precisely the approach I took to the project I am sharing here:

> *"The research process itself is conducted in such a way as to honour the voices of the participants…and facilitate the participants' increasing agency in their collective theology and practice."*[1] —Mary Clark Moschella

Consulting the material held in the National Archives of the United Church, in particular the fonds[2] containing the survey results of Faith Talk (2002) and Statement of Faith Survey (2005), allowed me to corroborate my inductive findings concerning implicit theologies with the words used across the church's explicit theologies. Likewise, the recent publication examining theologies expressed in our institutional life and work, *The Theology of the United Church of Canada*,[3] echoed those I was reading from the lived faith of congregations. Being granted the McGeachy scholarship allowed me time to write and produce materials which I hope will continue to invite and facilitate participation in critical reflection on the lived faith, the 'operative' implicit and explicit theologies among us.

It is important to say that I do not consider these initial reflections to be fully representative of the diverse expressions of the vitality of faith in the United

Church in British Columbia and beyond. By employing a method of participant observation in this project, a preferred method in the field of practical theology, I acknowledge that the strength of this method is also its weakness: it reflects all the voices at the table but only the voices at the table.

Most significantly absent from the conversation thus far is the Indigenous church which, though long integrated (BC Native Ministries) into the life of what was formerly known as the British Columbia Conference (Pacific Mountain Region), and thereby implicitly present in what is discussed here, has not spoken into this conversation with its own voice from the vantage point of its own new chapter of the indigenization of its structure and thereby its theologies. Other under-represented voices in the conversation include those of racial minority United Church congregations in British Columbia. Long before the challenge to advance the denomination's commitment to becoming an inter-cultural church through addressing the need to become an anti-racist church was articulated at the 43rd General Council (2018),[4] the BC Conference struggled to make real its commitment to racially diverse conversations. The poverty of the work represented here reflects the distance yet to travel toward that goal.

Though by these and other means limited, this text is a testimony to the faith that animates the ministries of the United Church of Canada in British Columbia. It is a descriptive snap shot in which many in the Pacific Mountain Region immediately recognized both themselves and those around them. In addition to *seeing* themselves represented in the work, those who participated in the workshops for which this material was originally developed were keen to *understand* those who differed from them. By mirroring ministries back to those engaged in them, including the theological threads to which those ministries are connected, this text and its accompanying resources attempt to address the expressed desire for greater mutual understanding within the theologically diverse communities of faith in this denomination. The aim is not merely to identify and delineate theological worldviews, but also to raise and celebrate the lives of faith in focus here, faith inherited and shaped over centuries of conversations like the one this text invites. The further hope is to build capacity for broad-based engagement in that conversation and thereby contribute to our denomination's ongoing construction of critical contextual theologies for our time.

The process of "reading" theologies from the ground up, from the way faith is expressed in actions as well as words, is a long-established practice in the United

Church and a common contextual approach to the study of theology. As noted above, it is reflected in the recent work of our church's scholars in *The Theology of the United Church of Canada*, in which what we sing and what we decide, what we preach and what we protest, together becomes the material which expresses our understanding of who God is, what the church is for, and what human life is about. This is commonly how we do theology in the United Church: we interpret and articulate the ways in which our life together echoes, animates, and contributes to the ancient faith to which we are connected.

Beginning with "lived faith" like this is also a means of beginning to undo the colonial practice of privileging some voices over others and of viewing authority hierarchically. In other words, the methodology is not value-neutral; it privileges the conversation over the desk. Moreover, it is demanding. Contextually attuned theology is engaged theology. It carries a commitment to mutuality, where listening and learning is as important as speaking and teaching. Culturally adaptive conversation, in which patterns of speech and silence are taught and learned, are themselves a means of incrementally developing and practicing norms of shared life, of constituting new communities. In this way, not theology alone but working out our theology together can be transformative, a way of shifting and redistributing the weight of words and silences and the worlds those words and silences reflect and animate.

Focussing on theological difference, as this work does, in no way suggests that this difference is equally important to other manifestations of diversity.[5] There is nonetheless an opportunity here to approach difference in a way that applies beyond this work. A critical objective for me in this work is to chip away at the presentation of difference either as something entirely superficial which obscures some deeper commonality to be reached below the surface or achieved on a higher plain, or as somehow the product of personal preference or taste. My treatment here of the variety of expressions of lived faith in this denomination reflects a deeper commitment to see and approach diversity as not only the deep grammar of how things are, but the agency (material and energy) for how things might be. This is a theological statement as well as a sociological one: the One who has created and is creating, does so by way of divinely multiform self-expression—by being a one made of three. I engaged the project described here as an opportunity to practice taking difference seriously, not as a description of our communities, but as the material by which futures are intentionally constructed and reconstructed.

Learning to approach difference this way—not as variation on a theme, oddity, or obstacle, nor as aesthetic or utilitarian—is a profound reorientation for the Western mind. It remains on-going work personally and across the church.

In a monumental project of practical theology, the Theology and Faith Committee of the General Council, in 2002 and again in 2005,[6] asked the church what it believed. The results were stunning. In poured hundreds of responses on behalf of thousands of individuals, representing countless conversations over many months around tables large and small across the church, evidence that people of faith want to talk about God. Moreover, these responses were testimony to the capacity of our church for two critical tasks: theological reflection on our life together and conversation across lines of difference. Both lead to transformation—a critical and ongoing reshaping of our theologies and an even more critical remaking of the human community. This latter transformation, of course, foreshadows the hope of the Christian church.

The way in which the fact of our theological diversity plays out on the pages of the *National Post* or the *Vancouver Sun* or among the usual suspects featured in the front pages of the former *Observer*[7] completely obscures that capacity. We both distract and misrepresent ourselves by framing theological conversation as a zero sum game across one dimensional lines. What follows here takes its lead not from debates and divisions as they have been featured and provoked, but rather from the deep confidence I have in the church's capacity to bear the burden of its array of theologies with grace, as blessing not curse. This confidence is based on the theological abundance I have witnessed and by which I have been shaped in the various places out of which our theologies arise, from the committee table to the communion table, the task force table to the dinner table.

This is not, however, an apologetics for the status quo. It is true that we know our theologies implicitly better than we can articulate them explicitly. This is no fault of our scholars of explicit theology who have gifted us over generations through teaching, publishing, preaching, and serving the courts, commissions, committees, and councils of the church. Nor is it the fault of lay people who are shy of theology for reasons various and longstanding. No diagnosis of the failing is relevant here. The point is that talking about faith is an art that can be recovered. Faith is both where theology begins and what it is designed to serve. The church asks theology for help when it needs to talk. It makes sense that we should be asking for it now. I have seen evidence that we can build our capacity for that conversation together.

Finally, there is a responsibility to locate myself in the conversation. I acknowledge that this project is in itself an expression of "lived faith," a sample of the very thing it attempts to read and interpret. Beneath it and throughout it, is evidence of my own 'operative theology,' formed by a lifetime in this denomination and experience of two of its sibling denominations. More evident than my theology perhaps, and linked to it, will be my relational epistemology, by which I mean that I believe we know what we know by way of our shared life. In fact, these are intimately related. Implied in the theology this project represents is an understanding of God which is communitarian, incarnate, and creative, making both manifest and possible a life together we have yet to experience in full, but is a constantly in-breaking source of hope. In so far as faith is wider than any human life, but animated by those lives in fragments of a whole, my work over the past few years in an attentive reading of fragments cannot help but have given me an incrementally wider view of that astounding, immeasurable collective fabric of faith. In this way, my work is confessional, a testimony to an abiding, deepening, and inextricably shared faith in the Holy Mystery who is wholly love.

If the church, in any of the five expressions or variations thereof I have mirrored back to us here, is by grace the body of Christ, it will be by its very nature a salve not only to itself but to the world. The shapes and activities which communities of faith take on in our time may or may not be as novel or innovative as we have predicted of late, but in so far as they are in themselves manifestations and agents of the abundant life convincingly expressed in our time and place, I believe they necessarily will be appreciatively and explicitly variegated. In this way, it is simultaneously and constitutionally both what the church does and who the church is as a body-made-of-difference (*ut omnes unum sint*) that becomes the salve to a world wounded by its inability to be the same.

Janet Gear
Cambridge, England
2019

Undivided Love

Notes

1. Mary Clark Moschella, "Practice Matters: New Directions in Ethnography and Qualitative Research" in Nancy Ramsay (ed), *Pastoral Theology and Care: Critical Trajectories in Theory and Practice*. (Oxford: Blackwell, 2018).
2. United Church of Canada Archives, United Church of Canada Committee on Theology and Inter-Church and Interfaith Relations, Fonds 568, 2018.135C - box 9 - file 8, Faith Talk 2002 and 2019.093C - box 1 - files 6 and 7, Statement of Faith 2005 survey and responses.
3. Don Schweitzer, Robert Fennell, Michael Bourgeois (eds), *The Theology of the United Church of Canada*. (Waterloo: Wilfred Laurier Press, 2019).
4. United Church of Canada, *Proceedings,* General Council 43, 2018, 134.
5. I do not wish to contribute to docile celebrations of difference-in-general which both obscure the painful realities borne in bodies deemed "different" and undermine their agency to dismantle the status quo. Though the politics of difference is beyond the scope of this text, it is never unimportant. I attempt here to break with the pattern of treating difference as merely aesthetic, interesting or beneficial.
6. Referring again here to Faith Talk (2002) and the Statement of Faith survey (2005).
7. *The United Church Observer* took the name *Broadview Magazine* as a rebranding in April, 2019.

Introduction

The Project

FOR A PROLONGED AND INSECURE MOMENT IN THE MID-2010S, IT SEEMED to me as if every congregation I knew of had employed a consultant. Out of concern for their future, these congregations and their leaders gathered to ponder the question, "What is God calling us to next?" This turned out to be an extremely difficult question. A large part of why the question is so difficult and why the good efforts of the consultants may at times have come up short, is because asking a committee, congregation, or denomination as a whole the question "where is God calling us?" assumes we all speak the same language about God. The question rests on the assumption that we share a compatible understanding of what we mean when we say, "God," a shared understanding of God's activity in Christ, by the Spirit, for the world, a common understanding of what the church is and what it is for.

In truth, there are in many communities of faith multiple theologies, multiple understandings of God and God's relationship to the world and the church. These distinctions are of course very difficult to discern, because they are not easy to articulate. For various reasons, most of us do not 'talk theology' when we get together to plan the next Board meeting or to meet with property developers. Some feel ill-equipped to do so. Some with long memories worry about orthodoxy, offense, and opposition. Yet when a community of faith turns its face toward the future, its particular outlook reflects these distinct underlying, often implicit, theologies. These theologies are what we could call "lived theologies," because they reflect how we live or seek to live our faith. These lived theologies are tethered to our faith in the very God whom the church trusts is leading, beckoning, or accompanying us into the future, but they are most often unarticulated, living below the surface of our actions and aspirations.

What if we were to surface the theologies "operative" in the faith of our communities? Rather than being stalled by anxiety about the future or pulled in the direction of trends, we might pause to make *explicit* what is *implicit* in how faith is being lived among us. Perhaps then, a congregation's faith might guide its future. A vision, mission, or strategic plan might emerge from the community of faith's "lived theologies" rather imitate what another community is doing or something a new book is suggesting. Perhaps we could learn to *read* the faith of the community in order to *lead* the faith of the community. Theology, after all, is meant to do just this; it is meant to interpret and articulate living faith in order that we better understand it. Theology in that way is always a second tier faculty, helping faith so that faith can lead. Some years ago, one region on the West Coast of Canada's United Church did just that: learned to read the various expressions of lived faith within and around their communities in order to let the operative theologies of that living faith inform their futures. We learned to *read* the faith among us in order to let faith *lead* our communities into the future.

The Learning

Over several years in one region of the United Church of Canada, workshops[1] in which these operative theologies were described were offered to church leaders, congregations, Presbyteries, Conference committees, theological students, and to the Conference as a whole at its General Meeting (BC Conference 2017). The intention was to equip leaders to identify the operative theologies within their communities of faith so that they might be better equipped to lead from the faith of the community *up* rather than from the latest trend *down*. We quickly learned that we could not begin with leaders but that congregants themselves were keen to identify their own operative theologies based on their own lived faith. The work of *reading to lead* includes and coincides with offering opportunities for people to recognize the way in which their own faith—whether long held or just developing—is articulated and celebrated as one among many expressions of lived faith. In terms of leadership, this discovery and appreciation apparently precedes the task of bringing a theological lens to the various challenges and opportunities captured in the phrase, "where is God leading us?"

For this reason, a good deal of what follows here is aimed at offering fulsome descriptions of each of five identified operative theologies in order that readers might have the same opportunity as the workshop participants had to identify their own dominant stream of lived faith.

Having found themselves on the "map" of operative theologies sketched across the landscape of the church's living faith, people eagerly embraced and deeply valued the opportunity to be presented with descriptions and testimonies of *other* theological worlds, and to imagine the relationships among them. Through this exercise, people soon recognized that there is no single "correct theology" from which several others deviate. Instead, a picture came into view of a variety of legitimate Christian theologies in communion with one another across the church, and possibly even on its thresholds. People took an immediate interest in learning and developing an appreciation of the spectrum of theological diversity in faith communities like theirs. The differences between their own theology and the theology of others with whom they share a church community or ministry team came into view positively. The variety of operative theologies could be seen not solely or primarily as a point of tension or disagreement, but of potential strength. Examples of such discoveries, insights, and theological collaborations uncovered through the workshops are used as examples in what follows.

After considering the array of theologies, how they are manifest in individual and collective lives, and taking into account the strength and liabilities inherent in each, leaders were ready to ask how the implicit theologies operative in the congregation they serve, their own included, shape or might potentially shape its ministry and mission. They were, in other words, prepared to *lead* based on what they had been able to *read* of the community's faith. It was those very leaders who asked for this text; it is presented here for them and others like them. The hope in presenting this material is that by sharing that same overview of operative theologies, similar occasion for discussion among colleagues and congregants might arise which brought workshop participants new insights and resources for leadership across theological difference.

The post-Christendom culture in which we find ourselves on Canada's West Coast and elsewhere in the global West is highly individualized. It places great value on personal choice, including personally tailored spiritual paths. When particular patterns and practices of Christian life have long since ceased being passed on and inherited from one generation to the next in a comprehensive way, individuals begin mapping and packaging their own spiritual lives. They might even construct their own spiritual truths by which to live. This presents a unique challenge to the church, but not one addressed here. In some ways, a workshop which identifies five variations of Christian theology found in congregations could have been experienced as a way of offering "spiritual consumers" a dispenser of separate features from which to assemble a preferred theological world to inhabit. This was neither the intention nor the result. On the contrary, the workshop confirmed the paths people were already on. Conversations at the *Theological Banquet* confirmed that the banquet does not need to be assembled. It exists. The workshops affirmed for people that their faith is not a self-made virtue but a gift of the Spirit for this time and place. The way faith is flourishing within and among us is not an innovation but a creative fragment of the faith shared by the church ancient and universal. The discovery of the way one's own faith echoes and animates something longer and wider than a single lifetime only confirms that even if theologies are under construction, faith is not self-made!

At the table, the adventure continues. Whenever and from wherever we enter such conversation, it is shaped by what we bring, just as we are shaped by what we encounter there. In this way, theology is always mutually constructive—(in)forming lives and being (re)constituted by them. Generously hosted, theological conversation invariably collects and employs the widest array of experiences, practices, images, explanations, and interpretations—those taught (doctrine), accepted (tradition), rejected (heresy), and fresh—from all its participants. The conversation creates a kaleidoscope of living faith which invariably inspires the life and work of the faith community. In this way, there is no contest between so-called "academic" theology and the "ordinary" theology we are reading from the ground up among communities of faith. Instead, there is an open table of incarnations of living faith wrapped in new and ancient words, images and gestures. Along with accompanying resources, this text is intended merely as an entryway into that conversation. The entryway was designed by and for a specific community—the United Church of Canada (primarily, the Pacific Mountain Region) in the mid-2010s. Tested beyond that community, it appears and hopes to be an entryway through which others are able to enter the conversation as well.

The Invitation

At the United Church of Canada's union in 1925, though we considered ecumenism a strength, some viewed our theological diversity as a threat to unity.

Our approach then was to stress what we held in common. Any unresolved theological differences the founders of this denomination held slipped beneath the doctrine section of the Basis of Union upon which all could agree. This text and its accompanying resources are based on the assumption that we are ready to surface the diversity that lives within and below our statements-in-common and our shared life as a church. It is founded on the conviction that genuine difference serves to strengthen us and that theology is here to serve us. This is an invitation then, to learn to read our lived faith, always ill-fitted in words, as an intimation of the imperfect legacy we share—a conversation of love and longing, of the near and the beyond, the intimate and the ineffable. This conversation makes theologians of us all—adventurers in the ancient practice of the church.

The material that follows is by no means the first of its kind. Arguably, since the apostle Paul offered early Christians a version of the popular body metaphor by which to interpret their own communities of faith, church leaders have been aided by typologies of faith and models of church. There is an overabundance of rich resources reflecting the relationship of faith to any number of personal and social indices: faith and learning style, faith and personality, faith and stages of personal development, faith and levels of psychological integration, faith and charism, faith and leadership theory, faith and generational theory, and the like. Likewise, there is a plethora of resources categorizing styles or models of church related to the same. What follows here is not an attempt along these lines; its aims are simpler. As instructive as such conversations are, we are not in conversation with a corresponding theory or framework at the moment. In some ways, in our commitment to read the faith of the church in order to lead the faith of the church, we are attempting something closer to the bone, something which demands more from us, more vulnerability and honesty.

What matters to us here is how people variously *live* their faith and how that *living* is connected to their experience and interpretation of the divine life at the heart of it all. The academic study and construction of theologies is a rich and lively conversation, and is in no way divorced from this invitation to read the faith of our congregations and communities from the ground up. Because theologies originate in *lives,* the words, images, and concepts put forward by such scholars and schools are ones we constantly borrow, in whole or in part, to wrap around and give voice to the living faith we carry and are carried by. However, we are very deliberately disassociating our interpretation of the living faith of our congregations from such frames of reference. The first reason for this is that these schools of thought cut across each of our streams of living faith, bringing their various theories of atonement, culture, ethics, and anthropology with them. So it is inaccurate to imagine, for example, all neo-orthodoxy to fall into one of our categories of lived faith, and all liberationist into another, and process into another. The second reason is that these various theological worldviews cut across the lived faith of the church because they are *live*, not fixed. Theologies are never intended, as they are sometimes used, as the means and measure by which to assess one another's fidelity to a favoured interpreter of faith. As *thought helping faith*, rightly employed, these theologies are at faith's disposal. They are meant to offer languages to borrow, not systems to adopt. Closer to poetry, they give us images by which to speak with one another about life in, with, and for God. Theological language is a treasure for the church and for people of faith or curious about faith. They are words which grasp after the truth we live by and the longing, hope, joy, and beauty through which that truth is revealed. Though some may be tempted to fit schools of thought into our categories of lived faith, they will be disappointed. The project here is *our own:* for us and about us. It concerns the living faith of our living church and extends an open invitation to explore that faith together. If we are able to suspend prejudice, to be curious about the lived faith of others, and non-dogmatic in ways of interpreting and expressing faith, the conversation remains beautifully and authentically multi-lingual and creative. We find ourselves immersed in the richness, depth, and breadth of a living faith, communally held.

In such conversations, quite apart from the question of theologies, another dimension of the shared life in communities of faith is likely to emerge: the reality of difference, in this case different expressions of lived faith. We discover that in noticing difference, we begin to equip ourselves for living as if difference were meant to be, which of course, it is. Difference is never about taste, accident, or choice. It is quite simply the fabric of living things: they are diverse or they perish. In becoming good at being multi-form, we are simply learning to contribute to, rather than to inhibit, life's flourishing. Even as we take this opportunity as a practice run at living together with difference, we are in no way equating the nature of theological diversity with other forms of difference. On the contrary, it is the hope that through each and every lens of lived faith, the very real struggles for life together will be seen more clearly.[2]

The Project

Finally, and most simply, whether we are considering ourselves, our congregations, and those hovering around their edges, a staff or board, or the region or denomination as a whole, to read lived faith is to enlarge it. More accurately, to read the faith of our communities is the way in which we acknowledge that faith is always larger than any one person or group can inhabit. Faith is a form of love for God approximated through human lives. Reading it together, we grasp a larger view of that which can only ever be an incomplete gesture, a fraction of an undivided love.

Notes

1. This refers to the *Theological Banquet* workshop piloted, produced and offered in and for the BC Conference/Pacific Mountain Region (PMR), 2015-2020 by Janet Gear with support from PMR's *Leadershift*.
2. HyeRan Kim-Cragg takes up the question of diverse lived experiences' bearing on shared life in *Interdependence: A Postcolonial Feminist Practical Theology* (Eugene: Wipf and Stock Pickwick, 2018)

Chapter One
The Sound of God's Name

The Language Faith Speaks

A FULL TEN STOREYS ABOVE THE CHANCEL OF ST. PAUL'S CATHEDRAL IN London is the Whispering Gallery—an architectural and acoustic masterpiece that enables whispered sounds to travel the full circumference of the cathedral dome. That much is true. The fiction is that the whispered sounds never completely die but travel eternally in inaudible waves. If this is true, the "happy birthday" I whispered there ten years ago is still circling around the dome.

Around and above the gallery are eight massive statues of early church figures. In an incredible demonstration of pastoral supervision, they sit perched in all their glory at the proud height of their immeasurable contributions to the church universal, peering over the cathedral below. It does not take much imagination at those dizzying heights to overhear their whispered confessions—multiple overlapping, historically asynchronous, and ongoing conversations of the founders and early adapters in the art of doctrinal faith. We know what a two-thousand-year-long conversation sounds like, because we are part of it. The faith of the church comes to us, in part, in the finely tuned precision of this conversation, delivered in creeds and confessions. From one generation to the next, their words are the texts, the containers, for the living faith we carry.

But we know just by looking at them—Jerome, Gregory, Basil, and friends[1]—that when the cathedral lights are out and the onlookers have gone home, the whispered conversation continues, replete with pauses, retractions, and exasperations. For them, as for us, there are just as many moments when words fail us. There are times when faith expresses itself not in a neat and tidy statement, but in a blind and blinding trust in the confounding mystery of it all. In these moments, it feels as if faith is carrying *us* more than *we* are carrying, or at least articulating, faith. Because the faith of the church comes to us not only in creeds and confessions but also in those pauses and queries, those "let me try to put it another way," "perhaps, it is more like this," moments, there are among us what we call "non-creedal" Christians who can't settle on quite the words to use for what for them is less an assent to belief as a surrender to it. Like other united and uniting churches, the United Church of Canada is officially "non-creedal," by which we mean that on the occasions in which faith is confessed (adult baptism, confirmation, and membership to orders of ministry, for example), it is just as acceptable to use our own words as to employ the creeds of the church. We understand them both to be equally proximate and provisional ways of wrapping words around mystery, variously revealed. We refer to those words as *theology* and to the place they arise from as *faith*.

What both creedal and non-creedal Christians have in common with one another, and with that circle of stone saints still whispering among us, is faith. Faith turns out to be infinitely larger than all of us. It is at the same time both intimately ours and yet not ours at all. Faith grows in us and flows through us but is neither our possession nor our achievement. Faith speaks the particular language of love given to us by our ancestors, whomever they may be, in the dialect of our time and the idiom of our experience. For Christian denominations, that language is one we share across time and space in the great company of believers, pilgrims, disciples, and followers of the Christian church. In this way, when we speak of what we believe, we are speaking not of *our own* faith but of our particular expression of a *shared* faith. Just as stardust is in our cells, faith is an echo of the ancient breath of Pentecost in our own bodies. Faith is ours for as long as we ourselves have breath—a divine gift for us to hold in the little fragments of our days, ours to carry and to be carried by. To speak of faith is to join a conversation larger and longer than any lifetime. It is to whisper into that dome, to add our voice to two thousand years of words within the Word. This text is an invitation to bring your faith to the conversation, find your place at the table where faith is the feast and all are welcome.

The Sound of God's Name

*On the day
when you are wearing
your certainty
like a cloak
and your sureness
goes before you
like a shield
or like a sword,*

*may the sound
of God's name
spill from your lips
as you have never
heard it before.
May your knowing
be undone.
May mystery
confound your
understanding.*[2]
—Jan Richardson

This poem beautifully describes the appropriate posture for speaking about faith. Theology is ultimately an audacious and impossible task, a task that should both compel and disarm us. It is no small thing to speak and account for the holy names that "spill from our lips" and land among us. And it is of no small consequence whether all those names, and the lives they claim and call, can live together well and to what end.

We have consistently told ourselves in the United Church that we have no theology and that we do not know what we believe, if we believe anything at all. This is untrue in every respect. We are neither uninterested in theology, incapable of theology, afraid of theology, nor deprived of theology. That fact that what we believe is not uniform but varied means we are burdened with theologies, not bereft of them[3]. That we are at times tongue-tied may well be true, but this is not for lack of theology or lack of faith. Words are never the first language of faith; life is.

This makes faith, not theology, the starting place. Theology is secondary. Theology is always at the service of faith, running behind it, trying to express it, to share it, to make sense of it. Faith leads, theology follows. Faith is always at the heart of the way we live as children of God, the way we walk in the way of Jesus, sanctified by the Spirit who gives us life. Theology's job is to give us language to speak about such things.

The Christian faith is an incarnate faith—a faith in the Creator of a living creation, One embodied in the people of Israel, incarnate in the person of Jesus, and animated in the living church. It is a faith that lands first in matter, in the body. The Word becomes flesh, and is known in the way our lives carry it, individually and corporately. So the question, "what do you believe?" is a beautiful echo of the question, "how do you live?"

The way faith is wordlessly lived out, in very small ways as well as very large ones, is what is known as "implied" theology, or our "lived," "demonstrated," or "operative" theology. This implicit theology is no less theology than doctrine is. Most congregations in uniting and united denominations like ours house multiple theologies, multiple understandings of who God is or what we mean when we say "God," multiple understandings of God's relationship to the church (what we mean by "church"), and to the world.

These lived or operative theologies implicitly express how we live as a church, corporately and personally. In other words, what we believe is somehow lived or brought to life, even if it is not verbally articulated. For example, very simply, lived faith is what determines which prayers we cut out of the Sunday bulletin and save or to which blogs or podcasts we subscribe. It determines which sermons or anthems speak to us, even with which minister we connect. Lived faith is behind why we might prefer serving the refugee committee to joining the worship committee, or *vice versa*. It determines which webinars we attend, and which books are by the bed. Operative theologies might have everything to do with why the young adults who cross the globe for a mission project may not be the same young adults who cross town to attend the Taizé services. It might even determine whether you seek solace in the garden, regularly give blood, or write to your local member of Parliament. Obviously these things have to do with many factors, but above all, or perhaps beneath it all, these micro actions of lived faith have to do with the particular contours of our own faith, its implicit theology.

These various implicit theologies at work in and beyond our congregations can be teased out of the faith-fuelled activities and actions through which they are expressed. In other words, we may learn to read expressions of faith-in-action and to recognize different implicit theologies associated with them. What follows here are descriptions of the most distinctive features of five of those operative theologies in communities of faith. These theologies are not being overlaid onto congregations from elsewhere. Rather, they are descriptions of the way faith is lived personally and corporately among us. These are theologies read *out of* the lived faith of our church, not *into* it.

Admittedly, it is not always possible to know precisely what beliefs about God propel or inspire particular actions or activities. This is art, not science, and a messy art at that. Yet, if we consent to imprecision for the sake of what we might discover about one another, it turns out that it *is* possible to begin with how faith is lived—how it is demonstrated, how it becomes actions rather than words—and to tease out from those actions the threads of belief about who God is and what God is like. In giving those threads language, and contrasting them with other beliefs teased from other actions, we allow theology (words about God) to be at the service of faith (trust in, or longing for, God by this, another, or no name).

To say that we have "no theology" is for some a way of saying quite the opposite: that we have too many theologies for their taste. For them, all this theology makes things muddled and muddy where they seek clarity. This same claim is for others an expression of desire. They wish the beliefs and actions of the whole denomination more closely resembled their own. For many, this claim of having no theology reflects the fact that the rich complexity of living faith our denomination has grown and inherited over its lifetime does not match the common perception of what a "real theology" should be. No relief for these complaints is offered here. What follows is for those who are able to stomach the reality of our multiple theologies. It is for those who are open to considering each of them a genuine expression of a living faith. There are no winners or losers here, no subtle victory or subliminal put-down. There is also no promise of peace and harmony; these cannot be delivered by way of teaching but only by way of a change of heart.

Underground

As we engage the work of theology by bringing heart and mind to the task of better understanding our shared faith, we quickly discover that united and uniting denominations are difficult places to be a theologian. It is important to understand why this is the case. Ecumenism, the context which gave our denomination birth, is both a gift and a challenge. It is simplistic to imagine a melting pot for, or umbrella over, the diversity of theological positions we inherited as a denomination built through amalgamation, because no such thing exists. What we have instead is rather more like a subway map.[4]

Figure 1: Tracks

The urban imagination is able to picture an underground system of train routes. There are some tracks along which every train travels, but there are also trains running on tracks going in different, even opposite, directions. There are stations where one train may be disembarked and another boarded readily from the same platform, and there are stations where certain trains have never met. Such is the complexity of convictions, commitments, and confessions that lie beneath our denomination, indeed our Reformed Christian tradition as a whole. Complexity does not necessarily require simplification. To simplify complex organisms is to destroy them; it is to un-bake the bread. Theologically diverse communities of faith are blessed by their complexity and the vitality that complexity promises.

In reality, the subway map is much more organic than lines of steel convey. Over time, of course, some of these "tracks" begin to inform, even *re*form one another, but the image of tracks serves to illustrate an underground theological network of beliefs, or "theo-logic." Visualizing this network metaphorically maps the relationship between our understandings of God, church, and world. To imagine different tracks is especially important in conceptualizing the reasons for both incompatibilities and sympathies across the theological landscape. We are able to imagine why those boarding the train at the station of *one* understanding of God will disembark on a platform of church unlike the platform where those riding a *different* train of divine agency are standing. Were there a solitary track, this task would be less complicated. In a creedal tradition (Lutheran, Presbyterian, Anglican), methodically relating each station to the next makes sense. We call this systematic theology for a reason; it understands the system. Having inherited an organic, ecumenical network of tracks, this approach makes less sense. For this reason, we first venture above ground to read the lived faith of our denomination where patterns and practices are beautifully apparent. This lived faith gives us a clue as to the subterranean "track" along which those beliefs travel. We call this above ground work contextual or practical theology. Above ground and below ground work are equally important. By beginning with how faith is lived, however, we remember that these theologies are never merely inherited ideas but ways of life, ways of love, ways of following Jesus, of giving glory to God, of aligning our lives with the flourishing of life in the Spirit.

Reading the lived expressions of faith in the church as practical theologians do, is about reading the way a life, maybe yours, maybe someone in your congregation, or someone you know outside the church, is fuelled or inspired by faith through observing the particular form faith has taken in that life. We read what our faith is inspiring us to do. Beginning with that lived expression of faith, it is possible to trace how it shapes and is shaped by the ancient inlay of tracks beneath the surface. A better metaphor here is an organic one. Imagine the flower and fruit of faith above the surface connected to a living root below the surface.

Figure 2: Colour wheel

Using this organic metaphor for a moment, we are able to describe and illustrate five operative theologies associated with the lived faith of the United Church. In the description of each, we are intentionally over-emphasizing the distinctions between them, highlighting the particular leaning, the strength of character of each. It is extremely important to remember, however, that these are not exclusive features; these are the dominant feature of each. No operative theology has a territorial claim on a particular expression of faith. Rather, all five expressions of lived faith contain all the features of the other four, to a lesser degree. The importance of keeping this in view cannot be overstated. Just as every colour on the spectrum is made up of all the rest, so too are each of our five theological "colours" made up of all the rest. Here we are pulling out and displaying a dominant hue or energy merely for the task of distinguishing between them.

For example, all are *evangelical* in some way—bearers of the good news; all are anchored in the practice of liturgical and communal life (*ecclesial*); all are *missional*—outward-looking in love of neighbour; all are engaged in the world—*the oikos* (*ecumenical*)—in reading and responding to its yearning to more closely resemble the kin-dom of God; all are deeply *spiritual*—prayerful, intention, attentive ways of being present to the holy—the transcendent and immanent presence of God. If this were not the case, the operative theologies connected to these expressions of faith would not be Christian theologies. Each one is a Christian theology and each lived faith explored here bears all the marks of the church. There is no hidden hierarchy or judgement here, no progression from elementary to advanced, or from genuine to marginal theology. We will soon see that no single theology has any greater shadow than another. All are faithful, all are rich, all pray, sing, work, and witness. All have roots and current expressions in the United Church. All lead deeper into life in, and with, and for God. Those interested in the question of who is in and who is out will find no help here. The spectrum we are focussed on is better conceived of as a circle than a line. We are not interested in the edges of exclusion but in nurturing the depth of, and relationships between, operative theologies within communities of faith and among those curious about them. It is good to pay attention to thresholds, to where and how people enter and exit a community of faith across the five expressions of lived faith, but this is a generous inquiry, not a suspicious one.

Figure 3: Distinct roots

Staying with this organic metaphor, we might imagine each one of these distinct lives of faith as the result of a seed that fell on good soil. They grow differently above ground because their roots or beliefs below the ground are also different. We *see* difference above ground; we *understand* difference by going below the surface. The complex root system under each lived faith has a distinct set of beliefs, an internal theological logic. It is in these roots that we see the way a lived faith is connected to a coherent operative theology—a theology that holds together beliefs about God and how God acts in the world. We are not suggesting that the roots *determine* the flower; only that in the symbiotic relationship, the operative theology is hidden from view. We pull up the roots it in order to understand the faith better.

Though we are keen to understand the roots, we remember that we always begin with how faith is *lived*. By asking ourselves, "what is my faith most leading me to want to do?" we begin to form a picture of the distinct character of lived faith captured in each of our categories. For example, there those who would answer the question by describing their commitment to share their faith, to give testimony to what Jesus has done and is doing in their life, particularly in order to help those without faith to find faith (evangelical). This is distinct from those who would answer the question about what their faith most inspires them to do by describing their commitment to their church community and to the way the relationships and the opportunity to serve and to worship together anchors their Christian life (ecclesial). When others think about what their faith inspires them to do, they have trouble imagining who they would be or what they would be doing without faith, because it is simply what they do day to day in helping others as a nurse or social worker or foodbank volunteer (missional). Some will very specifically point to their faith-informed activism. They would not be propelled or energized in climate action or human rights without faith in God's promised future of peace and justice (ecumenical). And there are those who answer the question about what their faith leads them to want to do by describing their orientation toward the world as a sacred place and their desire to live in harmony with all things and in the divine life (spiritual). Sometimes, providing images of these activities and asking people to choose one is the most instinctual way of identifying the strongest inclination in a lived faith. Though we may carry all of these to a greater or lesser extent, our response to an image (of an intimate bible study, the passing of the peace, an Emergency Shelter, a demonstration, or a labyrinth) is a good indicator of our heart's knowledge.

By unearthing the theological roots or tracks beneath each of these categories of lived faith (what our faith most leads us to want to do), we glimpse the otherwise hidden "theo-logic" of each. For example, for each stream of lived faith, we uncover how various understandings of how God acts in the world (divine agency) are related to the church's vocation and to Christian identity.

Lived Faith	What is God doing?	How?	Church's Core Activity	Christian Identity
Share Jesus with others	God in Christ saves and transforms lives	Through the atoning sacrifice accepted in heart of believer	Share the gospel	messenger
Worship and learn about God together	God in the Holy Spirit is revealing the eternal embodied presence of Christ	Through baptized and gathered community, sacraments, ministries	Proclaim faith generation to generation	servant
Go where the need is	God is healing and blessing lives and communities	Through the presence and actions of neighbour-disciples	Commission love of neighbour	neighbour
Work for social change	God is mending the world	Through those responding to the call of radical social transformation	Enact hope through justice, peace, reconciliation	partner
Open my life to holiness and wisdom	God permeates all creation and beckons the soul into life	Through creation and its unfolding	Nurture spiritual path	pilgrim

Table 1: Theo-logic

We learn that there are those who primarily *live their faith through bringing news of Christ* to those who do not know him. For them, God's agency is rooted in the atonement which brings new life to the believer. They offer the world the gift of God's saving word (**evangelical**). There are those who primarily *live their faith through participation in communities of proclamation, sacrament and self-offering*. For them, God's agency is experienced in the risen Body of Christ, the church. They offer the world the enduring presence of the church from generation to generation (**ecclesial**). There are those who primarily *live their discipleship in love of stranger*. They experience the divine agency of healing or salvation brought to life in the sent people of God, and offer the world acts of compassion (**missional**). There are those who primarily *live their faith by joining the struggle for fulness of life*. For them, God's kin-dom is experienced in a divine summons to social transformation. Their offering to the world is an enacted hope for justice, peace, and reconciliation (**ecumenical**). There are those for whom God's transcendent agency is rooted in radical incarnationalism. They *live their faith in attentive relationship to the sacred in the ordinary* and they offer the world ancient paths of wisdom and illumination (**spiritual**).

We will meet in these pages people of faith whose lives express their faith in different ways. Each expression is indicative of an operative theology. Each expression offers the church particular gifts. Recognizing that within or beneath the gifts are distinct understanding of God and God's relationship to humanity, church, and world, we *begin with the distinctive feature* of each form of lived faith and probe the roots to understand the beliefs that shape and are shaped by that particular expression lived faith.

Seeing the Believing

At a Thanksgiving dinner at my home some years ago, someone suggested we take a group photo. Creatively, my nephew took leadership by standing all fourteen of us in front of the large mirror in the dining room. Awkwardly at first, and then disarmed by humour, we smiled into the glass as he surreptitiously captured our image with a waist-high iPhone. How often do we see ourselves alongside others in quite that way, each of us looking both at ourselves and at the group as a whole, seeing ourselves as others see us and watching others as they too watch themselves? What we are attempting here is somewhat the same task. We are collectively peering into a wide mirror, seeing ourselves alongside others who are doing the same. It is both awkward and disarming. It will never capture the whole of who we are and nor is it intended to do. Hopefully however, it will provide a snapshot reminder of one of the most important tasks of leadership: to see, including to see ourselves among others.

In the following pages, we will be introduced to people and communities whose lived faith is fuelled by the five operative theologies I have seen reflected in the life and work of this denomination. Like colours in a rainbow, these theologies are distinct only momentarily. The longer one looks at any of them, the more their colour begins to blur and morph, as if a kaleidoscope has turned to reconfigure the pattern. Each is far more complex and nuanced than descriptions they are given here. These representations are meant not to capture the whole, but to highlight features that will help us recognize those who inhabit and animate particular expressions of faith, particularly those different from our own. They are to help us see one another. For the sake of clarity, we have labelled each one of the categories, not with a definition but with a one word description.

Category	Lived Faith
Evangelical	Share Jesus with others
Ecclesial	Worship and learn about God together
Missional	Go where the need is
Ecumenical	Work for social change
Spiritual	Open my life to holiness and wisdom

Table 2: Names for lived faith

To see one another through the lens of operative theologies helps us to interpret the life and work of our communities of faith. For example, perhaps you have had the experience of two board members not seeing eye to eye about stewardship. They appear to disagree about finances but we might be aided in our leadership by viewing the tension as a collision above ground of differing operative theologies below ground. Perhaps deep within the core of their faith and possibly never articulated as such, they hold different understandings of how God is active in the world. One might be what we are calling "ecclesial" and have an implicit understanding of divine agency, which views the activity of simply *being church* to be the primary manifestion of Christ's presence in and for the world. Another might be what we are calling "missional," whose implicit theology of divine agency understands Christ's presence to be manifest by anyone, anywhere who serves another through acts of compassion. When the board is faced with the question of whether or not to refurbish the aging church building, these two board members will vote differently. One is not being a traditionalist or materialist, hopelessly attached to a building. The other is not neglecting their inheritance, not some autonomous activitst. Moreover, neither is simply being stubborn. If we consider how each of their lives of faith is implicitly rooted in an understanding of God and God's agency in the world, their differences are not idiosyncratic; they are connected to the operative theologies beneathe the surface of the boardroom conversation. For one, God's enduring presence on the earth is in the Risen Body of Christ, the church—not the building but the covenanted, sacramental, worshipping, teaching community whose best home is in a sacred space. Of course that person will vote to raise funds to put on a new roof. Why wouldn't they? For the other, God's presence is in the hands and feet of the community of disciples whereever they go and whomever they meet. Why upgrade a tattered chancel when you could fund a shelter? No church consultant is going to change either of these minds, because it is not a matter of mind. It is a matter of heart, a matter of faith—faith connected to implicit understandings of who God is and what God's relationship is to the church and to the world. It is by no means straightforward to host these variant hues of lived faith when they collide at the board table or on the ministry team. Bringing these implicit, subterranean beliefs onto the table, sets a banquet of faith by which to both better understand and nourish the church and its ministries.

Reading operative theologies matters because theology is the language of our living faith, a way to lend understanding to the convictions and commitments that are often unspoken but deeply felt among us. We have already claimed that these theologies give expression to everything from how we worship to the choice of the committees we serve, the sermons we preach, the Sunday school lessons we design, the books we read and teach, the community we grow, how we live, what we do outside the church, and what we do in the sanctuary. They are lived out in our favourite hymns, and what we re-post on Instagram, who our closest colleagues are, and what we fear about others. In this way, these theologies shape us and shape our church.

For example, in a congregation where the language and lens of diverse operative theologies had been learned, the minister was able to help two members understand one another's contrasting commitments—one to an UNDRIP[5] workshop and the other to the seniors' friendship circle—as two distinct ways of living their faith, rather than two "personal priorities." By referencing the learned language of the way an *ecumenical* operative theology differs from an *ecclesial* one, the congregants were able to recognise and appreciate one another's lived faith. This is precisely the objective of this exercise: a way of seeing that leads to understanding.

In this attempt to read and understand the lived faith and operative theologies across the church, there has been no attempt made to tease out any continuity with the United Church's denominational roots at union. It is not difficult to see, however, that the Spirit appears to have animated lives of faith in similar directions then, as now. We are struck, in other words, not by the *continuities* but the *resemblances*! The lived faith of our denomination's founders included ardent revivalists (evangelical), Christian educators (ecclesial), missionaries (missional), social reformers (ecumenical), and while always home to those rooted as much in personal as they were in corporate religious experience (spiritual), later grew and drew a post-liturgical renewal population of aesthetically and experientially-oriented members. Yet faith, being a living and shared thing, does not *progress* but rather *grows*. It has taken on particular forms over the decades which are always contextually influenced and which, in some ways, are unique to this denomination.

To a certain extent, even the words and descriptions of the people we meet here will be flattened to fit the page. This is a serious limitation of categorization. The testimonies will lose their nuance and variety as they are slotted between articifical boundaries. We will of course find ourselves thinking, "well, yes but," "well, not exactly," and "not in every instance." We will have to consent to not finding ourselves and communities precisely reflected on these pages. Theology attempts to put our faith into words, but those words are always an approximation not least because faith's first language is life. A further liability of typologies like this one is that, in the wrong hands, they can lend themselves to stereotyping and pigeon-holing. The objective here could not be farther from this. If we find ourselves labling others, we have misused the work presented here. The work instead lends itself to reverence and respect for what the Spirit is animating in the lives of others. By observing how faith is lived, we are reminded of how faith is never motivated by opinion or aspiration but always by relationship with the divine life. Faith is always holy ground, a glimpse of human life communing with the holy.

There is yet another tendency when faced with a conception of reality that divides a community into different groups as this may appear to do. The tendency is to want to put the community back together again, to deny the importance of any distinction at all. This is potentially the most problematic resistance to an exercise like this one.

One and Not the Same

This is a bold declaration, that with respect to our expressions of lived faith and the theologies to which they are variously tethered, we are not all the same. Indeed, we are *not* all the same in the end. We are different in the end and that's the point. We might all be faithful in the end (or not) but we are not all the same in the end.

To some ears, that statement is deeply troubling; it feels fundamentally unfaithful. For those who carry a profound and prayerful desire for Christian unity, being preoccupied with our differences is experienced as a dangerous undoing of what the Holy Spirit is creating among us. In these instances, the desire to subvert our differences rather than surface them stems from love; it stems from the deep hope and belief in the promise that in Christ all may be one. Far from problematic, this prayerful commitment is a gift to this conversation. Likewise, a yet scarcer gift: from an extremely rare depth of wisdom few people have attained and of which Jesus is an example, unity can be glimpsed on the far side of difference. This glimpse or vision of oneness is what we might call love in its purest form. This love has the capacity to protect individuality and difference on its way to creating wholeness or oneness. This oneness is never synonymous with sameness. It never resists difference because love collects and shelters particularity rather than obliterating it. The trinity is a beautiful metaphor of this reality—a one that protects the three.

I want to distinguish both of these—the longing for unity in Christ and the vision of the reality of oneness—from other ways in which we might find ourselves insisting that we are all slightly different versions of more or less the same thing, or maintaining that we are all saying the same thing in slightly different ways. No matter how much we see ourselves represented in each of the five different categories or even in each other, none of us belongs to all categories equally! Every one of us has a dominant or foundational orientation in our life of faith. It is important for us to recognize that orientation, not for our own sake, but because it influences how we see others. Our own dominant orientation, quite literally, will "colour" our perspective, with or without our knowledge. In other words, self-knowledge is critical. To "take the log out of your own eye" is not simply about recognizing our faults; it is about seeing and understanding ourselves well enough not to project ourselves onto others. It may be counter-intuitive to insist that self-knowledge leads to better knowledge of others, or that naming difference is necessary for bridging it, but these are critical principles to embrace for our life together in community. The divinely crafted architecture of difference is not decoration on the surface of our humanity, but the very test of it.

The statement "we're all the same deep down" may sound inclusive and generous. Unlike the commitment to unity or the vision of oneness though, in fact it may spring from somewhere else. It may spring from a self that has not seen itself, an undifferentiated self that imagines everyone to be merely another version of themselves. In this way, to say "we're all the same" is another way of saying, "we're all like me." Differences are never minimized by denial. When we pretend differences do not exist, we erase not just the differences but also those who inhabit them. In our desire for unity, our work becomes first to learn to see. There is no more difficult work within or outside the church than this, no more important work than this acknowledgement of one another. It bears the weight of the greatest commandment. To love one another is first to see one another. We cannot love what we have failed to notice.

As we venture into this difficult territory of navigating difference, this holy ground of learning to see, we remember that difference itself is a manifestation of the divine life. We acknowledge too that difference is bridged or transcended in two directions: in depth and in proximity.

Figure 4: Colour spectrum cone

The more closely we work with people whose theology differs from our own, the more the edges between these worldviews soften. The deeper the faith and the more practiced the spiritual life, the more these boundaries begin to dissolve.[6] We know that in Christ we grow in both these directions—deeper in God and closer to one another. These are, in fact, not two directions, but one.

Margaret Wheatley wrote that, "it is not our differences that divide us but our judgements about each other that do."[7] I believe it is true that judgements are the wounds that become infected and threaten the life of the body. This is why paying close attention to each operative theology's particular strengths and liabilities is so important. We will be less prone to judgement when we have considered our own limitations alongside other's strengths.

Every operative theology or stream of lived faith has a shadow. We will see in what follows that the antidotes to the dangers inherent in each stream's shadow are found in a completely different one. This leads us to consider the way in which our shared life is in itself a gift of and for new life. We come to recognize that combinations or collaborations, or community as a whole, become the corrective to the temptations inherent in operative theologies we inhabit. We discover that individually and corporately, we are not safe from our collective shadows without a peculiar voice at our side! Difference is not just interesting or merely colourful. Difference can be conceived of as salvific, just as the Pentecost story illustrates: diversity is the wild, self-correcting package in which wholeness comes. Christ's life-giving agency among us is as multivalent as creation itself. Why would we imagine it to be otherwise?

Table Settings

An extended metaphor throughout the following chapters is that of a banquet table. The workshops on which this text is based use this metaphor as a way to invite people together, as if to a shared meal. Superficially understood, the experience of being Christian in a non-creedal denomination might feel a little like serving oneself from a buffet of beliefs. Far from this notion, the reality of the non-creedal, or as one of my students preferred to call it, "supra-creedal,"[8] community of faith, is that the banquet on offer is a true feast. The conversations at the banquet tables are a genuine bring-and-share of lived theologies. They engage stories, words, images, prayers, curiosities, and longings related to personal and communal traditions. Those raised in feasting traditions know that it is not the independent offerings of those gathered, including their ancestors, that creates the feast, but the *sharing of them*. At the theological banquet workshops, at times, we are quite literally seated with those of like operative theologies at tables displaying distinctly coloured cloths for our discretely labelled cohorts of lived faith: evangelical, ecclesial, missional, ecumenical, and spiritual. Other times, we are set among the diversity of theological streams. In both instances, understanding deepens. Faith is affirmed and strengthened among the like-hearted, and theologies are stretched and challenged among the dissimilarly-oriented. In every case, it is lives of faith that are being shared, not ideas or positions.

Hosts of these conversations may be surprised by the ease with which most people are able to identify their "theological home base." The way they *live* their faith leads them to the table at which they share in common how they *understand* their faith, their implicit theology. Providing images, testimonies, stories, prayers, hymns, and examples of lived faith typifying each of the five categories of lived faith allows people to identify their dominant theological home. However, no one's faith is ever entirely monochrome, neither over their lifetime nor at any given moment within it. Recall that we are inviting people to take a *snapshot* of their lived faith, not a video, and to see what stands out within a single frame. It is true that our faith is a living thing and therefore complex, fluid, and multivalent. Nevertheless, those who are able to consent to rather heavy-handed distinctions and simple charts for the sake of clarity are readily able to identify their home base. Clergy are the notable exception. Because their vocation is in most cases ecclesial, they have assumed an ecclesial lived faith and see things through an ecclesial lens. For some, this may not be their theological home base on their off time! Clergy need to read between the lines of their day-to-day occupations in order to determine how their faith is most naturally and authentically rooted in God.

There are various moments at which a community might be called to the theological banquet. The community may be attending to its mission, governance, relationships, or ministries. In every case, the conversations like those sparked at these tables represents foundational work, offering a place to begin, not to end. The intention is to affirm the lived *faith* of those in the community, to deepen an appreciation of theological *difference* within a community, and to build capacity for *theological* interpretation of community life. By observing and engaging the way faith is lived in a community, implicit operative theologies become evident. As we see in what follows, the leader or leaders are commissioned not only to read the lived faith of the community and those curious about it, but to nurture that faith in the variety of ways it is manifest.

At each table, there is room for honest self-reflection about the particular strengths and liabilities brought to the community of faith *through* their particular expression of lived faith. Every stream brings many gifts but each one has a strong suit. We have identified the gifts of each stream based on countless conversations at theological banquet tables over many years. These are gifts that people seated at their table of lived faith recognize in themselves and in others like them, but the descriptions here are far from complete. By far the best way to identify the strengths brought by each expression of lived faith is to consider the lives of those who live them beautifully and well. Whatever of Christ we see in them, whatever gift of the Spirit they share, or light their life casts, could well be an echo of their lived faith, their place of deepest connection with God. We learn, for example, that chief among the evangelical's gifts is the ability to create intimate relationships of prayer and community, that the ecclesial's gift is committed service, that the missional's strength is concrete action, that the ecumenical's gift is sophisticated analysis, and that the spiritual's strength is disciplined practice.

We also take stock of the shadows we are in danger of casting. No one likes to think about these, and it is very difficult not to become defensive when we are confronted with an unfavourable view of ourselves. When we hear the descriptions of what these shadows cast, we are not inclined to own up to any of them. Invariably, the shadow that seems the nastiest to us is most likely the one that belongs to us! A shadow is not a weakness. A weakness is an underdeveloped strength. A shadow is not where good under-performs; it is where good goes bad. A shadow is the shape of demise, the undoing of what is good. Like strengths, each one of our expressions of lived faith has a distinct shadow: each demise wears a different guise. In the descriptions of the shadows, we refer to the dangers inherent in them. The words *shadow* and *danger* are used almost synonymously. The shadow is most often hidden from ourselves and others; we know it only by the damage it does. That damage is dangerous; it interrupts the flourishing of life. We don't see, for example, that the shadow of exclusivity is in danger of bringing judgement, or that faithlessness endangers a community shadowed by over-pleasing, or that dangerous dependencies are caused by the shadow of easy-fixes, or that ideological battles mask despair, or that narcissism lurks in the shadows of inquiry. We cannot see a shadow, but we are able to sense the danger of its impending harm.

If we are a little horrified by our look at the shadows of each stream, we should be. They hold the opposite of what we believe God is calling us to do and be—the opposite of our strength or gift or of what the divine life is doing in us for the sake of the whole. Though the danger of casting a shadow falls equally across the categories of lived faith, it is never inevitable. Identifying shadows is in order to minimize the way we unintentionally diminish the light of Christ within and around us. Shadow work is spiritual work, personally and corporately, and exceeds the work we begin here of simply identifying the dangers that lie in unexamined shadows. We speak of the antidote to the *danger* of a shadow doing *damage*. The antidotes are not self-corrections. They are introduced from the outside, in this case from the beauty of others. For this reason, we refer to diversity as the Spirit's design of a self-correcting whole.

What follows imitates the experience of being among those we know or may come to know in communities of faith in united and uniting traditions like the United Church of Canada on which this work is based. The organization of the chapters is designed to introduce each of the five operative theologies as if by meeting those gathered at the banquet. Each chapter begins with testimonies to lived faith. These are glimpses of how particular lives are animated by faith in ways we may recognize within ourselves and others. Having met these streams of lived faith in person, we then attempt to both deepen and expand our understanding of them, and to fill out the picture of what a collective or communal expression of each of the five categories of lived faith might be like.

The structure of the text allows for it to be read in two directions: from top to bottom, and across parallel sections within it. In this way, a reader is able to be immersed in a theological world by reading complete chapters, or alternatively, to contrast specific aspects of each stream of operative theology under headings like 'distinctive features', 'current trends', or 'gifts and strengths', by reading these chapter subdivisions. In either direction, the result will be the same: merely a taste of what is a communion of living faith. In this way, the text is meeting its objective simply to set the table for a conversation where faith leads, and theologies follow—theologies under constant construction, formed by and informing lives of faith around every table at which we gather. Hosting that conversation becomes the privilege of the faith leaders who choose the same—who choose to be led by the faith of the communities they serve, trusting that those lives of faith are the "sound of God's name" for this time.

Undivided Love

Notes

1. The statues depict early church (both west and east) bishops, saints, and doctors of the church from the third to fifth centuries CE: Ambrose of Milan, Jerome, Augustine of Hippo, Pope Gregory I, Basil of Caesarea, Athanasius of Alexandria, Gregory of Nazianzus, and John Chrysostom.
2. Jan Richardson, "Blessing that Undoes Us," *Circles of Grace* (Orlando: Wanton Gospeller, 2015), 172. https://www.janrichardson.com.
3. Michael Bourgeois makes this argument beautifully in "Awash in Theology: Issues in Theology and The United Church of Canada," *The United Church of Canada: A History*, Don Schweitzer (ed), (Waterloo, ON: Wilfrid Laurier Press, 2012), 259-78.
4. Metro Maps by Vecteezy. https://www.vecteezy.com/free-vector/metro-map.
5. UNDRIP refers to the articles of the United Nations Declaration on the Rights of Indigenous Peoples (2007) and to campaigns related to them, including their legislation in provincial and federal law.
6. Reference to colour spectrum cone figure illustrative of the blurring of colours on surface through proximity and the dissolution of distinction through depth. Figure is based on "Hue, saturation and brightness cone." Gil and Natalie Dekel, 2007, PoeticMind.co.uk.
7. Margaret J. Wheatley, "Turning to One Another: Simple Conversations to Restore Hope to the Future." (New York: Berrett-Koehler Publishers, 2002), 36.
8. Samuel Grottenberg coined this phrase in reference to subordinate standards.

The Evangelical Banquet Table

Chapter Two
Meeting Evangelical Lived Faith

To proclaim Jesus, crucified and risen, our judge and our hope.[1]
—A New Creed, UCC

What I wrote when I was eighteen years old is still true: "I know that God will give me the strength to do whatever He [sic] wants of me. I know that all I have to do is walk with Him and I will never get lost again. I just want to stand before you and make a public commitment to this: I want to do whatever God calls me to do. I want to say, "Jesus, I love you." I've found that I'm more traditional than I once thought I was. I've found that I'd prefer to gather around the piano or organ and sing some of the old songs we don't sing any more than to gather around a candle in silence... Teaching people about Jesus who don't know about Jesus: what other reason do people come to church in the end? It has to be about the love of God. —Craig Perry[2]

CRAIG IS GIVING VOICE TO AN AUTHENTIC SPIRIT OF EVANGELISM AT THE heart of his faith. His testimony is beautifully centred on a deeply personal relationship with Jesus, an obedient love that anchors his identity. At the heart of his testimony is a moment of conversion, a "yes" to following Jesus that does not resemble the process of faith development or discernment more typical of others whom we meet in the following chapters, but comes with urgency, passion and conviction, "my life, no matter what I do with it, starts again here and now with

You." The joy and deep peace at the heart of this conviction is palpable in Craig and others like him. They inhabit a strength, unruffled by angst, as they freely choose thankfulness as a daily offering for what has been given, and commit to share this irresistibly *good news* with others!

We witness this expression of faith again here:

> *Candace comes into the church office with a request for the choir or congregation to sing "Shine, Jesus, Shine" in worship. It is the anniversary of a life-saving, life-changing moment many years ago for Candace, and she would like to give Jesus thanks for coming into her life and turning it around. Candace knows no one will raise their arms above their heads with her as they sing but that doesn't bother her. She joined this congregation because of the kindness people offer her, her son, and one another. She feels close to Jesus among them. She knows that the miracle of new life and birth of hope that happened in her own life can happen in the lives of others. She finds comfort in worshipping with people who pray for others like her whose lives can be changed through faith.*

And again here:

> *Calvin says that the most influential book in his theological education was by C.S. Lewis. He was disenchanted with liberal theology and found his faith re-ignited in the company of YWAM (Youth with a Mission) friends he met on campus as an undergraduate. Calvin is a passionate blogger who finds good company among young ministers (pastors) of all denominations. His ministry is centred on prayer and devotion to scripture. He has recently started a 'p.i.t. stop' [prayer-in-transit] drop-in group where people can "unburden to Jesus the [stuff] that happened to them (or because of them) that day." Calvin is part of the "pastors in public" team, an ecumenical group of ministers donning tattoos and crosses who maintain a public presence in community coffee shops and pubs as a form of Christian witness. He is on the Board of Cruxifusion.*[3]

Chapter Two Meeting Evangelical Lived Faith

Who are the Evangelicals?

Lord, I come to your awesome presence
From the shadows into your radiance
By the blood I may enter your brightness
Search me, try me, consume all my darkness
Shine on me, shine on me.
—Graham Kendrick [4]

The table of evangelical lived faith is the most diversely populated table at the banquet—generationally, racially, internationally, politically, and theologically. They become a community in our schema by virtue of their *lived faith*: they *share the good news* of salvation in Jesus Christ. Who do we encounter across this wide diversity of self-proclaimed evangelicals at the theological banquet? We might group them into three sub-categories: legacy evangelicals joined in spirit and name to the still-remembered tradition of evangelism (and evangelicalism) popular in earlier decades of our denomination, evangelicals originating outside this denomination who have joined it by way of immigration or choice, and those who have joined us by way of refuge.

> The gospel is the central thing: the work of Jesus, God's Son who frees us. Everything else hangs on that and is a response to our own understanding of the Kingdom first being born in our own hearts. —Rev. Heather Joy James, Oakridge United Church, Vancouver

We begin by meeting those who lead or belong to evangelical faith communities, many of which have made a deliberate "re-branding" to reflect this identity. Believing "anything is possible in Christ," they live their faith in a concerted commitment to find attractive, meaningful ways to invite people into authentic and intimate communities where Jesus is known, loved, and worshipped as Lord and Saviour.

> Jesus' life, death and resurrection is of first importance, and has the power to transform us, our communities, and the world. We strive to be a living model of Christianity—a

multigenerational, neighbourhood community, gripped by the gospel of grace, seeking to reach and serve our multicultural society for his glory.[5]

The evangelical lived faith is the faith of the *messenger* of glad tidings, the one who eagerly shares the gospel with others. The language of these evangelicals is passionate and direct, unapologetic and personal. For some, it carries an intentional corrective directed toward a denomination believed to be in need of Christ-centred revival,[6] but we are not confusing that concern with our evangelical category of lived faith. Broadly speaking, we are considering the wide range of leaders and lay people, whether or not they harbour any particular overt or covert critique of other theologies, whose primary way of *living their faith* is to make known the saving power of life in Christ. The portrait of Calvin above typifies the way in which many of these legacy evangelicals find a community with whom they share models of ministry innovation through relationships with the wider evangelical movements, nationally and internationally. While their community is wide, it is also intimate. Young evangelical Christians especially take very seriously their commitment not simply to tell about Christ but to *live in Christ,* including the practice of living in intentional Christian community where support for a life of prayer, devotion to scripture, charity and mission are supported by friends and family. We can make no assumptions about their social values or their views on the theologians *de jour*. It is true that they are more likely to read Eugene Peterson than Joan Chittister, but the *centrality of the good news of salvation and the commitment to share it* is the defining feature of this category, nothing else.

> This community of faith has the message of God's love.
> Others need it. When they see our love, they will know God.
> —Rev. Everest Kao, Chinese United Church Vancouver

Another group of evangelicals at this same table at the banquet are those at home with an evangelical lived faith of gospel praise, prayer, invitation, and testimony whose faith was shaped by evangelical missions of our own and other denominations. They may have immigrated to Canada or be first, second, even third generation Canadians. Christians from all over the world with Methodist roots, for example, often but not exclusively, find themselves at home at the evangelical table. The intimacy of their life with Jesus and the centrality of the atonement to their faith are features of our evangelical category of lived faith. Whether or not they are living their faith by actively bringing that saving message to others or by living a life of faith-informed uprightness before God in response to this message is not so easy to determine at a distance, but their profound sense of being blessed by God through Jesus' sacrifice is foundational to their faith and they speak this language of love fluently.

Our portrait of Candace above is typical of those whose life journey has brought them to Christ by way of the intersection of their own hardship and the Christian witness of an evangelical lived faith. Evangelicals intentionally situate themselves in precipice places in the community where testimony in word and deed to salvation in Christ—the promise of new life and forgiveness—matters most. The evangelical banquet table therefore hosts the real and raw life experience of those whom Jesus has saved: saved from substance use, saved from criminality, saved from abusive relationships, saved from alienation and condemnation. For them, new life in Christ could not be more real. For Candace, and for others, the simple profession of faith in Christ's sacrifice for their own salvation is something to be shared and celebrated. Because this message features prominently in art and music, evangelicals at the theological banquet table include a disproportionate number of performing artists. Singing or playing hymns and praise songs, gospel, country, and popular Christian music, for themselves as devotion or for others as testimony, is one of the ways evangelicals live their commitment to share the message that "His love saves me." So Candace, and others like her, are not merely asking to sing their favourite songs when they introduce praise music to others; they are living their faith, a faith animated through telling about what Jesus has done for them and can do for others. The words of the songs are true; they are, in and through song, *their* words offered to those who, like them, need what Jesus brings.

> My three passions in ministry are directing the Gospel Choir, leading The Word is OUT!! LGBT spirituality discussion group, and most of all, as a follower of Jesus, helping others discover and live to their full potential in the body of Christ. I celebrate when people can love Jesus Christ with all of who they are, with honesty, integrity, and authenticity. It was

a painful journey for me to get here; I want to help others on this journey. —Rev. Curt Allison, St. Andrew's Wesley United Church, Vancouver

The third group of evangelicals are those who find their way to this table from denominations they have left not by way of emigration but by way of seeking call or refuge. In all but the most radical contemporary incarnations of evangelical churches and denominations, a person may be sincerely welcomed as a sibling in Christ but not be seen as equal to others or wholly acceptable. Women seeking equal opportunity to offer ministerial leadership may move from evangelical churches into the United Church, among others, to live their call. They bring their evangelical passion with them and are at home at the evangelical table. Likewise, LGBTQI2S+ persons and those offended by their reception in some evangelical communities seek refuge elsewhere. Though not all communities of faith in any particular denomination are of one mind about theologies of human sexuality, the denomination's policies mean that siblings having left evangelical churches variously seeking leadership opportunities, acceptance, or safety often find their way to us. Recalling the metaphor of the underground subway, there is no question that this journey is a complicated one for these theological refugees, but for those like Curt and others who navigate it, it is possible to praise Jesus in a denomination like the United Church, for example, as one liberated from theologies of condemnation experienced elsewhere.

It is an eclectic table, the evangelical table, characterized by the way in which those seated there demonstrate among themselves the very spirit of welcome and invitation by which they gift the world. Around the table are those as diverse as the few we have met above: the leader of an affirming ministry with an theological degree from Bob Jones University, a newly admitted minister to the denomination from Nigeria who is passionate about believers' baptism and eager to share the gospel in the context of North American consumerism and materialism, two young families who together host an intentional Christian community of ordered ministers sharing a house, grounded in prayer for the neighbourhood and for one another that each may grow in the fruits of the spirit, and a Chinese congregation who gathered at an "Abide in Jesus" Retreat Day to pray for the renewal of their congregation, trusting in God's miraculous providence to bring the twenty new members they are seeking. In all, they are a diverse, Jesus-centred,

Chapter Two Meeting Evangelical Lived Faith

there-is-a-saving-word-to-share group with friends beyond, and deep roots within our denomination.

It is true that the traditional or core evangelical community gathered at this table share in common such things as joining the majority of the Christian world in maintaining male language and imagery for God, being inspired by I. J. Packer, John Stackhouse, John Stott, or N.T. Wright, as well as the still favourite, C.S. Lewis,[7] or being fed by national and international evangelical alliances, including the United Church's own *Cruxifusion* network. It is important to say though, that when beginning with lived faith, we do not differentiate orthodoxy, neo-orthodoxy, liberalism, post-liberalism, or anything else. There are plenty of typologies that do that. Many lead to squabbles, including among us. Our project here is different. It is about how faith leads, not about which theology wins. The evangelicals at the theological banquet live their faith as eager messengers of God's saving love in Jesus.

What's in a Name?

To publish glad tidings

We choose the name *evangelical,* because people whose lived faith is profoundly and personally Jesus-centred and focussed on sharing Christ with others, find themselves at home under this banner. The name suitably expresses their lived faith as receivers and givers of the news of God's "glad tidings" in Christ. We are using the term evangelical here, as we use all the terms associated with the operative theologies we are exploring, as a nametag, not a definition. We need no reminder that evangelism belongs to *every* Christian. We are using the term here as a label for this particular expression of lived faith in which *sharing* the centrality of *salvation* through the cross of Jesus is the *strong suit*!

We will see that every category of lived faith we name has baggage to overcome! The disadvantage of labelling this category evangelical is that many who do not locate themselves here have concerns, prejudices, and stereotypes associated with the term. Some prejudices are legacies to be reckoned with; others are judgements to be dispelled. It is true that evangelism is associated with Western cultural imperialism for a reason; it is grossly inaccurate to link it with slick and shady salespeople of the gospel.

Beyond its appeal to those who claim this name at the theological banquet, there are other advantages to using the term to describe this expression of lived faith. Though very early in its life, the United Church of Canada was careful to define from among a variety of meanings and objectives associated with evangelicalism, the *kind* of evangelical church we were, it *most certainly* and *unapologetically* identified itself as such.[8] Though the term clearly means something different yet again, some decades later, as a label for this particular incarnation of lived faith, the continuity of commitment to share with others the good news of God's love made known in Christ remains. Moreover, using such a large and live term gives us opportunity to continue to reflect contextually and constructively on its meaning and legacy.

Flashback

> The United Church in 1925 was not a liberal church, or a social gospel church, or a modernist church, but, in the self-descriptive language of the time, an evangelical church in the heritage of the Protestant reformation of the sixteenth century.[9]
> —Phyllis Airhart

Looking over our shoulders very briefly to help us to understand who might be seated at the evangelical table at the theological banquet, we remember that we are looking here not necessarily at continuity between our contemporary evangelicals and those who founded our denomination, but rather at the resemblances between those who express their faith as messengers of Jesus' saving power today and the similar orientation of our ancestors' lived faith in earlier generations. We are reminded also that using the term evangelical as we do here is complicated both by its history (how it has been used in our denomination) and by the history associated with it (the weight of its heritage for good and for ill). Our denomination began with an evangelical *raison d'être* and has worked and worried its unhappy entanglement with imperialism from the outset. Looking back at the issues which emerged for evangelical lived faith then may illumine some of the dimensions of its current vitality and variants.

While the founders were suspicious of conservative evangelicals, they completely embodied the evangelical lived faith in their stated objective to bring Christ to Canada. Exactly *how* that was to be done led to the alienation of some evangelicals. One of the most important things to know about our history is that we did not create the tension between conservative and liberal evangelicals; we inherited it. We are a church which put an "and" between the commitment to "bring glad tidings of salvation" and offering "dominion-wide service."[10] So began the theological dance the ecumenical church was choreographing along with us, a bit of jazz which attempted to be inclusive of discontinuous moves: evangelism AND social service; evangelism AS social service; and social service AS evangelism. Those least happy with the innovation were conservative evangelicals. That the denomination's domestic mission to "bring Christ to Canada" was abandoned and its overseas mission "to win the world for Christ" along with it, those committed to conversion-oriented evangelism understandably felt their church had lost the plot. Some at the evangelical table today are those who identify strongly with disenfranchised ancestors like the former United Church Renewal Fellowship (UCRF). It would be wrong to assume that very many of the evangelicals in the church today would reignite those mission goals in a way that echoed the first chapter of the denomination's life after union. With only very few exceptions, growing colonial consciousness has for generations forced both renovation and reconstruction of the evangelical mission as distinct from its social service sibling. There appears to be confidence, in places like Cruxifusion (a descendant of UCRF), that there is room for an in-house conversation both about the distinctive commitment to evangelism *and* potential renovations within it. So, for example, at a recent Cruxifusion gathering, John Stackhouse's commitment to a Christian Canada[11] found an appreciative audience even while questions of sexual ethics, religious pluralism, and Christian imperialism, commonly raised on the floor of General Council, were also voiced. Still, the impulse of the evangelically lived faith at the theological banquet table predominantly views the secular as devoid of, and in need of, meeting Christ and confessing faith in him, a worldview not held the same way at other tables at the banquet.

One Line Credo

I believe in the good news that Jesus' sacrificial death saves all who believe in him, offering them forgiveness of sins and everlasting life.

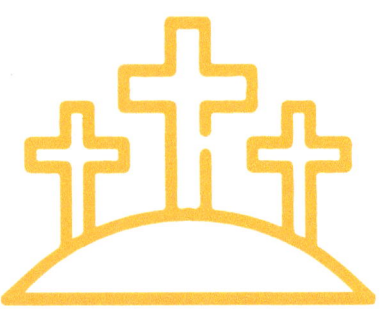

Figure 5: Evangelical symbol

If we were to capture this core belief in a symbol,[12] it would undoubtedly be a cross, not a saccharin cross but one supporting a crown of thorns or set on a Good Friday hillside.

The colour is gold or yellow, conjuring joy. Liturgically it carries Easter and the centrality of atonement, in particular.

Distinctive Features: Intimacy and Atonement

> [L]ooking to Jesus the pioneer and perfecter of our faith,
> who for the joy that was set before him endured the cross.
> (Hebrews 12:2a)
>
> He himself bore our sins in his body on the cross, so that, free from sins, we might live for righteousness; by his wounds you have been healed. (1 Peter 2:24)

Among the distinctive gifts of the evangelicals is their intimacy with Jesus through prayer and personal experience, their passionate conviction that Christ's atoning sacrifice offers new life and freedom, and their knowledge of and reverence for scripture. They are joyful, often musical, messengers of the promise of new life in Jesus and are sincere and hospitable in inviting and creating intimate and authentic Christian community, sharing Christ in word and in deed.

What is distinct about this stream is the *emphasis on bringing the saving word of Christ's atoning sacrifice to the non-believer*. Because we cannot take for granted anymore that people in Canada, or other similarly liberal Western societies, know anything about Christ, this group has a renewed sense of call and purpose. We know this by the term, "post-Christendom evangelism" which focusses both on finding new, and reinvigorating established ways to introduce Jesus to those whose faith is misplaced in materialism and consumerism, or is quite simply unrealised.

One trend among evangelicals is away from focussing on one-to-one relationships in which to introduce Christ to others and instead toward being a witness to and participant in God's redemptive power at work in "the neighbourhood." This orientation toward a more engaged evangelism is what we are calling the 'missional' stream in this schema, those whom we meet in an up-coming chapter. Mission and evangelism are inseparable siblings.

When asked to self-identify with one of the five theological streams presented, those who find their way to the evangelical table do so by recognizing themselves in the theological roots beneath the description of the lived faith. Though at first glance, this seems counter to the exercise of *first* identifying the lived expression of faith before reading the operative theology with which it is associated, it makes ultimate sense to do so in the case of evangelicals, because it is the *message itself* which is central to their lived faith. They are the *messengers*, so of course the message is key. The central activity of the evangelical heart is believing and sharing the salvific (saving) message that in Jesus' death we are reconciled to God. While some embrace and others reject substitutionary atonement, all evangelicals at the table place it at the centre: God's love is known in Christ who endured the cross for us.

Credo Unpacked

Unpacking a credo is not about testing for Christian orthodoxy. It is not about what is and is not believed, but where the focal touch-point is for faith to come to life. It is about following the grain of what *matters* in lived faith and borrowing the language of the church's faith to make that *implicit* conviction, *explicitly* theological. What matters to those at our table of evangelical lived faith is that they are grateful believers in, and thereby testifiers to, Jesus' saving love. Atonement matters to evangelical lived faith, not because it is a central tenet of Protestant faith (though it is that), but because their life in God is most palpably experienced in sharing the reality of *salvation*.

In the United Church, the belief *that* Christ saves has never been tied to a single interpretation of *how* Christ saves. Soteriologies cut across the denomination and across the operative theologies of lived faith represented by the metaphor of the theological banquet. What we are calling an *evangelical* lived faith in our schema is not officially tied to a particular soteriological model (substitutionary, satisfaction) but the **centrality** of belief in God's saving act through the death and resurrection of Jesus for Christian faith is unequivocal. This sets the evangelical table apart from those whose faith includes this same soteriological claim (in any model) but is *most meaningfully animated* by their connection to God elsewhere, like in the community of disciples, the intricacies of on-going creation, or the promise of the future kin-dom, for example. The credo is simply the one-dimensional language for the flesh-and-bones experience of life in God.

No Protestant needs reminding that a credo does not prescribe behaviour. Clearly, not everyone at the table of glad tidings will approach social and political issues the same way. Whether dealing with other faiths, with gender diversity, with the history and future of Christian mission, with marriage, or with public education, those familiar with the internal debates within the evangelical world at large, and in our own denomination's past, will not be surprised to see this table working out what it means to be saved in Christ. Their table is a microcosm of the Protestant church at large working where interpretations of scripture, creation, and human life are held in tension, challenged, and reconstructed.

> What is God doing?
> > God, in love and by grace, is sustaining, ruling, redeeming, and judging the world.
>
> How?
> > Through the atoning sacrifice of Christ on the cross, his bodily resurrection, and his eternal reign as Saviour.
>
> What does it mean to believe in Christ?
> > To turn to Christ, believing that in him I am reconciled with God eternally.

What is the church for?
> By the Holy Spirit, the church is empowered to share the gifts of the Spirit through discipleship and witness, sharing the gospel so all who believe may make Christ known to others.

What is the Christian life?
> As a believer who has taken Jesus into my heart, I am saved by God's action in Jesus' reconciling death and resurrection. As a Christian, my identity is as one who has been given new life, a grateful and joyful messenger of life-saving good news.

Christian identity:
> Messenger

Christian character:
> Saved

Why I read Scripture:
> The divine inspiration and supreme authority of the Scriptures, the Word of God, are trustworthy for up-building faith and governing conduct.

Distinctive focus related to sin and grace:
> Sins are forgiven through Christ's atoning sacrifice, freely given, a sign of God's grace.

Key biblical texts:
> John 3:16 For God so loved the world
> Romans 8:28 All things work together for good

Gifts

> *He walks with me and he talks with me*
> *And he tells me I am his own*
> *And the joy we share*
> *As we tarry there*
> *None other has ever known*[13]
> —Charles Austin Miles

When the more than three hundred and fifty members of the then BC Conference divided themselves into home groups based on their lived faith and operative theology, and were asked to bring back to the whole body of those gathered a symbol that reflected their own sense of their distinct gift to the church, the evangelical group brought Jesus. This was at once both shocking and delightful—scandalous and foolish, one might say. On one hand, how could they be so bold as to think only they had Jesus and every other table at the theological banquet was bereft of him? On the other, how perfectly fitting that the evangelicals, unlike any other table, brought the message itself, the one who abides in their hearts, the one without whom they are lost: Jesus. In that beautiful moment, it was not an arrogant corrective but an uncomplicated, even innocent, and excitedly generous gift that came into the room, the perfect symbol of the evangelicals' faith.

The gifts of the evangelical faith to the church are many. Evangelicals have given their lives to Christ. They are serious about Christian living and build communities of support and accountability to help them maintain their commitments to Christ. Their lives are centred on scripture and prayer and they are knowledgeable about both. They have a profound sense of belonging to others in Christ and treat all people of faith as siblings. To those outside the faith, evangelicals are eminently hospitable. They take seriously the power of their witness to introduce others to Christ. They are generous, often tithing their income and living simply. They have an eye to those who are in need of Christ and Christian community, namely young people, especially university students away from home, new immigrants and new neighbours, people experiencing incarceration, and those attempting to maintain sobriety. Evangelicals know how to welcome, how to praise, how to witness to Christ's presence and power in their lives, how to teach and preach the faith, and how to pray with and for those seeking to know and love him as they do. They work ecumenically, having close associations with evangelical alliances and colleagues within and outside their own denomination who share their lived faith and operative theology.

Dangers and Shadows

As we are reminded of in 1 Corinthians, the gifts of faith, fruits of the spirit, are always in danger of corruption. When a blessing spoils, it wounds within and without. We call this a shadow. We use Jungian language not because we have abandoned Christian language, but because we do not have an equivalent term in our lexicon. Sin is something different; classically understood, it refers to distance, internal and external, between ourselves and God. A shadow is an undoing, not a gap. By exposing the shadows at each table at the theological banquet, we help to mitigate the danger of acting from within them in ways that bring harm to ourselves and others, undoing the love that by grace abides within us.

When the unique gift of the evangelical comes undone, it casts a shadow peculiar to its gift. The undoing of the messenger's invitation and believers' intimacy becomes the inverse of welcome and belonging, manifest as exclusion: if you have not claimed Jesus as your Saviour, you are on the outside. This is the shadow that leads to judgement and even condemnation, making the evangelical appear self-righteous. There is a sense of "are you one of us?" about the evangelical's posture toward those with other expressions of lived faith, something not so prevalent at other tables at the banquet. When the evangelical fruit has spoiled, the scripture becomes a measure rather than an inspiration, Christ becomes *theirs* rather than *everyone's*. It is easy to mistake zeal for virtue, making even the evangelical's gift of joyful enthusiasm a potential hiding place for the shadow of superiority. These shadows are not actions on which other may pass judgement. These are a confidential mirror for the evangelicals alone, the particular spoilage of exclusion, judgement, and condemnation. Each of us will have a turn to wrestle with our own shadow.

Antidote

> Let each of you look not to your own interests, but to the interests of others. (Phil 2:4)

An antidote is literally a "give-against," a gift with the ability to counter what it comes up against. In the body of Christ, the gift to counter what is ailing in us is found in another part of the body. The antidote to the evangelical's shadow is found very close to home in its impulse toward service, the outgrowth of its own hospitality and generosity, its missional sibling. Why? When we are confronted by the reality of people's lives, our sense of what is Christ-like and what is not becomes less idealistic. It becomes challenged and softened by the complex reality of people's lives, not weakened. To mistake discipline for rigidity is a dangerous error. Discipline, even in prayer and study of scripture, is *in order* to be supple, not instead.

A piece of denominational history can be read through the lens of this antidote. When the realities of life were encountered through evangelical missions, the arrogant, cliquish, and judgemental assumptions carried in the shadow of that evangelical impulse were challenged. The church discovered that when the fruits of the spirit in love, hope, and charity are evident, it becomes problematic to remain convinced that Christ is absent where his name is not spoken. When there is evidence that lives have been broken in the hands of Christian institutions, it is impossible to maintain an unaltered interpretation of salvation in Christ. When the legacy of that harm is appropriately and widely acknowledged, it is difficult to imagine neutral territory where his liberating name can be spoken afresh. What then does proclamation of Christ's triumph over evil sound like? All these questions have shaped the constructive theologies that are operative at the tables of lived faith in our church. They are there because our evangelical impulse led us directly to them, out in the world, where evangelism wants to go. When evangelism listens as well as speaks, it encounters Christ in a different way. Its *singular* reliance on the authority of scripture rather than its *primary* reliance on the authority of scripture gets in the way of that listening.

This is not to say that evangelism's antidote is to abandon evangelism for social service and to capitulate to theologies it cannot embrace. It is to say that for the evangelist to be free of their shadow, the messenger needs to be accountable to the world in which the gospel message lands, not merely to the heart where it is claimed. Christ is no doubt our judge (but we are not).

At the theological banquet, the evangelical needs the *missional,* the one with both feet firmly planted in the world where hearts turned to Jesus become neighbours turned toward each other.

Notes

1. "A New Creed," The Manual of the United Church of Canada, 20.
2. Used with permission, this is an excerpt from Craig's testimony from the panel presentation (May 26 morning) at the BC Conference Annual Meeting, How Big is Our Tent? University of British Columbia, Vancouver, May 25-28, 2017.
3. Cruxifusion is a network of United Church of Canada leaders proclaiming Jesus Christ as Lord and Saviour whose origins in 2010 constituted a relaunch and rebirth

4. of the former Renewal Fellowship, Community of Concern and National Alliance of Covenanting Congregations. http://cruxifusion.ca.
4. Graham Kendrick, Shine, Jesus, Shine. Makeway Music, Tunbridge Wells, England, 1987.
5. Cambie Village Church in Vancouver, B.C. is a congregation of the United Church of Canada's Pacific Mountain Region that has undergone a rebranding in support of its evangelical mission to reach new Christians. Its 2020 website's look and content reflects the expression of lived evangelical faith embraced by its leaders. http://www.cambievillagechurch.com/.
6. The reference here is to a movement and community within the United Church committed to neo/orthodox Christo-centrism (Jesus Christ as Lord and Saviour), respectfully offered as a corrective to perceived slippage from Trinitarian theology. This movement is defined doctrinally or theologically and thereby falls across rather than within any of our categories of lived faith. We see it in what we designate here as evangelical, ecclesial and missional leaders, most clearly expressed in the Cruxifusion network of "Christ-centred ministry personnel within the United Church of Canada."
7. Though not reflective of the population of global evangelical Christians, both popular and traditional evangelicalism in the west is dominated, almost exclusively, by white men.
8. Phyllis D. Airhart, A Church with the Soul of a Nation: Making and Remaking the United Church of Canada (Montreal and Kingston: McGill-Queen's University Press, 2014) and John H. Young, "Evangelism in the United church of Canada: Templeton to Emerging Spirit," Touchstone 27 No. 1 (2009), 26-35.
9. C. T. McIntire, "Unity Among Many," in Don Schweitzer (ed), The United Church of Canada: A History, (Waterloo: Wilfred Laurier Press, 2011) p 22.
10. Airhart, A Church with the Soul of a Nation, xvii.
11. John Stackhouse reflected on his experience at Cruxifusion in 2019 in the following article: "A Splash of Fresh Water," in Faith Today Evangelical Christian Fellowship Magazine, July-August 2019.
12. All symbols in this text are designed by Tressa Brotsky of Pacific Mountain Region's Leadershift staff team in support of the production of Theological Banquet workshop resources, 2020.
13. Charles Austin Miles, In the Garden (1925)

Chapter Three
Living Evangelical Faith

Congregational Snapshot

We're on a mission—to know Christ and to make him known. Nobody's perfect. Everybody's welcome. Anything is possible in Christ. We are a Bible-based church committed to making disciples. Local. Authentic. Real relationships.
—Cambie Village (United Church), Vancouver

THERE IS NO SINGLE CONGREGATION OR KIND OF CONGREGATION THAT typifies the evangelical stream, but there are features within some communities of faith which demonstrate their evangelical lived faith. These include their articulated *purpose* to bring Christ to those who do not know him, along with related commitments like the centrality of scripture for anchoring one's life in Christ, focus on small group, invitation, public presence, praise, testimony, and prayer. Of course, all these feature in every congregation, but they have a life-saving "make Christ known" orientation in the hearts and hands of evangelical communities of faith.

Obviously, websites and Facebook pages, Instagram posts and roadside signs are the most public places for evangelical communities of faith to evangelize. The website that simply states John 3:16, "for God so loved the world," is the classic version of plainly stating the "good news" of salvation in Christ. The very popular banner-line appearing on church buildings and webpages, "To Know Christ and

Make Him Known," adopted from the evangelical church alliance, is a statement of purpose for the church, not a message of salvation for the passer-by, but appears to serve to self-identify, if not to *share* good news that here, among these people, Christ will be met and made known.

In some congregations, the evangelical lived faith is inhabited by a particular ministry or in the person or persons of the ministry team, rather than in the congregation as a whole but nonetheless shapes the congregation's faith in an evangelical direction. For example, the beautifully evangelical lived faith of the "pastor" of a congregation located on the campus of the University of British Columbia has the congregation's support (and a regional church innovation grant) to offer the *Foxes and Fowl* ministry located at a Graduate Student pub on UBC's campus. Advertised in the university media, this gathering attempts to reach those who wouldn't make their way to church but are curious about who Christians are. This typifies an evangelical "fresh expression" of church insofar as its aims are to share what life in Christ is about with those who do not know him, with the intent to build community and connection beyond the reach of the local church. The goal is not to bring new members to the church (ecclesial, in our schema) but to testify in word and *presence,* to what life in Christ means in day to day living. Insofar as those who gather are new to Christianity, it is an *evangelical* ministry of the congregation. If it is simply a better place for Christian students to be than in Sunday morning worship, it is a fresh expression of an *ecclesial,* not *evangelical* ministry in our schema.

A low-barrier or culturally adapted gathering space is typical of evangelical churches where informality is an attribute of the worship settings. Other leaders may trade in their sermon and pulpit for this coffee-in-hand style "talk" from a three-legged stool, but it is the substance that makes something evangelical, not the style. In an evangelical faith community, the message engaging people's everyday concerns in mental health, relationships and family, personal finances, ecological threats, or loneliness will be shared as if those receiving the message are hearing the gospel for the first time: *this* is what new life, salvation, recovery, a new beginning looks like when Jesus is Lord. This message will be echoed in the music as well. Music reflective of evangelical lived faith in a congregation may be either or both traditional hymns and praise music. The lyrics will focus on individual salvation and love of Jesus, the core message of the evangelical heart. These songs are typically in the first person singular (*"my faith," "Jesus and me,"* versus *"our faith*" in "*God's world*"). Giving one's life to Christ is a personal experience and remains a deeply personal relationship for those with an evangelical lived faith, as in for example:

> Blessed assurance, Jesus is mine!
> O what a foretaste of glory divine!
> Heir of salvation, purchase of God,
> born of his Spirit, washed in his blood.[1]

as well as:

> This is the air I breathe
> This is the air I breathe
> Your holy presence living in me
> And I, I'm desperate for you
> And I, I'm [sic] lost without you[2]

The popularity of praise music, coffee (or beer) and three-legged stools among *some* evangelical congregations in denominations like united and uniting traditions is not to be confused with congregations who adopt evangelical-style worship but maintain a lived faith, which is not evangelical in the ways we are describing it here. We will see in the next chapter why praise lyrics are often a mismatch for an ecclesial lived faith which in our schema is *corporate* in identity and *communal* in approach, not *personal* in identity and *public* in approach.

Because Scripture is the uncontested authority of faith for evangelicals, bible study is central and most popularly taken up through the Alpha Course.[3] An evangelical faith community will have an active prayer life, as both a sign of faith and a practice of faith. Praying the scriptures particularly, is a way to develop a holy or Christ-like heart and mind. This focus on prayer, and the personal nature of the practice of devotion makes the evangelical lived faith not unlike the spiritual lived faith in this regard. Though many other features of these expressions of lived faith make them the most dissimilar to one another of any in our schema, this overlap in prayer life is a fertile place for the Spirit's innovation among us!

We are highlighting here distinctively evangelical features of some congregations, but not imagining they are found in *exclusively* evangelical congregations. Predominantly evangelical communities of faith, of course, will include expressions of the other streams of lived faith, and of the ecclesial and missional streams, particularly. The underlying lived faith can be discovered by asking, "what does this congregation's faith ***most*** want it to do?" If the answer is "bring people to Jesus," or "make Christ known," it is evangelical in this schema.

Sacraments

> For God so loved the world that he have his only son that
> whosoever believes in him will not perish but have eternal life.
> (John 3:16)

An important aspect of the lived faith of any congregation is its understanding of the sacraments. How do sacraments express an operative theology tied to a particular expression of the lived faith? In one response to the Theology and Faith committee's survey, Faith Talk, a respondent sums up the evangelical's experience of the sacraments this way, "God sent His son to die in our place. We partake of sacraments in remembrance of His sacrifice for us."[4] Here is classical atonement theology plainly stated. A communion liturgy for an evangelical will stress the reality of human sin, the need for forgiveness, Christ's atoning sacrifice on our behalf, and our indebtedness, praise and thanksgiving to God, for a gift freely given in love. While this theology appears in many hymns in *Voices United*, communion hymns do not refer explicitly to the atonement. Evangelical churches will sing older hymns from within and outside the UCC, and contemporary Christian music:

> Till on that cross as Jesus died,
> The wrath of God was satisfied –
> For every sin on Him was laid;
> Here in the death of Christ I live. ...
> And as He stands in victory
> Sin's curse has lost its grip on me,
> For I am His and He is mine –
> Bought with the precious blood of Christ.[5]

Baptismal liturgies will also employ imagery of death and resurrection, being cleansed of sin and born again, and becoming Christ's own.

Chapter Three Living Evangelical Faith

Trends and Sources: What Else is Going on?

> An effective way in our church to introduce people to a lasting faith in Christ.
> —Alpha participant

The trouble with a snap shot is that it does not capture movement. In truth, all these operative theologies are dynamic and connected to a web conversations and communities spanning the global Christian community. Just how much bearing these wider conversations may have on those seated at our evangelical table at the banquet depends on their particular context: are they a young ordinand called to an entrepreneurial church plant, or newly admitted to the denomination from the Christian Alliance, or a long-time member of Brighouse United in Richmond, British Columbia? This diverse population with an evangelical lived faith will not necessarily be reading the same posts or the same books. Nevertheless, we might flag here a couple of trends which may shape the fluid landscape our evangelicals are navigating: the missional[6] or *Fresh Expressions*[7] movement and the post-evangelical movement. These two trends intersect with the traditional or core evangelical community.

The Sent-church Trend

Of the more active evangelical conversations, is the one related to experimentation with entrepreneurial or innovative ways of sharing the gospel with those who have not encountered it. A couple of umbrella terms shelter this trend: missional or mission-shaped ministry[8] (not to be confused with our "missional" category which refers to those with hands-on lived faith) and *Fresh Expressions*. Launched in the early 2000s in Britain, the *Fresh Expressions* movement is a missional revitalization effort designed with both the *evangelical* objective of reaching those untouched or unreached by current expressions of Christian faith manifest in traditional forms of church, and the *ecclesial* objective of planting or revitalizing communities of faith. This movement is now so broad and varied that it cuts across several of our categories of lived faith and we will encounter its influence again in the chapters on the ecclesial and missional categories in our schema. For now, we can acknowledge that this is both a "going out" (evangelical/missional) movement for those with evangelical spirit, and a "come and see" (ecclesial) programme in the hands of the established church. Only the former is of genuine interest to the evangelical lived faith.

Unlike the evangelical church in the United States, and missionally-trained lay leaders in the UK however, evangelical leaders in denominations like the United Church are by and large paid accountable leaders responsible for congregations, seldom free to test their genuinely evangelical (and entrepreneurial) wings. Unless furnished with funding for a *Fresh Expression*, they preach "being sent" from the confines of "being home." Had they their druthers, some would most definitely take the notion of being *sent* to testify to Jesus' life-saving gospel in hand. A handful of ministers have had the opportunity to do just that through evangelically motivated social entrepreneurial partnerships and start-ups funded by the Edge[9] and other sources. In ways both flashy and modest—as barber or baker or neighbour, as artist, comedian or social entrepreneur—being a witness to life in Christ is being embodied in shapes outside the congregational model. It is fair to say however, that for the most part, the way evangelical lived faith is nurtured among lay people in our denomination is relatively more harboured than sent.

Being a *deeply* congregational church, the United Church's evangelical lived faith doesn't naturally stray far from the faith community. Being "sent," as evangelicals are encouraged to be, is difficult for most unless they are gifted with an evangelical lived faith. Being *equipped* to be sent, however, is not. Thus, the popularity of discipleship programmes designed to form followers of Christ as *sent people*. We see this approach to evangelism beautifully and expressly reflected, for example, in the publication by North Bramalea United Church congregational ministers, Debbie Johnson and Jamie Holtam's, *Bullseye*.[10] The evangelical principle of introducing people to Jesus through our person, not just our words, is foundational to the text. So discipleship has a deliberate and distinctive evangelical thrust in this literature and in many similar texts.[11]

Within and beyond our own context, the *Fresh Expressions* and missional movement surface the perennial question which echoes the early decades of debate in our denomination regarding what kind of evangelical church we were: evangelicals of proclamation or of presence, of word, or of deed?[12] The same breadth of evangelical expression and theologies of mission exists in the *Fresh Expressions* movement as our own expressions and theologies of evangelism took in the early decades of our denomination. Like the *Fresh Expressions* movement itself, the trend in calling others to new life in Jesus has two faces: innovation (in spreading the word) and discipleship (for living the way). Innovation is about *how* people encounter Christians in the neighbourhood or society, and discipleship is about *what* they are encountering of Christ in us. We will see these two faces appear across several categories in our schema, in particular in their ecclesial form in the next chapter.

Bridges Back and Forth

In the evangelical world, there are those rooted in traditional evangelical faith whose theology has shifted such that they fall under the self-proclaimed label *post-evangelical*. These people are sometimes regarded as belonging to the *emergent church* (an American term). Though many of the longer term evangelicals at the theological banquet do not identify with the theologies associated with the post- and emergent trends, those same trends build a bridge from evangelical traditions to united and uniting churches and may indeed bring people directly to our *evangelical* table.

For the most part, the theological conversations among post-evangelicals are anachronistic for our denomination which may be regarded as somewhat of a post-evangelical forerunner. That said, there are those at the evangelical table at the theological banquet from evangelical churches or whose theology is actively under construction, for whom the post-evangelical conversation is timely and apt. Among such evangelicals are those genuinely asking questions and resolving issues related to religion and science, human sexuality, mission in an inter-faith context—questions most long-established people in denominations like ours no longer ask quite the same way.

A bridge the other way, these post-evangelical writers are of interest to those at other tables at the theological banquet, thereby creating conversation with evangelicalism not otherwise happened upon. For example, we see post-evangelicals like Nadia Bolz-Webber,[13] Brian McLaren,[14] and Rob Bell,[15] for example, being of interest to our *ecclesials*. Post-evangelicals who have embraced science or process philosophy as theological conversation partners, such as Donna Bowman,[16] Phillip Clayton,[17] or Thomas Oord[18] are most likely to appeal to our *spirituals,* rather than to many of our evangelicals. In this way, post-evangelicalism is just that, a movement that departs from evangelicalism such that it does not intersect with many of our evangelicals. However, the conversation allows for some evangelicals to find a place at the theological banquet and for other tables to bridge to theirs.

Lived Faith	Sharing the good news of God's love mae known in Jesus with those who do not know him
What is God doing?	God, in love and by grace is sustaining, ruling, redeeming and judging the world
How?	Through the atoning sacrifice of Christ on the cross, his bodily, resurrection, and his eternal reign as Saviour.
What does it mean to believe in Christ?	To turn to Christ, believing that in him I am reconciled with God eternally.
What is the church for?	By the Holy Spirit, the church is empowered to share the girfts of the Spirit through discipleship and witness, sharing the gospel so all who believe may make Christ known to others.
What is the Christian life?	As a believer who has taken Jesus into my heart, I am saved by God's action in Jesus' reconciling dweath and resurrection. As a Christian, my identity is as one who has been given new life, a grateful and joyful messenger of life-saving good news.
Christian identity	Messenger
Christian character	Saved
Why I read Scripture	The divine inspiration and supreme authority of the Scriptures, the Word of God, are trustworthy for up-building faith and governing conduct.
Distinctive focus related to Sin and Grace	Sins are forgiven through Christ's atoning sacrifice, freely given, a sign of God's grace.
Key Biblical texts	John 3:16 Rom 28:8
Strengths	Intimate, Invitational, authentic, knowledge of scripture
Shadow	exclusivist
Antidote	Diverse exposure: missional

Table 3: Evangelical

Chapter Three Living Evangelical Faith

Notes

1. Fanny Crosby, "Blessed Assurance" in *Voices United* (Toronto: United Church of Canada Publishing House, 1996) 337.
2. Marie Barnett, *Breathe*, Vineyard, Sugar Land, TX (2001).
3. Alpha is highly successful, international evangelical Christian education course originating in 1977 at Holy Trinity Church Brampton in London, England. Though contextually adapted, it is founded on the commitment to "bring the lost to Jesus Christ."
4. United Church of Canada Archives, United Church of Canada Committee on Theology and Inter-Church and Interfaith Relations fonds, Fonds 568, 2018.135C - box 9 - file 8, Faith Talk 2002.
5. A popular evangelical song introduced in some United Church congregations as a communion hymn is Stuart Townend & Keith Getty, *In Christ Alone*, Thankyou Music (Adm. by CapitolCMGPublishing.com excl. UK & Europe, adm. by Integrity Music, part of the David C Cook family, songs@integritymusic.com), 2001.
6. Missional theology here refers to the legacy of Lesslie Newbigen (The Gospel in a Pluralist Society, 1989) and David Bosche (Transforming Mission, 1991) and their influence on Bishop Rowan Williams in the endorsement of the Fresh Expressions movement in the Church of England in the early 2000s. Inspired by this and other work (particularly in the USA), the "missional movement" is an enormous trend across the church.
7. *Fresh Expressions* is a movement originating in the Church of England and Methodist Church UK in the early 2000s directed toward creating churches for a post-Christian social context. https://freshexpressions.org.uk/ and https://freshexpressions.ca/.
8. Note that in United Church circles, the American missional movement is as, or more, influential than the British movement. This includes the work of missiologist Darrell Guder and the Princeton Theological Seminary as well as evangelical leaders including Alan Roxburgh, Craig Van Gelder, Alan Hirsch, and others.
9. The Edge and its affiliated Embracing the Spirit are networks for resourcing and funding entrepreneurial and other experimental ministries and missions in the United Church of Canada, modelled after Fresh Expressions. https://edge-ucc.ca/.
10. Debbie Johnson and Jamie Holtom, *Bullseye: Aiming to Follow Jesus* (Toronto: United Church Publishing House, 2015).
11. Another popular example of evangelical commitments embraced by congregational life is Mark Greene, *Fruitfulness on the Frontline: Making a Difference Where You Are*, (Downers Grove, IL: Intervarsity, 2017).
12. Phyllis Airhart, *A Church with the Soul of a Nation*, esp. "The Search for a Faith for Sociable Souls," p 102-125.
13. Nadia Bolz-Weber is a pastor and theologian in the Evangelical Lutheran Church, author of several books including, *Pastrix: The Cranky, Beautiful Faith of a Sinner and Saint*, (New York: Jericho Books, 2014).
14. Brian McLaren is an American post-evangelical leader, author of many books, including *Faith After Doubt* (London: St. Martin's Essentials, 2021).

15. Rob Bell is an American evangelical pastor and foundational emergent church figure, author of several books including *Love Wins,* (San Francisco: Harper One, 2011).
16. Donna Bowman is a process theologian with evangelical roots, author of several books, including *The Divine Decision: A Process Doctrine of Election,* (Louisville: Westminster John Knox, 2002).
17. Phillip Clayton is a process philosopher and theologian with evangelical roots, prolific writer, editor and author, including *The Predicament of Belief: Science, Philosophy, and Christian Minimalism,* (Oxford: Oxford University Press, 2011).
18. Thomas Oord is an evangelical independent scholar and writer of, for example, *God Can't: How to Believe in God and Love after Tragedy, Abuse, and Other Evils,* (Grasmere, ID: SacraSage Press, 2018).

The Ecclesial Banquet Table

Chapter Four
Meeting Ecclesial Lived Faith

We are called to be the church[1] —A New Creed, UCC

It is not too much to say that the church saved me. Not in a dramatic one-time-event but in small regular embodied experiences of the gospel—embodied in concrete community— that gave me a place to belong without condition—a community that saw gifts in me and named them and called them out and gave me a place to practice them and hone them and offer them. It was the church: the tangible love and presence and challenge and call of the community that raised me in the way of Jesus... It is the joy and privilege of my life to serve the church and to be part of proclaiming that gospel, of offering that life-giving gift I have received to future generations.
—Michelle Slater[2]

IN HER TESTIMONY, MICHELLE IS BEAUTIFULLY DESCRIBING THE FAITH OF an ecclesial. She is giving witness to a faith anchored in the Body of Christ and manifest both in what she receives from, and gives to, the church. She refers to the church as "home" and as "family." Earlier, Michelle speaks reverently of the sacraments and reflects on the power of sacred music. She identifies her childhood minister as someone who was a central figure in her faith formation, so much so that she followed her example. Not surprisingly, Michelle is an ordained minister of the church, someone with deep respect for the orders of the church and a high sense of the calling and setting apart of those who minister in Christ's name, who embody Christ's church.

Another testimony looks like this:

> Shirley wears a UCW Life Membership pin on her blazer lapel. She taught Sunday School from 1960 to 1985. During that time she served first as an Elder of Session and then on the Board. Personally supportive of every minister the congregation has called, Shirley responded to the growing pastoral care demands of the ageing congregation by starting a seniors' ministry team in 1984, and a Caring Committee in 1987. For fifty years, Shirley has baked for teas and knit for bazaars, washed up in the church kitchen, typed committee minutes, worked at potlucks and Thrift Sales, visited shut-ins, written cards to new parents, new confirmands and the bereaved, read Scripture and served communion, attended Bible Study, and pledged generously. She is one of thousands of women who have done the same.

And another:

> Casper is an engineer in his mid-thirties. He chairs the Board in a congregation he joined less than three years ago after moving from the United States with his young family. Raised in Boston, he went to a Catholic school. Casper connected immediately with the minister; their families have become friends. He and the minister share leadership at "theology on tap" nights. Casper brings two members of the congregation to church who no longer drive. Since joining the congregation, he has also arranged for a new website design and an update to lighting in the building. He speaks eloquently about stewardship, and energetically supports the fundraising run for mission. Though he may not be familiar with the term, a generation ago Casper would have belonged to a group who identified themselves "as one that serves."[3]

The expression of lived faith in these testimonies of the church is obvious: service to the church as a place of identity and belonging.

Chapter Four Meeting Ecclesial Lived Faith

Who are the Ecclesials?

Let us build a house where all are named.
their songs and visions heard, and loved and treasured,
taught and claimed as words within the Word.[4]
—Marty Haugen

Michelle's testimony above provides us with a portrait of an ecclesial: formed in love *by* the church, for loving service *to* the church so that it may flourish into the future. Beautiful continuums weave their way through the ecclesial identity: past, present, and future; giving and receiving; self and community; gift and call. To serve one another, to serve Christ, to serve the church: this is one motion for the ecclesial. The ecclesial stream is made up of Christians who somewhere deep within them have been gifted with the beautiful ancient faith of the One Holy Catholic and Apostolic Church and trust that by the grace of God, the Risen Christ is at work in the world through what the church does simply by being the church.

Ecclesials are on your Boards, your worship committees, in your choir, and on your property committee. They serve committees and courts at every level of the church, and are often in paid accountable ministry. Ecclesials nurture the faith of children and youth as children's ministers, youth and young adult ministers, Sunday school or church club leaders, camp counsellors and their volunteer trainers. In working with congregations and learning to read the operative theologies among them, a sure way to identify the ecclesials is to consider who has keys to the rooms or cupboards in the church building, who deadheads the flowers out front, and who knows where the ladder is. We call them volunteers; they are more accurately servants.

It goes without saying that the majority of people on our pews are ecclesials. This group is so large, its subgroups are worth noting. To see the ecclesials in a more nuanced way helps us to follow the various threads which connect the variations in their lived faith to their operative theologies. Using Faith Talk[5] responses as subtitles below, we see that the ecclesials' lived faith can be animated in four directions: service (*God's family working together*), learning (*discipleship; people who practice Christian faith*), worship (*prayer and praise*), and community (*belonging*). We'll look at these more closely, by focussing on lived experience.

God's Family Working Together

Shirley's portrait above exemplifies a faith lived through service to the Body of Christ—the core identity of the ecclesial. She expresses her faith as *labour* dedicated to build up, to host, govern, share, to care for, to form, and to maintain for the next generation, the covenanted family of faith who gathers at Christ's table of welcome and new life. Most ecclesials will recognize themselves here. They, like Shirley, are the servants of the church, without whom none of us would be here.

The trouble with the word "servant," particularly when taken out of the gospel context, is its relationship with the misuse of power. We must acknowledge that servants and service are not neutral terms but tainted by the historic and on-going realities of involuntary servitude and both under-paid and unprotected service industries, particularly among immigrants, disadvantaged classes, and races, and among women and others inhabiting female gender roles. Given that women shoulder the majority of volunteer work in congregational life, referring to them as servants is extremely problematic. This, in addition to theologies of sacrifice which dominate the church universal, combine to make the church a knotty place for genuinely ecclesial women to express their faith and not be taken advantage of or taken for granted. This must be closely monitored in the growing popularity of hospitality and seniors' ministries which depend disproportionately on a female voluntary labour pool.[6] Properly understood, the imitation or inspiration of Christ is an imitation of *fullness of life through the offering of life*, not an imitation of servitude or sacrifice leading to diminishment. The ecclesial "volunteer," as we call them, is a servant first of Christ, and is united with the Spirit in love for the community of God's beloved people, one whose life flourishes, not deteriorates, in service.

For one shaped by covenanted identity and relationships, there is joy in *shared* work and meaning in *good* work. Though they may be deeply connected to a particular community of faith, it is the church universal ("*God's* family") to whom they belong: if they were not in *this* congregation, they would be in another. A striking example of the ecclesial servant's faith is expressed in the response to the question, "what images, concepts, or practices sustain your faith?"[7] with these three things: the bible, church buildings, good work. The integration of faith and service could not be better expressed.

Often the "good work" to which ecclesials contribute is in support of others beyond the congregation in the neighbourhood or across the world. This generosity through stewardship and support of the church's mission is integral to the ecclesials' lived faith. When it is hands-on and *central* to their lived faith, our schema will place them with the missionals. When it is manifest in justice-seeking and global relationships, we place them with the ecumenicals. When it is simply part of doing what the church does, it reflects the lived faith of the ecclesials.

It is demeaning and ignorant to claim that this expression of lived faith is "for people who like to be busy." Anyone who likes to be busy (and there are many in the church) are busy in every aspect of their lives; they do not need the church to keep them busy. They are busy at church, because they have the Spirit-led gift of loyalty and service to the church universal. Ecclesials are the servants of the church, the glad contributors to the covenantal community to which they belong.

When ecclesials look at the theological banquet, they are sometimes struck with a tinge of resentment. Side by side with the other experiences of lived faith, they have to ask themselves how they were "gifted" with service to the Body when others were given a walk in the woods or the gratification of saving a life! The pastoral responsibilities in surfacing differing operative theologies include attentiveness to such feelings and a capacity to draw out the rich theological interpretations of each stream for the affirmations of faith in each one.

For these ecclesials, the church is the *diakonia*, the servants, God's family *working* together.

Discipleship; People Who Practice Christian Faith

Learning faith and living faith are inseparable. A classic (and currently re-embraced) term, "discipleship" and a newer (inter-disciplinary) term, "practices," capture the integration which is foundational to *formation* of faith, a growth of faithfulness through apprenticeship. For this subgroup of ecclesials, faith is the lived experience of inhabiting the faith, of becoming Jesus' followers, of learning and practicing what it is to be a Christian, of modelling or embodying Christ, individually and corporately. This formation cannot happen without the church—without Scripture, preaching, teaching, and serving. Where else does one learn to be Christian but among them? For many of these ecclesials, the church is the temple, the community set apart from competing values and norms, the place of learning and formation in the way of Christ. Even those who draw a more porous line between the church and the world nonetheless hold different expectations of the Christian community to those of society at large, and both expect and ensure that the church is teacher of Christian life, not simply a place of Christian worship.

> Earl is a retired school principal. He attends church regularly, and serves on the Ministry and Personnel Committee. He prefers academic lectures to participatory bible studies but attends both. He reads widely, from Kwok Pui-Lan to Walter Bruggemann. Though he wouldn't use the word 'disciple' of himself, Earl is both a Christian and a life-long learner, and therefore expects the minister to be a good teacher, a learned preacher, and a model Christian.

Teachers, leaders, and preachers are ecclesials of this sort, living their faith as guides, inquirers, and practitioner/disciples of the Christian life, the Way of Jesus. Here is where the theological schools, centres, and learning circles find themselves—teaching and learning faith as service to the church and world. Here also are the camp leaders, children's ministers, youth ministers, and their volunteers.

Because discipleship practices span the theological banquet of lived faith, we might question why this orientation is lodged here. Beneath the lived faith of the practicing disciple is an implicit theological root wedded to the community of believers. These ecclesials are in church not first because they seek to belong to a family of God's beloved people, but because they are oriented toward growing in faithfulness and Christian virtue. They take their Christian identity seriously in every aspect of their lives and value the place in which it is taught and modelled.

> "I figure that if I pray, I'll learn what prayer is. Right now, I haven't got a clue." Bronwyn is bringing her children to church school because she was raised in church and is grateful for the love that surrounded her as a child and the inspiration she received there to want to do something good with her life and to try to make the world a better place. She is back in "Disciples" class "trying to figure out what was underneath all that good stuff I absorbed as a kid."

The roots of this expression of ecclesial faith are often well interpreted by theologies of Christian virtue and social ethics,[8] Christian practice and discipleship,[9] and in both inherited and emerging expressions of the church as a counter-cultural community of faith formation and practice. For these practicing, disciple ecclesials, the church is *didache*, a community of apprenticeship and learning.

Prayer and Praise

> *In a congregation on Vancouver's North Shore, the introductory bars of the anthem are played while the choir moves from among the pews to the chancel steps. The choir itself is larger than many congregations. I count eighty-seven of them. The youngest is twenty years old; the eldest are octogenarians. There are three generations of several families in the choir and some who have sung on these chancel steps for over fifty years. What does your faith most make you want to do? "Sing," a forty-one-year-old widow replies, smiling. Behind every face, here as in every choir, there is a story that makes every note of praise an act of faith as well as an act of worship. To the left and to the right stands the community in whom these choristers experience the love of God, in front of them a disarming view of the Body of Christ whose open faces are so often the privilege of the preacher alone. These are ecclesials whose ballast of faith is worship. Whether on the pew, at the lectern, at the piano, or in the chancel, ecclesials don't "attend worship;" they "worship."*

These particular ecclesials are difficult to spot unless they are leading worship, yet there are many of them on the pews. They serve on worship committees and contribute to worship leadership, liturgical arts, sanctuary up-keep and care of the sacraments. They attend worship services when away from home and hum hymns by heart. We find a new generation of them now in monastic communities, drawn to daily worship, dipping back into Methodism for prayer books and memorized liturgies. Most who hold a worship-centred operative theology at the theological banquet are ecclesials, though they share this orientation with some spirituals. For these ecclesials the church is the *liturgia*, the act of communal worship.

Belonging

> *Jenny is a thirty-year-old immigrant to Canada from mainland China where she attended a church in Nanjing. On her first Sunday in Vancouver, she walked to the closest church to her home. It happened to be a United Church. Because churches are where Christians gather on Sundays, she fully expected the sincere welcome into the community she received there.*
>
> *Chloe met the minister of the church where she began to go to AA after moving from Winnipeg to Nanaimo. She liked the minister's humour and her non-judgemental tone when she spoke with Chloe about her journey to sobriety and her struggle with self-acceptance and gender identity. Chloe didn't intend to join the congregation, because she wasn't sure she would "qualify" as Christian. The minister said there was no test, that "it's like a family-we-all-wish-we-had," and it was.*
>
> *Abeo was five when he came with his mother to the congregation who sponsored them as refugees fleeing persecution in Nigeria. At the annual meeting a year later, he added to the tree of life prayer poster, "I love my family at St. Andrews."*

The lived faith experience of these and others like them is an important culmination in considering the operative theologies of ecclesials. Most ecclesiologies (theologies of church) begin with the activities of the church, the *how* of worship, hospitality, service, proclamation. But the experience of belonging is of the church's purpose, the *what*. There is a great deal of critique in contemporary church literature about the concept of "belonging" and "family" and the corresponding preoccupation with hospitality and tendency to form impermeable communities of likeness, clique, or kin. Suspending that worthy caution for the moment, it is important to acknowledge that many people on the pew, in moments or over a lifetime, live their faith simply by receiving an unearned gift of love and belonging, the grace of God embodied in a community that has accepted them. The world is not a welcome place for many; a few among the world's unwelcomed or lonely find their way into the arms, acceptance, and affirmation of God's love embodied in the holy friendship of the community of the Risen Christ. Their faith in God is rooted in this concrete experience of love. Whether or not they "give back" as some are so eager to insist, is irrelevant. These ecclesials are not like other ecclesials; their faith is based on what they have received as beloved of God, not on what they appear to be contributing to the on-going life of the Body of Christ. For these ecclesials, the church is the *kononia*, the community of God's love. They are ecclesials in our schema by virtue of their identity as belonging to the Body.

In all, through the words offered by ecclesials across the church, we have a picture of the sub-categories of those who meet God in the gathered community of Christ's Body, the church: those who become the Body by virtue of service to it, those who take on the form of the Body by way of practicing discipleship, those whose experience of corporate worship with the Body is their holy ground of lived faith, and those whose connection with the Body is primarily in receiving the blessing of belonging.

What's in a Name?

I am the church. You are the church. We are the church together.[10]
—Don Marsh

The ecclesial table at the theological banquet is populated by those whose lived faith is inextricably linked to loving and committed service in and with the gathered community, in whom and with whom they experience the presence of God and grow in faith. We should be very clear that the category "ecclesial" does not refer to those whose faith is *in the church*. Like those in each of our five categories, their faith *is in God*. In this instance, God is met, worshipped, and loved in and through service to the Body of Christ. The name "ecclesial" is selected deliberately, because it does not mean "church," a word so often associated with the building or institution. By contrast, the ecclesial, or "assembly of the faithful," nametag is very much about *coming together for faith*, for learning faith, proclaiming it, expressing it in action, nurturing it in the young, and safeguarding its self-offering. Moreover, it is about doing all this *together*. The ecclesial cannot be ecclesial alone, only as part of the *assembly*. So, all of this faith-sharing activity takes place within the gathered community (assembly) of faith, the Body of Christ, which would not exist but for those who, by the work of the Spirit, serve that Body. Remember, the nametags are not definitions. For the sake of argument, all models of church (of which there are many) animated by an ecclesial lived faith wear this label. The ecclesial label, like the "evangelical" nametag, carries negative associations of its own. Every name in this schema has been battered and frayed in some way or another. After decades of decline in the western church, perhaps no other category feels quite as maligned as this one which disproportionately bears both the woeful legacies of institutionalized Christianity and the scars of our critical self-examination.

Flashback

As we like to tell it, the dominant storyline of the denomination's early decades highlights the construction of church after church, the creation of congregation after congregation, across the country. It is true that this church-building enterprise had evangelism in mind and a heart for mission, but the stories we tell of a church in every school catchment, and of Sunday School children spilling out of their classrooms, spells the ecclesial version of the denomination's history. This "shovels in the ground" history is without doubt the anthem of the ecclesial stream, the story of passing the faith from one generation to the next. In truth, the confounding grief of not being able to keep this apparent momentum up is the deep grammar of this same story, one that can be read from the complicated syntax of perpetual decline and the valiant efforts to teach, make attractive, revitalize, and reorganize what it is to be the Body of Christ in Canada. Since letting go over seventy years ago the mandate (though admittedly and tragically not soon enough some of the efforts) to Christianize Canadians, the United Church in British Columbia has not done much evangelical and missional pioneering. The denomination undertook "new church development" projects where demographics pointed to possibilities for congregations to flourish, but until very recently (inspired by Fresh Expressions and mission-shaped-ministry initiatives) we have not adopted a renewed evangelical church-planting project along the lines of pioneering or missional ministry.[11] In fact, the inward turn "from serving [society] to belonging [to one another]"[12] began over sixty years ago, making the church we have inherited one with rather a lopsided Christian calling.

All along, however, it has mattered greatly to church leaders that lay people know the faith in order to live the faith and pass it on. Early on in the denomination's life, the church identified a gap to be filled in biblical and theological knowledge and those trained to teach it.[13] Building lay training centres, beginning with Naramata in 1947, and developing a comprehensive all ages *New Curriculum* from 1949-62 represented fundamentally ecclesial commitments toward faith formation early in the denomination's life and contributed to its strength. BC Conference's commitment to resourcing ministries with children and youth outpaced much of the rest of the denomination and left its very ecclesial mark on several generations of outstanding leaders whose faith has shaped a lineage of disciples of the way of Jesus in this region.

The long and strong ecclesial stream is testament to lay people's life-long service to the church, built of stewardship campaigns, church governance and administration, the development of children, youth, and family ministries, church music and musicians, liturgical renewal, Christian education, and theological education. Records, archives, and collected oral and written histories of the denomination safe-guard this story, as do those who animate the church today—faithful branches of the one true vine. More than any other stream, ecclesial lived faith is passed safely in the minutes and reports, the policies and papers, the hymn books and curricula which the denomination has produced over its lifetime, artefacts of the Body being the Body.

Every generation of this denomination has known decline relative to national population growth, though not all generations were aware of it. The United Church's relationships with the world church, with Canadian and global society, and with its own members have variously and vigorously tested the ecclesial stream's capacity to endure. The effect of those efforts are evident in our time: many congregations are tired, most leaders are tested, the centre may not hold. Yet, faith continues to be inherited, formed, reformed, and shared in an as-yet unbroken stream of siblings and saints—the servants of the church and their distinctly Pauline self-understanding as members of Christ's Body.

An important part of that unbroken stream is each generation's own critical self-reflection about who is and is not shaping the Body in the wholeness into which it is called. From establishing "ethnic ministries" to pledging to become an "inter-cultural church" to challenging systemic racism, white privilege, and supremacy within the church, and from examining the roles of men and women in the church to transcending understandings of gender binaries, ecclesials have desired to have Christ contour the Body rather than allow the limited views within the body to shape the contours of their encounter with Christ. The history of the ecclesial stream is not simply one of "being the Body," but of "becoming the Body" in an ongoing and corporate transformation.

One Line Credo

I believe that God—Creator, Christ, and Spirit—is met and manifest in the beloved community of the church, the Body of Christ, in and for the world.

Figure 6: Ecclesial symbol

If we were to capture this core belief in a symbol, it would be the bread and cup or font and table. The sacraments belong to the Christian church universal, a unifying marker of the communion and calling we experience as the Body of Christ.

The colour is red, conjuring strength. Liturgically it is the colour of the birth of the church at Pentecost.

Distinctive Features: Identity and Community

One holy name professing,
and at one table fed,
to one hope always pressing,
by Christ's own Spirit led.[14]
—Samuel John Stone

Chapter Four Meeting Ecclesial Lived Faith

We remember that for each table of lived faith at the banquet, there is a primary place of relationship with God. This is the landing pad for our love of God, the destination or inclination of the Spirit's nudging within us. So this place of encounter becomes a way to live or express our faith: for the evangelical, it is the stranger to Christ; for the missional, it is the neighbour in need; for the ecumenical, it is the brokenness in the world; for the spiritual, it is the immanence of God. For the ecclesial, the primary place of relationship with God is the called and beloved community of praise, proclamation, love, and service—the church. Ecclesials are glad servants of the on-going life of Christ embodied in the gathered community of God's people; this is where their love of God lands.

Because the gathered community is involved in evangelism, mission, justice-seeking, and spiritual life, the ecclesial has a self-understanding of directly or indirectly participating in all these things. The life and work of the church is indeed their life and work, central to their identity as a person of faith or baptised member of the Christian church. It is therefore difficult for an ecclesial to imagine the reason for any of the other categories. Profoundly ecclesial church leaders may be quite dumbfounded by the whole idea of five operative theologies, five core callings or ways to live one's faith. Surely, the church is made up of *all* the categories, they claim, and to be an ecclesial is to be all the categories combined! Perhaps this befuddlement is a clue to the distinctive feature of the ecclesial. **For ecclesials, the faith community, its identity and its activity are inseparable.** Deep in their bones, they are members of the One Body, the Body of Christ, whom they serve for love of God. This is the beauty of the ecclesials: service is an act of self-offering to that larger body, a building up of the Body, rather than the pursuit of individual aims. The deep structure of baptism creates the grammar of the ecclesials' lived faith: a new community, a new identity, a shared life in the Spirit. Because the formation of this communal identity is a sacred trust and properly lived does not run contrary to the individual freedom in Christ offered to each person in the Body, it leads to a flourishing of life—both individual and shared.

From the outside, the distinctive feature of the ecclesials is **their relationship to, and investment in, the church being the church.** From within this lived faith, we understand that without the church, ecclesials are branches without a vine. Without this embodiment of the Risen Christ, the new community of God's holy people in which, and to which, to belong, there would be nowhere for their love of God to land, no manifestation of Christ to serve, nowhere to preach and teach, to pray and break bread, to share life, to offer care. For those in other categories of lived faith, this is just not so.

> I have a deep belief that we are all a part of the Body of Christ. In my upbringing in the church, there were so many people who cared, who taught, who loved, who served. Through that came the inspiration to do the same, to give back and to model that witness of living the faith with and for others.
> —Jen Cunnings, a Minister of Children and Families in Pacific Mt Region, UCC

If we were to pull on the thread of that love of God expressed through belonging to and serving the Body of Christ, it would be tethered to the lineage of faith itself. Faith is to be taught, modelled, shared, up-held, given in love from one generation to the next. Gathered at this table at the theological banquet are those whose particular, truly catholic identity has been shaped by the hymns and the creeds they know by heart, and the Moderators and minute-takers they know by name. The core features of the ecclesial faith include love for, and belonging to, the formative and transformative community in whom, and with whom, faith is experienced, taught, and incarnated.

Credo Unpacked

> Where two or three are gathered in my name, I am there with them. (Matt 18:20)

What do we believe God is doing that inspires people to live their faith in service to the church? We remember that in every category of the schema, the question about God's agency leans in the direction of life or salvation. "What is God doing?" is shorthand for "how is God being a life-giving, life-redeeming, life-offering God?" In the case of the ecclesials, God is being God in and through the church. Exactly how we imagine this happening is aided by the way in which the witness of the early church captured in Acts and the Epistles, and later in the creeds of the church, is echoed in our lived experience. Various versions of what God is doing in and through the church are creatively combined in the constructive hybridity of beliefs to which a lived ecclesial faith is tethered in our denomination. Without systematically aligning each ecclesial portrait above with biblical and doctrinal expressions, we can nonetheless acknowledge patterns that can be discerned in the collective ecclesial fabric.

What is God doing?
> God—Creator, Christ, and Spirit One—calls a community together who by the power of the Holy Spirit, becomes the Body of Christ, the manifestation of God's life-giving presence in and for the world.

How?
> Through covenanting with those baptized in Christ's name to create a new community in Christ, empowered by the Holy Spirit and commissioned into his ministry.

What does it mean to believe in Christ?
> To believe in Christ is to participate in his on-going life. It is to belong to him, become at-one with him through becoming one with his Body, incorporated through baptism into his Risen life and ministry.

What is the church for?
> The church is not *for* anything; the church's purpose is to *be* the church. Empowered by the Spirit to respond to, participate in, be led by, conform to, proclaim, teach, and make manifest in the world the Body of Christ, the church anticipates the Kingdom of God which by grace we experience in part through sacramental and shared life.

What is the Christian life?
> As members of the Body of Christ who experience companionship in the Spirit and covenantal communion with God, we are commissioned to, and formed for, a shared life of friendship in Christ, worship, discipleship and joyful service.

Christian identity:
> Part of the Body

Christian character:
> Servant

Why I read Scripture:
> Reading the Scriptures in community as texts that are revelatory of Christ's presence and purpose among us is central to shaping Christian life. Biblical stories remind me that I belong to a bigger story and bring meaning to worship, prayer, and discipleship.

Distinctive focus related to sin and grace:
> God's gift of Christ to the world is the grace by which we are given new life through forgiveness (justification) and faith which inspires us to conform to and bear fruits of Christ's life (sanctification) as his Risen Body, the church.

Key Biblical texts:
> 1 Corinthians 12:12 — Members of the One Body
> Matthew 18:20 — Where two or three are gathered

Because an ecclesial is not ecclesial apart from the church, the church will have offered the ecclesial the grammar of faith. You will notice Trinitarian roots here that are implicitly or explicitly fundamental to that grammar. Whether a person or congregation names God directly as God, Christ or Spirit is largely contextual. However, in sacraments and hymnody if not more broadly, this is the most self-consciously Trinitarian table at the theological banquet. The immanent Trinity (the nature of the relationships within God) is experienced and expressed in the ecclesials' lived faith more than in the ecumenical lived faith which stresses the economic Trinity (the nature of God's relationship to creation). There is a trend among some church leaders to reassert God's Trinitarian nature by using the term "the Triune God." This appears to be both a reflection of bourgeoning scholarship and renewed interest in Trinitarian theology and a way of identifying oneself with neo-orthodoxy in a context of evermore blurred theological traditions in Western Protestantism. Whether this language is a meaningful explication of the implicit theology expressive of the ecclesials' lived faith is unknown, based on the language offered through the Faith Talk responses over a decade ago before the term became increasingly popular in our circles. As all five of our categories of lived faith are Christian, they are all Trinitarian, though not identically so, as we will see. In addition to Augustinian formulae, Celtic theology offers Trinitarian language and imagery expressive of the lived faith of many ecclesials. However, most whose lived faith is best expressed in Celtic and Eastern theologies of the Trinity are seated in our schema at what we call the spiritual table.[15]

Gifts

Our ancestors in faith
bequeath to us experiences of their faithful living;
upon their lives our lives are built.
Our living of the gospel makes us a part of this communion
of saints.[16]
—*A Song of Faith*

The distinctive gifts of the ecclesials among us are many: articulate faith, welcome and care, worship and sacrament, and careful stewardship. Wearing as they do, a wider body than their own skin by which to love and serve God, they bear witness to the collective faith we are called to in Christ. Their formation as members of one Body can foster in them a counter-cultural displacement of the self-at-the-centre, a genuinely communal self-understanding that echoes the community of the divine life in whose image we are made. In this way, ecclesials are not teaching us to be a family (though we often use this language); they are demonstrating together what it is to be moulded into a *Body which shapes the self*, rather than a *self which contributes to a body*. Their love for God becomes the sinew, the connecting tissue, which holds the various gifts of the Body together. Collectively, they create tendons of connection, community, and belonging and they do so, through consistent, persistent acts of service to the whole. Their actions—in the kitchen, on the Board, in the choir, in children and family ministry, on the property committee, as ushers and greeters—build the nest that others, who may or may not see the Body ecclesials serve, may call home.

Gifts of God for the people of God. Ecclesials have worked generation after generation to shelter a place where faith in God—Creator, Christ and Spirit—is passed on with love, in word and in deed through embodiment of that love in community. Ecclesials know the traditions of the church's faith well enough to retain, reimagine or release them, all the while cognisant of their meaning and purpose. Above all, they enact those traditions—practice them together. By their own embodied example, ecclesials teach us to eat together, to remember Jesus, to pray and to sing and to give thanks, to read, share and become formed by Scripture, to welcome and care for one another as siblings in Christ, beloved of God.

It is right to give God thanks and praise. While they are the first to remind us that the church is God's blessing to the world, not the work of human hands, it is fair to say that without the lived faith of ecclesials, we would not be having this conversation. We are inheritors of the church that generations of ecclesials, for love of God, have nurtured and safe-guarded over centuries and across the globe. Considering the waves of persecution, dissolution, violence, and disinterest the church has experienced since its inception, this is not to be taken for granted. But it is not with a sense of accomplishment for what it has endured that ecclesials bear the battered name of the church in our time; they, more than any other stream in our schema, carry the communal contrition accrued through the chapters of grievous action and inaction by which the church universal is identified. Bearing both the scars and indictments of its history, ecclesials offer us the lineage of devoted guardians of faith. Their trust in God, and in what God is doing through calling and empowering a people to be Christ's Body, has sung an unceasing song of praise for millennia. True to its word, the ecclesials' gift to the church is the church.

Dangers and Shadows

But if I've not Love's understanding,
If I'm lost to Love's own songs,
My lovely words and thrilling actions are as Gongs.[17]
—Linnea Good

Both the dangers and the shadow for an ecclesial can be misconstrued as strengths. Animating a faith in God's abiding presence in the church through acts of service in and for that beloved community will of course be manifest in efforts to sustain that community, to protect it from internal and external threats. The danger here is that this commitment may slip off course; it might become the drive to succeed. Of course, we desire that the church endure, but when does passing on the faith inadvertently become the pursuit of parochial permanence?

We know of no other context in which to situate the ecclesial but the one marked by the insecurity of being a Christian church in the West at the turn of the 21st century. Even before the threat of COVID-19 closed church buildings in the spring of 2020, the struggle for vitality, even survival, within congregations was commonplace. Survival largely leans toward protecting the church's assets; vitality leans toward the invigoration of its ministries. Dangers lie in both spheres.

The old-fashioned term "maintenance," borrowed from our denomination's past, helps identify the nexus of the conundrum at the heart of the ecclesials' danger. In the early years, "maintenance" referred to the administration, fiscal management, and personnel which supported the work of the denomination. It was the counterpoint to "missions," and a necessity on which the work of the church's ministries depended. Making this distinction was complicated by a more contemporary view. Operations and administration came to be seen as ministries in their own right: a building redevelopment is a ministry, tenants are part of the ministry, the property has a mission, and assets serve as partners in mission. While the principles of the unified budget hold, in addition to the over-work of too few hands for too much activity, the greatest source of fatigue and resentment among ecclesials is rooted here: in the unacknowledged blurring of means and ends. They, of all people, understand revenue generation (what it takes to make ministries *happen*), but they also understand ministry *itself*. Calling property development *mission* when it is maintenance, or rentals *ministry* even when the tenants are teaching fitness, is not lost on an ecclesial. Moreover, it makes light of the core of their faith, which is to secure the teaching of the faith, not the building in which that ministry takes place. An equal and opposite danger to this is the lure of the maintenance when given such stature. Stewarding resources through property upkeep is not ministry, particularly if it is the only one still going on. Ecclesials know this; theirs are the first hearts to break when the carefully maintained properties and assets are not serving the Body of Christ in the world. But the temptation to sustain those properties and assets long after the ministry of the congregation has begun to flag is exacerbated by making maintenance indistinguishable from ministry and mission. This danger flirts with the ecclesials' strength, which is their hope that their legacy of passing the community of faith to the next generation will be realized.

We explore below three current expressions or faces of the pursuit of vitality in congregational ministry based loosely on the popularity of the missional movement and similar trends of practicing the faith: focus on **innovation**, on **discipleship**, and on **outreach**. Each has a unique danger.

Remembering that much of the church is insecure about the current state of affairs, genuinely not knowing what the best "new thing" to do or try might be, there are dangers related to **innovation**. There is the danger of an unwillingness to innovate but that danger is less prevalent than the seduction of novelty. There is a danger that novelty becomes attractive for its own sake; in the absence of other criteria, the church invests simply in those things which look different enough from the-church-as-we-know-it to qualify as "new ways of being church." Innovation needs ecclesials, those who carry the deep grammar of Body of Christ in their bones, to feel their way into new forms. The danger, of course, is that ecclesials feel blamed for the situation they face and thereby lack the confidence to reach deep into their faith to guide the church, and instead capitulate to whims or are excluded from the conversations about innovation altogether.

With respect to **discipleship**, the orientation among ecclesial leaders to take up the formation of disciples of Christian practice reflects the wisdom that we *act our way to new ways of thinking* in addition to *thinking our way toward news ways of acting*. What could go wrong with teaching the foundations of the faith through walking the way of faith? The danger in this occurs only when the context in which the formation is set is too small. If the backdrop is parochial, Christianity becomes a personal attribute, family identity, or lifestyle choice rather than the powerful and transformational call the ecclesial leader is hoping to extend to follow the way of Jesus into the world. The *purpose* and *context* of discipleship must be kept deep and wide for the ecclesial faith to flourish. While spiritual practices belong to every aspect of one's life (the orientation of spirituals in our schema), this does not mean that the biblically and doctrinally-based discipleship programmes should be domesticated for appeal. Certainly, cooking and walking can be core *contemplative* Christian practices (for spirituals), but they are recreational for ecclesials. An exception here would be Ministers of Children and Families who know how to bring the practices of faith home in habits, virtues, actions, and intentions. The ecclesials' shadow to appeal to the many may interfere with the trend to take up the rigours of being formed for discipleship in and by Christ's broken Body.

Finally, with respect to the reinvigoration of outreach ministry brought on by missional movements, here again the danger lurks inside the strength. The church is a "called out" community, an *ek-klesia*, formed as the Body of Christ for the world. There are dangers in using missional projects as strategies for growth rather than fostering them as an integral part of faith. Whether the outreach is faithful or strategic is a question which haunts many fresh expressions projects, particularly those launched as spokes of an ecclesial hub. The danger of a reinvigorated outreach by way of the missional trend rests in being driven more by the need to offer opportunities to do good and to feel good than to respond to perpetual and intermittent crises with the sustained and sophisticated attention required to do so respectfully and appropriately. Ecclesials are susceptible to this, as their shadow illustrates.

We remember that shadows are always only a hair's breadth from a gift. They emerge *because* of the gift, not in opposition to it. We've acknowledged that the ecclesials' experience of union with God through becoming and serving Christ's Body expresses itself in the gift of tireless stewardship of the life and work of the community of faith, including its membership, property, and vitality. This is experienced as the ecclesials' determination to endure, an expression of the lived faith that meets God and serves Christ through the gathered people of God across time and space. We hinted above at what happens when this determination to endure turns to desperation to endure. The temptation under duress is to remain active at any cost; the result is, quite literally, to lose the plot. When ecclesials lose sight of Christ's Body, they see only individual bodies. As people oriented toward welcome, hospitality, and community, the stress or threat of decline turns desperate ecclesials toward "needs-based" ministry. Ecclesials ask themselves what would make people happy. What would make them join? What would make them stay? What do they want? We know this is a shadow, because it leads away from life, not toward it. It leads very subtly to self-love, to a promotion of the merits of belonging to "us" without a sense of being conduits to Christ's life at the centre of the congregation's life.

Antidote

Come, walk among us, Holy friend.[18]
—Brian Wren

What antidote exists for the ecclesials' particular shadow, its orientation to endure through appealing to people's wants? What is at the root of that which manifests as human *want*? If we don't leave that question to psychology, it belongs to the ecclesial. The ecclesials' lived faith is tethered to the conviction that at the table, all will be fed. *All who hunger, gather gladly. Jesus Christ is living bread.* When ecclesials are grounded in the sure knowledge that it is not by them whom people seek to be fed, but by Christ embodied among them, Christ who transcends their inadequacies and makes food of friendship to feed the hungry with good things, they will not fall into the shadow of their own self-reliance. They will not assume to be and do themselves what Christ has only ever meant them to be and do through him. When the ecclesials lose their way, they need the good news that the "new thing" God is doing is renewing them daily to be the Body that is more than the sum of its parts.

At the theological banquet, the antidote to the shadow of the *ecclesial* is the authentic, daily renewed, scripturally-informed faith of the *evangelical*. Centred on the message of the gospel on which the faith is founded, worry and distraction about how to become popular enough to share the gospel is displaced by the confidence that comes from believing it. Faith is not magic; it may not renew the church the way we imagine or envision, but without it, there is no point in doing anything at all.

We are speaking here not of the rather polarizing efforts to "put Christ back at the centre of the church" which is reflective of broad-based renewed popularity of neo-orthodoxy, though this may be a reflection of the antidote in some form. Rather, we are speaking of the genuine call to depth of faith (not doctrine) as the core antidote to a shadow that is cast over faith when it bears the scars of the institutional and human legacies of having missed the mark of the ecclesial lived faith's deepest desire: that faith be embraced, celebrated, grown, and passed on. Depth of faith will grow in the hands of the beautiful and authentic life-in-the-Spirit, typified by those who walk with Jesus (our evangelicals) as well as those who seek wisdom in Christ (our spirituals). The least likely meeting place on our spectrum is here: evangelical meets spiritual in offering an antidote to the ecclesial shadow of doubt and superficiality.

Notes

1. "A New Creed," *The Manual of the United Church of Canada*, 20.
2. Used with permission, this is an excerpt from Michelle's testimony from the panel presentation (May 26 morning) at the BC Conference Annual Meeting, *How Big is Our Tent?* University of British Columbia, Vancouver, May 25-28, 2017.

3. As One That Serves (AOTS) was the name of the United Church of Canada's national association of local men's ministry of service organizations, active from 1923 to the mid-1970s, and disbanded as a national body in 2019.
4. Marty Haugen, "Let Us Build a House," in *More Voices,* (Toronto and Kelowna: United Church Publishing House and Woodlake Books, 2007), 1.
5. United Church of Canada Archives, United Church of Canada Committee on Theology and Inter-Church and Interfaith Relations fonds, Fonds 568, 2018.135C - box 9 - file 8, Faith Talk 2002.
6. This point argued in Ann Morisy, *Journeying Out: A New Approach to Christian Mission* (London: Continuum, 2004), especially chapter 5, "The Suburban Challenge," 95.
7. Faith Talk 2002 archives.
8. Examples of virtue and social ethics influencing this generation would include Alasdair MacIntyre, *After Virtue* (Notre Dame: University of Notre Dame Press, 1981) and Robert Bellah, *Habits of the Heart: Individualism and Commitment in American Life* (Berkeley: University of California Press, 1985).
9. For example, Craig Dykstra and Bass, D.C, "A theological understanding of Christian practices," in M. Volf and D.C. Bass (eds.), *Practicing Theology* (Grand Rapids, MI: Eerdmans, 2002), pp 13-32, and Dorothy Bass' *Practicing Our Faith : A Way of Life for a Searching People* (Minneapolis: Fortress, 1998).
10. Donald S. March, *We are the Church,* (Chicago: Publishing Company, 1972).
11. Though revitalizing the church has been a constant concern in BC Conference for over fifty years, the *Water Project* in the 1990s and the *Emerging Spirit* campaign in the early 2000s brought missional and evangelical concerns to the attention of ecclesials.
12. Phyllis Airhart, *A Church with the Soul of a Nation,* 204.
13. This point presented in John Young "A Golden Age: The United Church of Canada, 1946-1960" and Sandra Beardsall's "Whether Pigs Have Wings: The United Church of Canada in the 1960s" chapters in Don Schweitzer (ed.) *The United Church of Canada: A History* and in Phyllis Airhart, *A Church with a Soul of a Nation,* p 172.
14. Samuel John Stone, "The Church's One Foundation" in *Voices United,* 331.
15. Catherine MacLean, "The Triune God," in *TheTheology of the United Church of Canada.* (Waterloo: Wilfred Laurier Press, 2018) 21-50.
16. "A Song of Faith," *The Manual of the United Church of Canada.*
17. Linnea Good, *The Greatest of These,* (Toronto: Borealis Music, 1992).
18. Brian Wren, *How Great the Mystery of Faith,* (Chicago: Hope Publishing, 1989).

Chapter Five
Living Ecclesial Faith

Congregational Snapshot

> We are now a family of which Christ is the head;
> Though unseen he meets us here in the breaking of the bread.[1]
> —Bryan J. Leech

"ALL ARE WELCOME." THE ECCLESIAL MAY ADD TO THIS SENTENCE IN A number of ways: to become part of God's family, to learn the way of Jesus, to worship with us every Sunday at 10:30, but these three words are ones which capture not the complete description, but the distinctive feature of the ecclesial congregation. The sentence means "join us." Remember, for an ecclesial community, faith is lived by being with and inviting people into a beloved community of the church. A congregation of ecclesials is made up of Christians who believe the Risen Christ is present to and in the world *through* the church. So what is there to do more critical than to continue to be the church?

Log-on to your congregation's website or Facebook page. What do you see? Is there an image there of the building which shelters the beloved community who meet together here and, by God's grace, experience new life? Or an image of the minister with children gathered around for a story of faith? How do you photograph the body of Christ? Countless hundreds of congregational websites and Facebook or Instagram pages display photo galleries that spell **ecclesial** through depicting prized church buildings, beloved faces unknown to the outsider, smiling volunteers holding paint brushes, rakes, or serving spoons, a calendar of events listing Bible study, knitters group, and an upcoming thrift sale. There may be announcements about meetings scheduled or cancelled, requests for volunteers or baked goods, and possibly a link to sermons. Some websites feature a portrait of a choir or simply an empty sanctuary with the communion table set. The minister and staff are displayed and described. All these words and images and the activities to which they point are hallmarks of an ecclesial congregation. They indicate a community whose lived faith is expressed in being for one another, and welcoming others to become, the living church. Yet each and all the images together cannot help but fail to communicate what can only be experienced in the heart of an ecclesial. Like water becomes wine, like bread becomes life, the community becomes the church. This cannot be captured on a page. Ecclesials find it hard to believe that only ecclesials understand an ecclesial website!

Given the challenges facing congregations stewarding ageing properties with fewer pledges, and committed to passing on a faithful congregation of Christ's church to the next generation, energy is focussed in two directions: on maintaining the physical space and on the quality and shape of what happens in the space—in worship, faith formation, and community life. In terms of the building, this involves sharing space (tenants), renovating space (capital campaign), or selling the space (amalgamation or relocation). In terms of what happens inside it, this means striving for excellence, or novelty, or both (appropriate budget and staffing). There is, for many, a painful discrepancy between those preoccupations and the experience of "companionship in the Spirit and covenantal communion with God," manifest "shared life of friendship in Christ, worship, discipleship, and joyful service" at the core of ecclesial lived faith.

The snapshot of the ecclesial congregation and leader includes this discrepancy because it is this gap between the call of the ecclesial and the immediate concerns and affairs of the ecclesial. In truth, the day to day demands of congregations and their leaders frequently obscure and distract the lived faith of ecclesials with pressures particular to this century and this continent.

Sacraments

One bread, one body, one Lord of all[2]
—John Foley

Chapter Five Living Ecclesial Faith

Charlotte Caron[3] presents four theologies of baptism which combine to create the web of roots beneath the ecclesial lived faith. Informing the lived faith of the *belonging*-focussed ecclesial, is an implicit theology of baptism which stresses the grace of God's freely given love to the baptized. The ***service***-oriented, family of God ecclesials may implicitly understand baptism as symbol of covenant, a theology which stresses the relationship we enter at baptism, one that demands something of us and is not simply a gift. The ***discipleship***-focussed ecclesials would share this view, and would include those who favour believers' baptism over infant baptism for this reason. They may also implicitly hold a theology of baptism which is not focussed as much on the individual as on the church as a whole. If the faith of the church expressed in discipleship is God's gift to the world, baptism is about building the church through grafting another life to the vine, Christ's ongoing life in the world. For the ***worship***-oriented ecclesials, any or all of the above theologies of baptism, and those below of communion, will connect their lived faith with roots deep in the rich soil of Christian sacramental theologies.

Given its orientation to the community of Christ, we expect baptism to be central to the ecclesial stream. An interesting inner contradiction emerges from deep within the ecclesials' desire for all to belong to the family of faith: baptism cannot be the focal point of welcome and identity if this creates the reality or perception of a two-tiered community (baptised and not). In reading the lived faith of ecclesials, the defining feature of the "church" through which God is present and active in the world does not appear to rest on sacramental initiation but on formation and belonging. This affirms observations made of Protestantism more broadly.[4] It may also be indicative of the ecclesials' experience of the sacrament of shared life within the congregation, something which includes but exceeds the formal sacraments and is felt more holistically in the activities of congregational life in its entirety.[5]

As with baptism, interpretations of the sacrament of communion vary. In all, communion itself is central to the corporate identity at the heart of the ecclesials' lived faith; the shared table is symbolic and demonstrative of the shared life in which they experience the unconditional love of God, formation in the way of Christ, and union through the Holy Spirit. The lived theology of ***belonging*** oriented ecclesials would be well expressed by celebration-style liturgies which carry the implicit theology of acceptance into a community of love, something for which to give thanks. ***Service***-oriented ecclesials are most likely to be drawn to those communion liturgies which stress community and covenant. In particular, the *formality* of the service of communion communicates the serious intention to keep covenant.[6] Liturgies that are remembrance-focussed and thereby bring Christ's presence close, including his friendship and ministry as well as his death and resurrection, would appeal to the lived faith experience of the **discipleship-**oriented ecclesials.

Trends and Sources: What Else is Going on?

While not universally so, it must be said that a distinctive trend, or better, *feature* among many ecclesials in this moment is grief. For ecclesials, the word "church" means them. Ecclesials bear the weight not only of inheriting "the church" at a time when it is rightly dismantling the colonial and imperialist foundations both beneath and currently alive within institutionalized Christianity, but also in a period of precipitous decline. For the ecclesial, the church itself is a revelation of God's redeeming love and purpose so the news that the church could disappear by intention or by accident is not an interesting evolution in Christian life, but rather a devastating failure to pass the church to the next generation. Moreover, it is a fissure in the holy ground on which they most meaningfully and powerfully experience life in God. Pastoral leaders know that this profoundly affects the lives of their ecclesials. A proposal to sell a church building or the elimination of roles and responsibilities through centralized governance are experienced as serious and compounded losses and failures. Their spiritual crisis stems not from the notion that God has failed them, but that they have failed God.

Not all ecclesials experience this moment as one of loss and crisis. Some feel energized by the possibilities and opportunities afforded by the hinge time in which they are experiencing their life of faith.[7] It is a time of reformation and revitalization in the Body of Christ and they are on board as servants of the shifting sands of ecclesial landscape. Both the grief and the vision live side by side, as we see in what follows.

The Third Thing

As we saw above in the congregational snapshot, given the stresses imposed by the current decline in church involvement, the ecclesial congregation's core commitment to faithful and vital longevity presents most congregations with two enormous concerns: not to lose the building and not to disappear within it. These are not as pragmatic as they appear. For an ecclesial, these are matters of faith—faith which is lived in service to the church. To address these concerns, ecclesials at every level of the church have been, and continue to be disproportionately engaged in four significant projects:

Not losing the site:

- Building developments (sales, property redevelopments, mixed-use building developments)
- Revenue generation (thrift stores, rentals, tenants, concert venue, spending cuts)
- Not losing the people:
- Worship and faith formation excellence and novelty ("Godly Play," "messy church," pub church, technologies, musicians)
- Hospitality and welcoming ministries (seniors, cafés, public space, gardens, social media)

These four tasks take an untold amount of energy and skill. A wide-angle lens on the denomination would capture innumerable consultants, permanent and contracted staff and volunteer hours spent on these activities increasingly over the past two or three decades. It is difficult for contemporary ecclesials to consider this a trend rather than a norm. Ecclesial church leaders (this is nearly redundant but there are some church leaders whose centre of spiritual gravity lies elsewhere on the schema) continue to search within and beyond the denomination for resources to aid them in addressing these two areas of concern regarding acquiring and maintaining the physical and personal resources for ministry. Their search invariably brings them to a third preoccupation. Beyond not losing the building and not losing the people, ecclesial leaders are committed to offering the church a source of vitality, an articulation of *why* to gather. They are always in an earnest and painstaking search for that "third thing," the purpose-driven energy or the mission which presents itself in every generation, every era, as the framework, approach, trend or theology which drives the other two concerns. In this way, ecclesials are behind everything from the new curriculum to tent-making to work-place ministry to woman-church to new church development to partners in mission to practices of faith.

This vitality or core goes by a few names in this moment, as in every chapter of the church's life. This particular moment's "third thing" or articulation of purpose embraced and advanced by ecclesials, is far from new. The interpretation of the church it offers is that of the church *belonging to God's mission* in the world, thereby challenging our view of mission as a *project of the church*. In this way, it argues, mission is a *divine "project"* of which the church is part. While in no way a new theology, it is being popularly embraced in our time. We are speaking here of the wide, varied, and overlapping scene of the Fresh Expressions and the "missional church" movement, including some aspects of the emerging church. Ecclesial leaders are studying these movements, following their leaders, and reading the associated literature not because the other two enormous pieces of work have been handled, but because some handle on the "why" makes the tremendous burden of "how" a meaningful endeavour. What happens when ecclesials encounter this missional ecclesiology in our context? Without being drawn into a comprehensive overview, a glance at the landscape into which ecclesials are venturing might be useful.

Keeping it Ecclesial

Our considerations about the ecclesials' two major projects above is a good entrée into the conversation about the emerging, pioneering, and missional church movements introduced in our look at trends in the evangelical lived faith. If the up-keep of the buildings and the labour for the ministries housed within them were secure, what would ecclesials do to be the body of Christ? Simplistically, that is more or less what happened when the Fresh Expressions movement was launched in the Church of England in the early 2000s under the leadership of Archbishop Rowan Williams. In an effort to turn faith communities outward, to remedy a dying model of church, and redirect its preoccupations, funding was made available for the church to be the church, freed from legacy buildings and beleaguered congregations. These were and are led by "pioneers" (British term) recruited to experiment with *new forms of ecclesial communities* which would attract people to the Christian faith who had not yet encountered it, and build ways of being the church free from the burdens of trying not to lose the site or the few people who gather there. Those drawn toward pioneering or church-planting (UK) or missional and neighbourhood Christian presence (USA) are largely lay leaders with entrepreneurial skills (or courage to develop them) combined with an evangelical lived faith. In denominations in which such lay people may be called into and trained for such ministry, these initiatives have taken root. In our denomination, however, the responsibility for instigating such initiatives lies largely with paid accountable ministers, fewer of whom have an evangelical lived faith than an ecclesial one, and all of whom are by nature of their office, responsible for the other two preoccupations related to the health and well-being of communities of faith: property and members.

Roughly speaking, two things happen when Fresh Expressions, pioneering, emerging forms of church, or other missional projects land in *ecclesial* soil: new ministries and renewed ministries. We can differentiate these two manifestations of the ecclesial embrace of the Fresh Expressions or missional trend by whether they have a secondary energy: some are more evangelical/missional and others are solidly ecclesial. We see Fresh Expressions-like ministry projects in this denomination in what our schema would name their more **evangelical/missional** form, for example, in planting new churches and offering new property-less ministries in the community. We see the Fresh Expressions movement influence in its more **ecclesial** form, for example, in offering programmatic and liturgical renewals like Messy Church services. Whether we see one manifestation of the trend or another depends largely on the leaders' lived faith (or courage to go outside it).

We see training and resourcing in *both* directions inspired by these two interpretations of what the missional movement has to offer the church. For example, the Fresh Expressions UK website includes pioneering training (for new forms of church) *as well as* support for church building projects and children's worship resources (for renewed ministries). Likewise, the United Church Edge (inspired by Fresh Expressions) website, for example, offers grants and coaching for "renewing" congregations *alongside* opportunities for "pitching projects," our denomination's equivalent to entrepreneurial pioneering. Either way, the operative theology motivating this movement is largely ecclesial: finding ways to pass a vital and faithful church to the next generation. Operative theologies are exactly that, they are the *modus operandi* of those who carry them. Of course an ecclesial will be ecclesial, even when attempting to embrace an evangelical project or a missional world-view!

When the lived faith or operative theology remains ecclesial, which it tends to do in the hands and hearts of most church leaders, no matter how Fresh or Edgy the third thing may be, we find ecclesial leaders embracing this literature and adopting or adapting network resources in three over-lapping areas related to ecclesially-motivated outcomes stemming from an ecclesial lived faith: innovation (of ways of being the Body of Christ), discipleship (to form and live as the Body of Christ), and outreach (to express the love of the Body of Christ).

Innovation

Very simply, ecclesial innovation refers to novel forms of church community and worship.[8] Included in this is the possibility of imagining a church in "pieces." For example, one could imagine stand-alone worship without connection to stewardship and mission (jazz church or other arts-based gatherings for worship), or a combination of faith formation and community without worship (pub church, dinner church, or a community of faith connected to physical activity or sport).[9] Estock and Nixon[10] refer to this as "un-bundling" the marks of the church. We might also use the language of hub and spoke to describe this trend: a region, network or congregation serves as the hub (including the financial resources, legal status if needed, etc.) and the spoke functions with some independence as a "trial balloon" for a new expression of anything from an ancient form of liturgy, to table-community, to community service, to arm's length or inter-congregational faith formation. Here, ecclesial leaders are enabling parts of the church to drive the vitality or missional core of the congregation or faith community by trying their wings without the cumbersome package that includes revenue generation and property up-keep, just as the Fresh Expressions movement envisioned. The hub remains devoted to securing the resources to hold a roof over a place of worship, community, teaching, and service while at the same time sending out spokes of ecclesial innovation for ministries not undertaken in the hub. Over time, the hub is potentially transformed from the spokes inward. Such ecclesials have benefitted enormously from generous financial support at the (former) Conference, Presbytery and national levels for such innovations. Providing financial means is one way ecclesials with little or no innovative spirit can fuel the fresh church while maintaining the inherited church.

By their nature, ecclesials will have an eye to and a heart for securing identity (in Christ) and building community through whatever the innovation might be. Often seeded by evangelicals, the new shoots of Christian community become ecclesial in our schema only insofar as they are corporate—have a Body—among whom to belong and to serve. It is not enough for ecclesials that individuals practice rituals alone or share testimonies on a personal blog. Nor does it line up with their lived faith to have a barber shop or bakery as living witness to faith (as it would an evangelical). To innovate as an ecclesial is complicated business and for this reason, rare by comparison to what we in our schema would consider evangelical missions like cafés, art installations, bookstores, and comedy shows—beautiful and novel ways of sharing the gospel which may or may not lead to becoming even a temporary expression of the Body.

Discipleship

Gaining momentum ecumenically over the past fifty years, the missional agenda is premised on the assertion that the church is an instrument of *God's mission*, not that mission is an activity of *God's church*.[11] The missional movement is an ecclesiological movement that seeks to align the activities of the church with God's activities in the world. In the hands of ecclesials, the missional movement is a discipleship movement. In its focus on equipping people for participation in God's mission, it builds disciples. For this reason, many ecclesial leaders whose lived faith expresses itself in faith formation are drawn to "missional church" literature, networks and resources. Nearly ten years after the launch of "Mission-Shaped-Ministry" in the United Reformed Church (UK) for example, its 2020 national program, "Walking the Way," is a life-long learning initiative which is "about being Christ-centred and seeing our discipleship lived out every day."

> *We are called to proclaim and embody God's Kingdom, yet sometimes it seems as if the Church has been side-tracked; over-concerned about maintaining our buildings and institutions, or organising the coffee rota, rather than focusing on the teachings of Jesus and working out what they mean for each of us as we try to live the Jesus way of extravagant love, scandalous grace and radical actions. It's time for change. It's time to walk the way.*[12]
> —Walking the Way, URC

In the hands of ecclesials, the movement inspired by an operative theology that interprets God's activity to be "at loose in the world," this movement will not immediately take people out of the building and into the streets (where our schema's missionals are, as we will see shortly). Rather, it turns its focus toward forming disciples for their lives of Christian service (in the world). Forming disciples requires teaching, modelling and practicing the faith—all reflections of the lived faith of ecclesials. Whether leaders use denominational resources like "Walking the Way" or Anderson and Bott's "Invitation to the Christian Life"[13] or popular resources on the evangelical Missional Church Network website, the focus is on faith formation, or more fashionably, "becoming disciples." In this way, when the missional movement meets genuinely ecclesial congregations, as one would expect, discipleship looks very ecclesial, focussing on practices of welcome, hospitality and worship. By embracing the missional church identity as disciples of Jesus, even those perennially ecclesial activities such as greeting, coffee hour, worship leadership, teaching, and the stewardship of congregational life can be recast and reengaged as acts of discipleship, along with discipleship activities of day to day life at home, in the community, and in the world.

Outreach

So does this "missional church" ever become mission the way we used to think of mission? We must remember that *mission* here refers to the purposes of God which commission the church to be a sent people, equipped as disciples in the world. Within the ecclesial lived faith, there is deep care for the world the church serves. Those who have a heart for community ministry are led to the good work of offering presence, care, and support to neighbourhoods where there is need. We will meet them in earnest in the next chapter on what we call **missionals** in our schema. Obviously, the denomination has never been without a fully operative missional lived faith in the sense in which we are using it in our schema—the lived faith turned outward toward neighbour. It is interesting to note however, that though the evangelical churches came later to community ministry, and to social justice in particular, than the reformed churches from which the United Church, in part, emerged, it appears to be from evangelicals that denominational are adopting it in practice as a core method or principle for new or renewed energy in congregational life. Here we see ecclesial leaders following, for example, the New Parish Collective[14] and Alan Roxburgh,[15] local and popular training leaders in the movement inspired by the missional ministry taught in the South African context, proliferated by the Anglican and reformed churches in the UK and USA,[16] but now made contextually sensitive to the western North American context and often identified in this literature as the post-Christendom context. This work inspires neighbourhood asset mapping and partnerships along with being a pastoral presence in the community (as we saw in the chapter previous on evangelical lived faith). In so doing, some such leaders are ecclesials who are leading their congregations out of the building and into the streets in what becomes a reinvigorated outreach ministry for congregations whose few and tired hands have slowly let it go. For others, identifying those beyond the congregation who participate in God's mission of care, healing and justice in their neighbourhood inspire and renew energy for partnerships not previously imagined. The theological diversity within the missional movement creates opportunity for the ongoing constructive, adaptive work every church leader engages implicitly or explicitly in reading the operative theologies of *both* the resources they are using *and* their congregations in order to nurture the genuinely *lived* faith in and of their communities. In other words, using missionally-inspired ministry directives for stepping-up outreach in an ecclesial congregation will look different from using missionally-inspired resources to launch a mission-first community of faith in partnership with social entrepreneurships and service agencies in the local community. In our schema, only the first of these examples would fall under the ecclesial banner; the second, under *missional*.

Beauty, Faith, and Justice

Finally, not all ecclesial congregations are influenced by the triad of innovation, discipleship and reinvigorated outreach stirred by the missional or Fresh Expressions era. A trend has emerged from within united and uniting churches and most dominantly in the long established ecclesial communions like the Church of England or Anglican tradition, which have long lived with the dynamic inter-play of what our schema is calling the **ecumenical** and the **spiritual** lived faiths. Here, the commitment to social justice deep within the denomination, if not actively engaged in the communities of faith, props the ecclesial heart open to the world, while at the same time those communities of faith are plumbing the depths of their faith with the help of the ancient sibling of faith—the arts. In this case, using the language of our schema, the congregation is probably more spiritually than ecclesially or missionally aligned. We will see below that congregations possessing a spiritual operative theology are embracing other core principles for vitality including contemplative life, intentional marrying of faith and the arts, and forms of worship appealing to embodied spiritual life such as forest church. Drawn more downward than outward, these congregations who are shaped by a spiritual lived faith have strong identities as sacred spaces and are more inclined to offer their communities sacred music and sacred space than pub nights and neighbourhood clean-ups. While the ecumenical and spiritual lived faith in our schema most definitely overlaps, it is in ecclesial communities—congregations—where this overlap is made manifest most beautifully: love calls us to attend to the realities of this world (ecumenical) and beauty is the master teacher of that attentiveness (spiritual).

In every respect, the leader must *read* the faith of the community in order to *lead* the faith of the community. How are ecclesials in the congregation being offered opportunity to live their faith in *service* to both the new and renewed life of the Body of Christ for the sake of the church's on-going life as a beloved community of faithful Christian servants? Is "messy church," gourmet coffee, beer with the bible study, or voluntary snow shovelling an avenue to deepen the lived faith of a community? Regardless of the *popularity* of movements, trends, and faces on the speakers' circuit, it is their *operative theology* that will either support, hinder, or muddle the ecclesial congregation in their beautiful commitment to love God in a shared Body and to see the church safely into its future for other hearts to hold.

Lived Faith	Being the Body of Christ together through welcome, worship, formation and service
What is God doing?	God - Creator, Christ and Spirit One - calls a community together who by the power of the Holy Spirit, becomes the Body of Christ, the manifestation of God's life-giving presence, in and for the world.
How?	Through covenanting with those baptized in Christ's name to create a new community in Christ empowered by the Holy Spirit and commissioned into his ministry.
What does it mean to believe in Christ?	To believe in Christ is to participate in Christ's on-going life. It is to belong to and become at-one with Christ through becoming one with Christ's Body, incorporated through baptism into Christ's Risen life and ministry.
What is the church for?	The church is not for anything;I the church's purpose is to be the church. Empowered by the Spirit to respond to, participate in, be led by, conform to, proclaim, teach, and make manifest in teh world the Body of Christ, the church anticipates the Kingdom of God which by grace we experience in part through sacramental and shared life.

Chapter Five Living Ecclesial Faith

What is the Christian life?	As members of the Body of Christ who experience companionship in the Spirit and covenantal communion with God, we are comissioned to, and formed for a shared life of worship, discipleship, joyful service, and friendship in Christ.
Christian identity	Member of the Body
Christian character	Servant
Why I read Scripture	Reading the Scriptures in community as texts that are revelatory of Christ's presence and purpose among us is central to shaping Christian life. Biblical stories remind me that I belong to a bigger story and brings meaning to worship, prayer, and discipleship.
Distinctive focus related to Sin and Grace	God's gift of Christ to the world is the grace by which we are given new life through forgiveness (justificaiton) and faith which inspires us to conform to and bear fruits of Christ's life (sanctification) as his Risen Body, the church.
Key Biblical texts	1 Corinthians 12:12 Matthew 18:20
Strengths	Commitment to service, belonging, faith formation
Shadow	consumer-driven
Antidote	Authentic community of the gospel: evangelical

Table 4: Ecclesial

Notes

1. Bryan Jeffery Leech, "We Gather Here," in *Voices United*, 469.
2. John Foley, "One Bread, One Body," in *Voices United*, 467.
3. Charlotte Caron, *Eager for Worship: Theologies, Practices, and Perspectives on Worship in the United Church of Canada* (Toronto: United Church of Canada, 2000) McGeachy Papers No. 7.
4. This observation about the reach of sacramentally-grounded faith beyond congregational life and practice is made by Phyllis Tickle in *The Great Emergence: How Christianity is Changing and Why* (Grand Rapids: Baker, 2008) and Diana Butler Bass' *Christianity After Religion: The End of Church and the Birth of a New Spiritual Awakening*, (New York: Harper Collins, 2012).
5. As observed also by William Kervin in "Sacraments and Sacramentality in the United Church of Canada," in *The Theology of the United Church of Canada*, 223-250.
6. Caron, *Eager for Worship*.
7. Among church leaders taking hold of the moment with creativity and enthusiasm is John Pentland in *Fishing on the Other Side*, (Toronto: The Edge, 2015).
8. Fresh Expressions https://freshexpressions.org.uk/ and Edge https://edge-ucc.ca/ websites offer some examples of innovation.
9. Examples found in Casper ter Kuile, *How We Gather*, https://caspertk.files.wordpress.com/2015/04/how-we-gather.pdf.
10. Examples found in Beth Ann Estock and Paul Nixon, *Weird Church: Welcome to the Church in the 21st Century*, (Cleveland: Pilgrim Press, 2016).
11. Reference here is to missional theology for a post-Christian context mentioned above, the legacy of Lesslie Newbigen (The Gospel in a Pluralist Society, 1989) and David Bosche (Transforming Mission, 1991) and their influence in Britain and the United States on contemporary evangelical and mainline missiology. For example, Alan Roxburgh, Craig Van Gelder, Tim Keel, and Darrell Guder.
12. Walking the Way (United Reformed Church) leaflet, https://urc.org.uk/images/WalkingtheWay/documents/A5-WtW-leaflet-2017.pdf , URC London, England, 2017.
13. Dave Anderson and Richard Bott, *Invitation to Christian Life*, (Coquitlam, BC: Becoming: Resources for Jesus People, 2014).
14. The New Parish Collective is a networked community committed to innovative missional ministries in neighbourhoods. https://parishcollective.org/about/. See also Dwight J. Friesen, Paul Sparks, Tim Soerens *The New Parish* (Downers Grove: Intervarsity, 2014).
15. Alan Roxburgh, see note 11. For example, his *Joining God, Remaking Church, Changing the World: The New Shape of the Church in Our Time*, (New York: Morehouse, 2015).
16. See note 11.

The Missional Banquet Table

Chapter Six
Meeting Missional Lived Faith

To love and serve others[1] —A New Creed

[W]e hear far too many stories that leave claw marks on our hearts. If we could end addiction today, we would. If we could prevent all forms of abuse, we would do that, too. But we can't. By being here, by opening our doors and welcoming people inside, we can then help them address their addiction. When people hide in the shadows, they face addiction alone. But when they come into the light, we can help them find a healing path. Nobody, regardless of their current state, should be walking this path alone.
—*Don Evans*[2]

DON EVANS SPOKE ABOVE AS THE CHIEF OPERATING OFFICER OF OUR PLACE Society in downtown Victoria and as someone whose lived faith bears the empathetic scars of "claw marks on the heart." In our schema, the missional heart is exactly this: the heart belonging to those whose lived faith brings them into direct contact with human suffering and social need. Missionals are found serving in community ministries and social outreach organizations. From emergency medical technicians (EMTs) to grief counsellors, street ministers to relief aid workers, the missional lived faith is drawn to aid people who suffer whether from illness, disaster, harm, or neglect. Missionals live their faith through what their hands are doing. Another testimony looks like this:

> *Margaret was raised in poverty by a single mother in Prince George. When she moved to Victoria with her professional (doctor) spouse and small children, she joined a United Church congregation. For over sixty-five years, Margaret has volunteered in the congregation's foodbank, in-from-the-cold dinners, teens-with-tots group, winter shelter, and refugee welcome. She says, "It's very clear to me that we don't all get the same breaks in life, and God wants us to even the score as best we can."*

And another:

> *Caitlin was raised in the United Church largely by way of its ministry with children, youth and young adults. At age nineteen, she was unsure of a direction in life until she heard an older church member speaking at Naramata Centre about her experience as a medical missionary in China in the 1950s. Though her post-colonial perspective on missionary work dissuaded her from following exactly that path, Caitlin was inspired to pursue a career in nursing. She considers every day on the ward an expression of her faith. She feels her work is a calling, "a way to follow the teaching of Jesus to heal and comfort, to love your neighbour."*

Mission-shaped faith is lived out in commitments to traditional social ministries and longstanding missions like First United Church in Vancouver and Our Place in Victoria. This stream also includes people on the pew whose faith is lived out in their vocational life in healing or helping professions, including public service, and military and hospital chaplaincy. Missionals include those who served the church's former missions and those involved in its on-going global partnerships.

Who are the Missionals?

> We are here to help each other walk the mile and bear the load.[3]
> —Richard Gillard

Chapter Six Meeting Missional Lived Faith

When people place themselves at this table, it is very clear that, quite apart from theological trends or congregational priorities, their souls have been oriented this way as long as they can remember. A missional is a missional no matter how or whether they congregate. They are the serving professionals on the pew, the outreach volunteer in the church or community kitchen, the director of a community ministry, and the team of younger adults launching a social entrepreneurial start-up.

Missional lived faith is a *doing* faith which means missionals are not congregating as often as they are out *doing* something with their faith. Only a portion of them might be visibly involved even in a congregation's outreach program, so we know only a fraction of the missionals among us. The rest are one or two degrees of separation from congregational life, possibly raised, parented, mentored, or inspired by a person or community of faith. Thanks be to God, they are out in the world, making someone safer, less fearful, well, or less lonely. For this reason, missionals don't usually register on the surveys of lived faith in our congregations and denomination as a whole. Many may sit to one side of congregational life. We may learn to recognize them however, when we encounter them as caring professionals, community ministers, social entrepreneurs, or outreach volunteers.

Caring Profession Missionals

> *Our daughter's soccer coach served as a prosecutor for the Crown Counsel. The things he attended to on a daily basis on behalf of child victims of violence would devastate any human heart. When someone blithely commented that "they simply couldn't do what he did; they would hate it," Nat replied, "It's not about what we like or hate; it's about what needs to be done."*

This is the confession of a missional. He mentions privately that doing "what needs to be done," is something he learned as a child in a Catholic family. Missionals like Nat are out in the community as ordinary or extraordinary professionals, guided there by a sense of vocation which some would call duty and others recognize as discipleship. Either way, it is a call to love: to heal, to protect, to accompany, to put oneself between another and the danger, struggle, disadvantage, loss or pain they are experiencing. When they are commissioned by a church, we call them missionaries, chaplains, or diaconal ministers; otherwise, they have no particular title recognized by the church. Moreover, it is unlikely that we know them very well at all. Even when these missionals have a Sunday off shift work or fire-fighting, and find their way to 10:00 a.m. worship, we may not know their names and faces. We are unlikely to recognize the effect of their vocations on their hearts and on their faith. We know little about the questions they bring with them from the law courts, hospital, or street about God's grace and mercy. Missional professionals are often modest and understated in terms of their lived faith, understanding their vocations and avocations simply as "just something you do to help out where you can." Their lived experiences, however, are a gift to the community of faith in ways that are often unrecognized and untapped.

Community Ministry Missionals

> *every siren is for you*
> *every door knock*
> *every phone call is you*
> *every hunched over rain soaked*
> *rig fumbling*
> *falling asleep while talking*
> *huddled beautiful mess is you . . .*
> *every shivering solitary*
> *hooded bruised unwashed*
> *lost soul junkie street survivor*
> *addict lost son*
> *beautiful baby boy*
> *it's you*
> *it's never you but it's always you*
> —Cheryl Bear[4]

As Cheryl's poem so beautifully testifies, where evangelicals have intimate community with small groups, and ecclesials have family with the gathered Body, missionals dissolve the distinction between stranger and son. We meet here another sub-group of missionals, those who are directly involved in social ministry. For missionals engaged in organized community ministries—whether in a residence, centre, facility, café, or on the street—the relationships they form in their life and work become their primary community of faith. So here again, we may not come to know these missionals personally unless we are engaged in those community ministries. No matter how frequently or infrequently they meet—the people with whom they eat, the people whose names and faces they learn, the people who work alongside them, and the people whose stories they share—*these* are their siblings in Christ and *this* is their community of lived faith. These missionals may be part of a congregation or may worship in the company of others in their place of work or service, but regardless of what others may imagine to be essential for faith formation, worship, and community life, many missionals who work in community ministries feel no lack of these things. On the contrary, they experience a profound consonance between their faith and their community. These missionals are situated "where the world's deep hunger and their own deep gladness meet."[5]

Entrepreneurial Missionals

> *This movement is engaged largely by post-Boomer generations. Typically, these enterprises focus on contributing to social good, healing the environment and making "enough" money to keep the venture going. This is called a "triple bottom line" approach. They sacrifice maximizing profit in the short term for the long term good of social and environmental impact.*[6]
> —Rob Dalgliesh

Motivated by can-do-kindness, energy to fix problems, and determination to clean up messes, some entrepreneurial millennials are partnering with churches or seeking funding from denominational sources to launch social and community ministries in the shape of everything from bakeries to hairdressing to construction to diaper services. They are unflappably confident, innovative, and ready to risk (a challenging combination for many ecclesials who are cautious care-takers both by nature and by implicit theology). Though we cannot make generalizations about how particular generations live their faith, because there is a distinct appeal among a subset of millennials of any faith and no faith toward an economy of social good, we are not surprised when missionals in and around our congregations include young social entrepreneurs. In fact, a large number of Fresh Expressions, Pioneering, Embracing the Spirit, Edge, or otherwise branded mission projects come in the form of social innovation and social entrepreneurship rather than congregationally based ministry-starts.

Through the lens of our theological banquet schema, we consider these social innovators to be third generation missionals, descendants of a strong denominational history of community ministries and missions. The lived faith that once drew medical personnel to outpost hospitals now draws foodies for a youth-at-risk catering business. For some, the United Church is their home community of faith. For others, the church is a partner by virtue of investment funds alone. On the far end of the spectrum, there are missionals who plant themselves in the communities whose needs they wish to address, forming an intentional Christian community around the mission, somewhat like the ancient tradition of the monasteries. These contemporary missional monastic communities are more widespread in the UK and the United States than in our West Coast United Church context, but some are experimenting with this model. Though the relationship to the church and the models of community involvement vary, the missional commitment is consistent: if there's a need, don't just sit there, *do* something. Missionals consider every sector of society—private, public, religious, and corporate to be potential agents of social good.

Congregational Outreach Missionals

> *Bob is a retired minister who has served for years on the Board at First United Church in downtown Vancouver's Eastside. Bob picks up unsold bread from a bakery franchise several times a week and takes it to a café he established decades ago where people who are homeless gather for company and food.*

In numbers large and small, communities of faith are blessed with missionals whose lived faith manifests in a level of outreach that far exceeds the norm. When congregations do not have sufficient outreach going on to match the giving capacity of such missionals, these folks will find or establish ways to live their faith both within *and* beyond the congregation's outreach programs. Not being ecclesial, these missionals may not serve on congregational boards or attend congregational social functions. Like Bob, they are serving the board of the shelter or downtown mission, perhaps organizing sponsorship and support for refugees within and beyond the church, collecting furniture for the newly housed, running the community dinners or volunteering at the youth drop-in centre which shares the church building. They may have begun their own "shelter-to-home furniture redistribution centre" out of the church basement, or acquired a store front to run a volunteer café. These missionals of extraordinary skill and energy are often among the most senior members of our congregations.

In many respects, because the lived faith of missionals is so clearly embodied in their *actions*, it is the easiest lived faith to read. The challenge is to recognize that it is lived disproportionately more *outside* the walls of our churches than within them. Theirs is part of a beautiful lineage of faith lived in love of neighbour that has long shaped this denomination's heart outward, and extends the helping and healing hands of every community of faith into its neighbourhood and beyond.

What's in a Name?

We are the hands and feet of Christ, serving by faith each other's need.[7]
—Jim Strathdee

Every lived faith has a mission or reason for being. Each incarnation of faith animates its sense of purpose or "mission" through its particular expression of participation in the divine life—as messenger, member of the Body, and in this case, hands and feet of Christ. In choosing this name for those with a practical, pragmatic, out-turned, hands-on faith, we are arbitrarily exclusively assigning these actions the title, mission.

We saw in the two previous chapters how the *missional church* program has captured the imagination both of evangelicals whose attention has moved from inter-personal conversion to social action, and of ecclesials whose energies for reinvigorating discipleship practices include turning outward toward the neighbourhood as a way to reframe congregational life and witness. Admittedly, we have somewhat confused matters by choosing the name "missional" in our schema for hands-on faith, given that term is also attached to this popular theological movement. An important distinction we want to make between the missional church movement and our own nametag, is that no one is in the missional category at the theological banquet by virtue of adopting an approach to theology, evangelism, or congregational transformation, but only by virtue of an authentically *lived faith* which expresses itself in hands-on relationships marked by empathy, healing, and care. Lived faith is precisely that: how we live, not what books or dominant church leaders have recently caught our attention.

To further complicate matters, the popular missional movement chooses the name "mission-*al*," in part, because it wants to distinguish itself from previous incarnations of mission! In our schema, we make no such distinction. For us, a mission-shaped heart is quite simply an outward leaning faith, one that leads to service of neighbour and stranger. Understandably, for those with a long Christian memory, the term missional will conjure images of missionaries and mission fields from which the postcolonial Christian church wishes to disentangle itself. In no way do we want to sidestep or bracket the colonial legacy, violence and trauma associated with incarnations of Christian mission in our own denomination and in the Christian church at large. We include the missionaries' lived faith in this category with all whose desire to heal and to help, cognizant of its legacy. The church as a whole must reconcile the history and legacy not of this *term,* but of its embodiment when it is appropriated by projects like imperialism, colonisation, dependency, or other aims. This makes the term "missional," simultaneously both deservedly honourable and legitimately objectionable. As with other nametags at the table, "missional" can be a bruised name to wear, though a beautiful heart to carry.

Flashback

A close read of the history of our denomination's lived faith reveals the strong pulse of its missional heart. Formed long after widespread international and ecumenical rethinking of approaches to mission had begun, this denomination has been very much influenced by the history and theology of Christian mission in the nineteenth and twentieth centuries. We need no reminder of the relationship of Christian mission to colonialism's lasting legacies, locally and globally.[8] Though strewn with failings and the suffering those cause, the story of our missional lived faith is punctuated by continuous reflection and self-correction. When the church moves "out of its buildings" and into the world or the neighbourhood, it is always taught, albeit painfully, from the outside in. Our denomination's theologies continue to be shaped by that on-going learning. Here again, faith leads; theology follows. Nowhere is this more critical than in the reconstruction of theologies and practices of mission from the Indigenous perspective.[9]

From the outset, having favoured sharing the deeds of the gospel over spreading the word of the gospel, we predictably fell into patronizing and imperialist approaches to mission. Being rightly challenged on that front, we moved to foster relationships of mutuality and partnership. This self-awareness and self-correction is now over a century old, but its work is on-going. Even before the work of the Truth and Reconciliation Commission in the mid-2010s confronted us with a yet graver impetus for that self-examination and repentance for our earlier approaches to mission, the shape of late twentieth century mission in Canada and internationally had taken on a different form to its earlier one. In the case of Canada, community ministries were increasingly contextually responsive to, and inclusive of, relationships of trust within communities with expressed needs and desires for social, economic, and pastoral support. They adopted a method of reflection on their action such that they grew increasingly oriented toward policy related to root causes, particularly with respect to urban poverty, housing, and social services.[10] Internationally, mission shifted radically toward support for indigenous movements of social transformation, the work we will see below under the name "ecumenical."

This history is important to recall, because currently the missional heart is most often a young heart. New or young Christians for whom the history of mission is quite literally all in the past, tend to approach mission with a perspective uncomplicated by this legacy of lament and un-learning. To them, speaking of mission means becoming excited again about the New Testament call to be a sent people. Borrowing this excitement largely externally from British and American churches, this missional revival of sorts will, for better and worse, not necessarily come wrapped in the denominationally-shaped cautions and conditions our own approach to mission includes.

One Line Credo

I believe that through Jesus' call to discipleship, God's love is incarnate in followers who show love to neighbour and stranger.

Figure 7: Missional symbol

The basin and towel have become symbols of Christian service most closely associated with community ministry and mission, indeed with the diaconate. They conjure the appropriately intimate nature of this lived faith. There is no way to be missional without touch or the relationships born through acts of compassion. Other representations of this hands-on lived faith include images of the Good Samaritan, hands and hearts, and Christ bearing the cross depicting the willingness to carry the burden of suffering for another.

The colour is purple, conjuring passion. Liturgically, it is the colour of Lent, the season of suffering and compassion.

Distinctive Features: Concrete Action

> They also will answer, 'Lord, when did we see you hungry or thirsty or a stranger or needing clothes or sick or in prison, and did not help you?' He will reply, 'Truly I tell you, whatever you did not do for one of the least of these, you did not do for me.'
> (Matt 25:44-45)

At the theological banquet, the missional is the person whose faith is lived in proximity to the immediate needs of strangers. For the missional, God is at work in the world through Christ's disciples whose compassion and love of neighbour heals and restores lives and quietly witnesses to the power of God's love. Being the *hands and feet of Christ* are words often shared from the missional table. The self-understanding seated here is one of hands-on, walking-the-talk discipleship.

Certainly, while care of others is a chief characteristic of the lived faith across the theological spectrum, it is the central characteristic of missionals.

Nurses, social workers, counsellors, teachers, medical researchers, fire-fighters, care-givers, military and prison chaplains, diaconal community ministers: missionals do what they do with their lives and labour not as "part of the church," but because human need calls for human response. We have heard the argument that this kind of lived faith is simply the action of "good citizens," but not necessarily of "Christian citizens." This claim is very cynical indeed. Reading acts of love from the ground of lived faith up, missionals write with their lives a theology of incarnation *par excellence*. That the divine life is taken up in human flesh not just once, but over and over again in the lives of those whose actions echo the love incarnate in Jesus of Nazareth, does not deny his life but, on the contrary, continues it. It is true that citizens may not "know we are *Christians* by our love," but that is because others love, not because love is merely civic. If we believe, as Christians do, that being made in the image of God means being made capable of a love imbued with life-bearing, life-saving, life-restoring self-giving, then all such love is *imago Dei*. Why wouldn't one who shares love with others not experience this (implicitly or explicitly) as a meeting place with God, and as such, the locus of their faith? Where others feel at-one with God or whole in themselves or at peace in the world through prayer or togetherness or justice-seeking or silence, missionals experience this in hands-on acts of kindness, care, healing, and presence.

What we see in missionals is in no way "good works" for the sake of salvation, nor as a display of righteousness or contrived humility. Whether they are inspired to take seriously the parables of Jesus, the example of their Christian parents, or are simply called to attend to the concrete needs of others, missionals are not in it for the glory or the heavenly reward. Whatever the motivation or context, for missionals, God is met on the holy ground where compassion becomes concrete.

Credo Unpacked

> We sing of God's good news lived out,
> a church with purpose:
> gifts shared for the good of all,...

> fierce love in the face of violence, ...
> human dignity defended, ...
> We sing of God's mission.[11]
> —Song of Faith, UCC

Pragmatic and practical, the lived faith of the missional is beautifully captured in the phrase describing saints as "poets of the imperative."[12] And so they are; missionals are tethered to God by having been given something needful to *do*. Believing, as they do, that God somehow uses them for divine purposes of care and healing in no way leads to an arrogance about their place in the economy of grace. Rather, there is humility in their sense of belonging to God's purposes. This trust in the invitational agency of divine compassion shapes the missionals' operative theology. Their tangible experience of proximity to suffering contributes to the thread of cruciform theology that runs through our denomination. This incarnational theology of the cross[13] is born among those who do not know triumph, those for whom the realism of cruciform love challenges notions of all-powerful or controlling love. No wonder it is Jesus' face, life and story to whom missionals most closely relate.

> What is God doing?
>> In the way of Jesus, God is healing and blessing lives and communities.
>
> How?
>> By the power of the Holy Spirit, the hands and feet of ordinary people continue Christ's ministry of compassion and healing in the world.
>
> What does it mean to believe in Christ?
>> To believe in Christ is to follow his teachings. It is to imitate his actions. Christians follow Jesus with their hands, as well as their heads.
>
> What is the church for?
>> The church equips and commissions disciples of Jesus to live their lives in concrete service to those in need in our communities and in our world.
>
> What is the Christian life?

As a disciple, as one led by the Spirit into my life's true calling to help others, I believe we each have opportunity to follow Jesus' example of caring for those who are sick and lonely, those who are alienated and in poverty. We can do this every day in very small ways wherever we are. Compassion is the heart of the Christian life.

Christian identity:
One of God's sent people.

Christian character:
Neighbour

Why I read Scripture:
I am instructed by the Hebrew Scriptures about looking after those in economic and social need and I'm inspired by the parables and stories of Jesus' ministry of healing, inclusion, and compassion. In the kindness people offer one another, I am reminded of God's love for this world, despite the distress some people endure every day.

Distinctive focus related to sin and grace:
God is like Jesus. Jesus held back nothing for the sake of others. In this way, he showed us that we are for each other: to love our neighbour is to love God. It is sinful to turn away from God by turning away from others. Grace is experienced as compassion: God's compassionate forgiveness when we fail to love and God's compassionate love moving through every life that is turned toward another.

Key biblical texts:
Matthew 25:44-45 — When did I see you hungry?
Luke 10:25-37 — God as good neighbour (Samaritan parable)

In this category of lived faith, we "unpack the credo" best by watching these lives in action. These are doers, not speakers, of the Word. What we find in this brief attempt to see the distinctive features of the missionals' operative theology is that it is deeply ethical, trusting in the good, and at-one with the good, at-one with the author of goodness and of life, not just "doing their bit," but in many cases offering their lives to others.

Gifts

> He might have been a wafer in the hands
> Of priests this day, or music from the lips
> Of red-robed choristers, instead he slips
> Away from church, shakes off our linen bands
> To don his apron with a nurse: he grips
> And lifts a stretcher, soothes with gentle hands
> The frail flesh of the dying, gives them hope,
> Breathes with the breathless,
> lends them strength to cope.[14]
> —Malcolm Guite

At the theological banquet, it is difficult to locate anyone who finds fault with missionals. Do we find fault with Dorothy Day or the Romero House? Any hesitancy to befriend them comes only from a sense of our having missed their mark. We cannot imagine a world without them and those like them. Their kindness to strangers needs no defence. As we are speaking of it here, unmotivated by any selfish gain, the lived faith of missionals is pure and beautiful. It reminds us of Jesus and inspires us to "go and do likewise."

In addition to an uncomplicated and uncalculated kindness, missionals bring the gifts of practicality and hard work. They are often skilled in what they bring to the church's contribution to the world: offering a congregation's outreach ministry experience in social work or nursing, or bringing to the community ministry knowledge of social housing policy, mental health or crisis management. They do not count the cost nor do they seek recognition for their acts of service or caring professions which are often among the most difficult places for many to be, places of deprivation, grief, and struggle from which others shelter themselves.

Not only do they carry those skills into the community, they bring that world of partnerships, collaboration, civic participation, and encounter with the realities of others into the church with them. In so doing, their operative theology shapes the theologies of the church, implicitly and explicitly. Through their actions alone, they protect the church from isolation, prevent us from romanticism about what it is to follow Jesus, from an exclusive perspective on whom God loves, from spiritualism about the gospel's call to love, and from an elitist version of Christian discipleship.

More than these benefits to having missionals among us, however, we are inspired simply by what the Spirit is animating within them—humility in service, respect for human dignity, and unflinching compassion in the face of suffering. Truly, we see Jesus' hands enfleshed in their own.

Dangers and Shadows

The dangers that lie close to the missionally lived faith haunt equally today's social entrepreneurs as they did yesterday's missionaries. Helping others is a tricky business, not least because humans are expert at seeing only what we want to see and believing about ourselves only what we wish to believe. How many times have "helping" professionals or "helping" organizations harmed in the helping because we have been more invested in the benefits to ourselves than been genuinely and sufficiently selfless in responding to others (or remedying root causes) for *their* sake, not ours?

Obviously, we know that humans are hard-wired to benefit emotionally from offering kindness to others. In Christian terms, we understand this as a reflection of the *imago Dei* or of the Christ within, enabling us to flourish with God, world, and within oneself through one outward turn in love of neighbour. This does not mean, however, that one should seek ways to do good for our own emotional gratification or spiritual edification, nor for any social or political reasons.

This danger seems all the more real in the face of ecclesial programs which promote meeting and helping neighbours as a way to re-centre the church on its mission. This is particularly so when those being *sent* out into the community are not missionals by calling or gift. They may not respond to perceived needs with the respect and empathy for others in circumstances of struggle, not to mention the humility, so typical of missionals and so often absent in others. These are dangers indeed, dangers which are mitigated by rigorous self-examination, mutuality, trust, and accountability which are hallmarks of more seasoned missional ministries held by ecumenical and social agencies, government partnerships, and advocacy groups where a history of failures is remembered and experience is a teacher.

All trends enjoying popularity can spawn celebrity status leaders; this is no exception. Especially in the United States, the popular "meeting God in the neighbourhood" movement has a rather charismatic, male-dominated hipster profile. This makes it appealing to some leaders, less in content (evangelical) than in form. The danger in this is obvious: superficiality. Its followers adopt not the core missional charism, but the three-legged stool and the beard.

We remember that a shadow is different from a danger or a weakness. A danger is like a piece of fruit rolling toward the edge of the counter, while a shadow is more like a fruit beginning to rot. A shadow is spoilage, not misdirection. Every seat at the theological banquet is equally fitted with a shadow of potential harm to itself and others. The missionals' is no greater or lesser than any other. When the gift of the missional (humility and non-judgement) begins to spoil, it regresses and loses its way.

There is a kind of chosen naïveté in the missionals' shadow—a habit of patching the wound without looking at the body. We are speaking here of the resistance to ask why, to think systemically, a way of becoming attached to the *problem* which gives us something we can *do* rather than to the *cause* which may force us to rethink who we *are*. When missionals are caught in the shadow of this lived faith, it may take the misshapen form of self-justifying charity rather than the path of life-altering relationships along which this lived faith always leads. We are fashioned for one another, so of course actions of concrete self-offering to strangers are satisfying. Being missional is even trendy across the church at the moment, as we have seen. When we decide we know what help people need, we risk repeating the very patterns of paternalism of which the missionary impulse is always in danger. We have all seen just how badly that can go.

Antidote

In examining the lived theologies at the theological banquet of the church, we remember that in every case, the antidote to our shadow is the light of Christ. In this light, the missional is able to pause on the questions posed by the realities of historically imposed suffering. Rather than insisting on making everything a bit better, they grow in their capacity for becoming at-one with God's own compassion through accepting the reality of inconsolability among some of the world's cries for help. The missional is freed from the shadow of self-reliance,

Chapter Six Meeting Missional Lived Faith

even self-as-saviour, by looking at the bigger picture, not the smaller one. They are helped by finding themselves at the table with others who care as deeply as they do about those who suffer, those whose wide read on the systemic injustice and violence entangling the earth requires them to have hope beyond their own making. With the ecumenical at their side, the missional is safe from the temptation to shrink the world to fit in their hands instead of loaning their hands to a much bigger world. It is possible for even the painful legacies of mission to be faced, for repentance instead of charity to be the foundation of relationships, and for aid to be offered with respect, but all this takes sophistication, a step out from the under the shadow of paternalism.

At the theological banquet, it is the ecumenicals' systemic read of the *causes* of suffering—including our own culpability—that shelters the missionals from the potential shadow of simplistic acts of self-serving kindness to others, acts that may carry inadvertent prejudices or deliberate ulterior motives.

Notes

1. A New Creed, *The United Church Manual,* 20.
2. Don Evans, "Comment: When I Walk to Work at Our Place, I Feel Empathy, Not Fear," in Times Colonist, March 19, 2019 www.timescolonist.com.
3. Richard Gillard, "The Servant Song " Voices United, 595.
4. Cheryl Bear is Community Minister at First United Church, Vancouver. She is from Nadleh Whut'en First Nation https://cherylbear.com/. She shared this unpublished poem as part of her reflection for St. Andrew's Wesley United Church on November 15, 2020. Made public through St. Andrew's-Wesley with permission.
5. Fredrick Buechner, Wishful Thinking: A Seekers ABC, expanded ed. (San Francisco: Harper Collins, 1993).
6. The Edge and its affiliated Embracing the Spirit are networks for resourcing and funding entrepreneurial and other experimental ministries and missions in the United Church of Canada, modelled after Fresh Expressions. www.edge-ucc.ca.
7. Jim and Jean Strathdee, "In Loving Partnership," Voices United, 603.
8. Hyk Cho, "Practicing God's Mission beyond Canada" 251- 278 and Loraine MacKenzie Shepherd, "United Church's Mission work within Canada and Its Impact on Indigenous and Ethnic Minority Communities," 279 -312, in Don Schweitzer, Robert Fennell, Michael Bourgeois (eds), The Theology of the United Church of Canada. (Waterloo: Wilfred Laurier Press, 2019).
9. Carmen Lansdowne has critiqued missional theology from an indigenous perspective in Bearing Witness: Wearing a Broken Indigene Heart on the Sleeve of the Missio Dei, Graduate Theological Union Dissertation, 2016.

10. Barry Morris has chronicled this movement in his book, A Faithful Public-Prophetic Witness Dynamics, Challenges, and Ambiguities of Success in Urban & Community Ministries (Eugene: Wipf and Stock, 2019).
11. "A Song of Faith", The United Church of Canada Manual.
12. This reference is to the work of Edith Wyschogrod, Saints and Postmodernism: Revisioning Moral Philosophy, (Chicago: The University of Chicago, 1990). It is a phrase often used by colleague, Sallie McFague, in her writing and lectures on the saints to refer to how the lives of those who respond to God's call (saints) make ethical demands on those of us who strive to do the same.
13. Though not a theology-from-below, the most obvious example of the impact of the United Church's contextual theologies of the cross is in the work of Douglas John Hall, in for example, The Cross in Our Context: Jesus and the Suffering World, (Minneapolis: Fortress Press, 2003). A more liberationist interpretation of a missional lived faith would be found in the work of Canadian theologian, Mary Jo Leddy, as in for example, The Other Face of God: When the Stranger Calls Us Home (Maryknoll:Orbis, 2011).
14. Malcolm Guite, "Easter 2020" Wordpress April 12, 2020. www.malcolmguite.wordpress.com.

Chapter Seven
Living Missional Faith

Congregational Snapshot

Don't *go* to church; *be* the church.[1]

A popular catch phrase captures the heart of the missional faith: "don't go to church; be the church." In other words, the church is not a *place*; it is what we are doing. If an ecclesial Christian understands the church as a Body, a missional Christian understands the church as an activity. So what would a congregation of missionals look like? Better, where and how do missionals *congregate*? We see *collective* missional faith expressed in community ministries and missions (heritage version), in faith-based social enterprise or missional communities (contemporary version), and manifest in radically transformed congregations. We'll look at some examples of each below.

Community Ministries

First United Church Community Ministry Society (First United) in Vancouver and Our Place in Victoria are long-established urban community ministries with large staffs and both public and private financial and organizational partnerships. There are many such community ministries across the church, staffed by ordered and diaconal ministers, professionals and volunteers. In every case, the reality of the local community calls the mission into being. In other words, because of *this* reality, we have *this* ministry or mission located in *this* place. The operative theology in a community ministry is that of being a servant people, sent out to be a presence of healing, comfort, and advocacy. Faith is lived, made manifest, in relationships which might span otherwise wide social and personal divisions including race and class. These divides are often bridged by shared story or history that creates genuine respect, empathy, and solidarity. This respectful and compassionate ethos means that these ministries are rarely, if ever, merely a paternalistic helping hand. Though it is an on-going challenge to reach an aspired operating principle of self-governance, these community ministries, including those which began as missions, have benefitted from decades of self-critique and rigorous self-correction in their approach to ministry in and with disenfranchised communities. As such, unlike some less seasoned congregational outreach programs, they are training grounds for others to learn the humility, mutuality, respect, and friendship through which community ministries animate life in Christ. Beautifully at-one with the divine heart, community ministries, ministers, and the communities themselves become faith leaders, mentors to the broader church. Congregational outreach committees with a desire to steer clear of the shadow of naïveté and away from the appeal of charity, are able to learn what missional lived faith looks like from the vantage point of the foot of the cross. An example of this is the intentional partnering of self-selected congregations and the First United Church community ministry in its Partnership Circles of mentoring and mutual support in sharing relationships and advocacy—cornerstones of missional lived faith.

Mission-Shaped Ministry

Recently, the long established model of community ministry described above has been popularized not from within our own denomination with its long and rich history of community ministry, but by way of those inspired by the missional movement's mission-shaped ministry in the UK and the United States. In our look at ecclesial lived faith, we established that mission-shaped ministry leads in several directions, including to church-planting and discipleship-focussed reinvigoration of congregations.[2] As we would imagine, mission-shaped ministry also leads to expressions of what we are describing as missional lived faith in our schema—projects, programs, and businesses responsive to the *practical* needs of individuals and neighbourhoods, including or especially those disadvantaged by negative economic and social realities.

With generous and ready investment by the denomination at all levels, examples of these ministries are beginning to emerge in our own context just as they did two decades ago in the UK. For example, the Edge network provides an example of re-imagining community ministry as social entrepreneurship. Becoming part of the wider national network of social entrepreneurs allowed the Edge to provide mentors from the business and non-profit sectors, to introduce young missional leaders in the church to a wide network of social agencies, partnerships, and entrepreneurs, and to encourage competition for investment. A recent gathering of this network drew several *incognito* community ministries, dressed in new partnerships and funding sources. It was not difficult to recognize the denominational roots beneath a featured business venture which brings social enterprise, government, and community together to tackle issues of low employment and environmental degradation on a Northern Manitoba reserve.[3]

In truth, these social entrepreneurships, like their community ministry forerunners, are the most authentic representations or incarnations of *collective missional faith* we could point to. Because they are so often peripheral to congregational life, however, we do not see them. The fact that the United Church has historically understood community ministry as an end in itself, not as a means to grow church membership or discipleship, means we will only encounter collective missional lived faith in action when we step away from the congregation into the community. Moreover, the fact that the many missional millennials are not in the places older generations of missionals expect to find them (congregations, voluntary social agencies, community ministries) means traditional missionals fail to find and connect with their younger counterparts in the new sector they are populating. Because these generations are missing each other, one of the strongest streams in the lived faith appears weak and fragmented.

Missional Congregation

There is an awkward dance of operative theologies in the missional movement and its mission-shaped ministries with respect to our schema. Some congregational leaders with an interest in the missional movement are hoping, with the help of the concept of *missio Dei*,[4] to recover with and for their congregation the self-understanding of the church itself, and every congregational manifestation of it, as a missional response to the context in which that church was planted. In terms of our schema, this commitment is distinctly ecclesial, based on a lived faith that understands the church itself as salvific. Because neighbourhoods have changed while church buildings remained fastened to their plots, some congregations are motivated to rediscover their neighbourhoods in order to reimagine what shape the good news might take there. If we understand that God's mission or purpose *needs* churches to serve God's intention for the world, or to "participate with what God is up to," we are talking about what our schema calls an *ecclesial* ministry of the missional movement. In other words, whether the congregation re-invigorates its outreach by way of a newly planted community ministry in the neighbourhood, or replants a piece of itself as a community of faith in the neighbourhood, by our definition, it will be an ecclesial ministry, a boldly Spirit-led trust that gathering people, whether to help or hang out, can be an intentional way of seeding new communities of faith for perpetuity of the Body of Christ in and for the world.

By contrast, there are congregations whose collective lived faith is indeed so missional that they have surrendered their inclination to perpetuate themselves. We know these communities of faith only by witnessing their formation or transformation. Perhaps it is a misnomer to call these "missional congregations." Ultimately, congregations are ecclesial or they would not be there. If we see missional congregations at all, we likely witness them becoming something else. They often look precarious, because they sit on the cusp of giving themselves away. For example, a community of faith in Vancouver sold their building in an affluent neighbourhood and moved for a time into a café across town where they could be imbedded in the very community with whom they felt called to be in relationship. A genuinely missional community has a lived faith that finds first something to *do* with their faith and whose identity is shaped not by who *they* are together (ecclesial) but *with whom* they choose to be in relationship (missional).

Another example of a missional community of faith can be read from the website of a United Church in the interior of British Columbia. The tell-tale missional page prominently displays phone numbers for crisis line, police, emergency mental health, reporting abuse, and a women's shelter. On another page, there is an announcement about the indefinite closure of a forty-year long thrift shop operation and the temporary cessation of a six-year-long hot lunch program. Why? In the absence of a shelter for those seeking permanent housing in West Kelowna, the church became the shelter. Such was its *kenotic*, self-emptying, missional heart. While many congregations use their buildings as outreach by renting or offering space to social agencies, this particular congregation's mission was different; it took place *in* their building but was not simply *of* their building. Collectively, the one-time congregation became a volunteer-run shelter, supported by a community of prayer and worship.

Faith isn't an idea; it is a meeting place with God. Sometimes we don't know a community's lived faith until it is lost. When circumstances led this same congregation to out-source the running of the shelter in their building, rendering them landlords of their lived faith, a crisis of faith ensued. Lived faith needs to live. Taking mission from a missional leaves their faith gaunt and wanting. Suddenly becoming bereft of their mission and thereby the flourishing of their faith and sense of at-one-ment or participation in the life of God put the faith community's life—not simply its longevity—in jeopardy. This same bereavement was felt by every missional individual and missional congregation when the spread of the COVID-19 virus in early 2020 led to church building closures, ending community meals, thrift shops, and other outreach programs which incarnate missional lived faith for so many people in and around our congregations.

A unique example of a long-established (thirty-year) missional congregation is the Longhouse Council of Native Ministry in Vancouver. Serving an urban Indigenous community, this is not a congregation with an outreach program; it is a contextually-based urban ministry animated by an inter-generational Indigenous community whose faith has been nourished and grown in the sacrament of shared life, shared circle, shared table, shared struggle, prayer, and teaching. It is a place where contextually-grown responses to the impact of inter-generational trauma on the community has several faces: wood carving training for entrepreneurship, twelve step programs, baptism, and communion. At the centre of this community's shared life is the reality of urban poverty and disenfranchisement; in the hands of the able minister and elders, the gospel responds contextually and directly to that situation.

In sum, perhaps the question "what is a missional congregation" is not the right question. Rather, we might ask, what is a faith community for a missional? For missionals, the faith community is the community with whom they share their missional lived faith—the elders in the circle, the men at the shelter, the teens in the drop-in centre, the other nurses on the ward, the other firefighters at the station, the squadron, the language class, the ones whose concrete need awakens their faith, the ones known by name and face and recognized in the breaking of the bread.

Sacraments

This is my body. (1 Cor.11:24)

The operating room, the roadside response, the safe injection site, the shelter, the refugee camp: this lived faith is bodily in the extreme. The intimacy with which missionals relate to others is matchless.

That communion is frequently, though not exclusively, celebrated as a remembrance of a bodily Jesus—who incarnates divinity as flesh among flesh, who touches wounds, and feet, and faces, who pours wine and breaks bread and shares it, whose violated body is tended by friends, who lives with, for and among people who are both like him and unlike him—is sacramental for the missional. To make the ordinary sacred and the sacred ordinary is not lost on those whose hands, more frequently than most, touch broken bodies and share bread among strangers.

Leaders with missionals in their congregations will turn ritual into sacrament by bringing the community together around a table of remembrance of the humanity and the humility of Jesus' ministry, death, and resurrection. Missionals are often living the reality more than the ritual. In this way, it is the missionals who shape our sacramental life as a much as the sacraments of the church shape their faith. In the day to day experience of the vulnerability and dignity of human life, where any place we meet becomes a table and anything we share becomes bread, the missionals among us commune with Christ in the kin-dom he both is and brings.

Trends and Sources: What Else is Going on?

> *"We are a non-profit human service organization that addresses the unmet needs of people who are underserved, vulnerable, and overlooked. We are a presence of healing, respecting the dignity of each person through a personal approach and diverse services."*
> —Haircuts from the Heart, USA

This is the millennial face of missional faith in action: a "non-profit human service organization," or what we might call a community ministry, designed in direct response to the immediate, physical needs of those who are "underserviced, vulnerable, and overlooked," with a *hands-on* ministry which is concrete, compassionate, and intimate. A team of professional hairstylists volunteer in a salon-on-wheels offering haircuts, non-judgemental listening, and human touch.

Here is a fresh and simple incarnation of the ministry of the ancient monastic infirmaries, turn of the century prison chaplaincies, or of the contemporary youth drop-in centres. These activities are all missional ways of living the faith. At its best, this is and always has been a beautiful manifestation of Christ's ministry among the harmed and neglected, and an often powerful, meaningful, and faithful frontier for Christian life and community.

Millennial Missionals

For communities of faith with a missional heart, an important trend to watch is what happens to missional lived faith in the hands and hearts of the next generation. For example, where formerly a community lunch was offered from a church basement, advertised by an A4 mauve-coloured paper "Welcome"sign taped to the door, now we see a "pop-up," Instagram shared, or sandwich board advertised café in the financial district! There, servers who for various reasons are challenged to find employment, offer *caffè macchiato,* focaccia bread paninis, and organic and fair trade menu items in a spacious narthex hosting space both to those who buy and those who bring-in lunch. This latter description of the *Moot Café* in London, England is only one of countless "meet people in the community and *offer them* community" versions of self-sustaining mission which has taken hold, inspired by the Fresh Expressions movement. Not all these missions are missions-of-service as much as they are missions-of-presence or social entrepreneurships, so they may not draw older generations of missionals to them, those who live their faith in uncomplicated proximity to urgent social need. But being fashionable and responding to need are not mutually exclusive. So when a designer version of mission-shaped ministry *does* respond to the concrete need of the most underserved, missionals will be there, just as readily as they are in the thrift shops and food banks.

In their hands, these ministries are marked by typical features of millennials: action-oriented, tech-savvy, team oriented, collaborative, and social. Quality and image matter to them. Whatever the project or program, it will likely launch with a splash and hold itself to a measurable impact. Like the *Moot Café* example, contemporary missional lived faith is often engaged in partnerships with social entrepreneurships related to food—farms, community kitchens, and cafés, but also related to the arts—visual art, music, and theatre. The shapes contemporary missional ministries take are varied but always involve being contextually aware, focussed on the needs of the stranger in our midst, and in contrast to service agencies, encompass the basics of communal life modelled by Jesus: eating and talking together in low threshold, inclusive gatherings. Unlike previous generations' institutionalization of community ministries, these missional projects are intentionally impermanent, fluid, and experimental. The word "community" certainly applies to them, but not in a permanent sense.

As a feature of missional lived faith in every generation, relationships in the community reinforce the missionals' civically-mindedness in ways that our institutions do not. Missionals of all generations are often the most genuinely publicly engaged and socially connected among us. After all, this is the lived faith of public servants as well as pop-up salons.

Though it goes by the same name as our missional category, we recall that whether in the UK from the early *missio Dei* work, through the launch of Pioneering Ministries, or in following Alan Roxburgh and the New Parish Collective[5] in the USA, the thrust of what a lineage of three decades of literature calls "missional" is about offering experiences of Christian faith and community to people whom the church has not yet, or no longer reaches. These faith-sharing objectives fall into our evangelical and ecclesial categories on the theological banquet schema. Deepening the roots of discipleship as it relates to mission-shaped ministry is popular among ecclesials committed to strengthening the faith of their community in preparation for mission. But our missionals live their faith on their feet. Though their contributions would be invaluable, they are not likely to attend the preparatory and reflective discipleship classes so appealing to ecclesials. Where the inspiration of the missional movement *does* touch our missional lived faith is illustrated by the salon-on-wheels and *Moot* testimony above: upping the ante on what relationships and sites of care, advocacy, and community look like.

Old-school missional lived faith in this context continues to lean toward autonomously-led advocacy, partnerships, and an increasingly systemic approach to addressing social determinants of health, housing, employment, and education. Among the newly inspired, missional faith is more likely to reflect the social entrepreneurial trend we see both internationally, and across other denominations. A hybrid of the old and new, some congregations are being offered a way to interpret their current outreach commitments and missional lived faith as evidence that they are *already missional*.[6] The intention is to build a missional congregational identity from the congregation's own operative theology up, rather than importing one from elsewhere.

The commitment to walk to the talk, combined with the idea of ministering without a congregation, is very appealing to young missional leaders who are overwhelmed by the prospect of managing the challenges of congregational life while catching the wave of innovation and radical reform invited by this mission-oriented moment in the church. Along with those of previous generations in missions, community ministries and outreach ministries who share a lived faith born of a call to meet immediate human needs, these leaders are not first and foremost congregational leaders, or what our schema calls ecclesials. Spirit-led to hear and to respond to the words "I am hurt,"[7] we find them far more inclined to find ways to shape ministry from their missional lived faith than to force their lived faith into an ecclesial mould.

Lived Faith	Being the hands and feet of Christ through acts of compassion to neighbours in need
What is God doing?	In the way of Jesus, God is healing and blessing our lives and communities.
How?	By the power of the Holy Spirit, the hands and feet of ordinary people continue Christ's ministry of compassion and healing in the world.
What does it mean to believe in Christ?	To believe in Christ is to follow his teachings, practically and concretely. It is to imitate his actions toward strangers and all in need.
What is the church for?	The church equips and comissions disciples of Jesus to live their lives in concrete service to those in need in our communities and in our world.

What is the Christian life?	As a disciple, as one led by the Spirit into my life's true calling to help others, I believe we each have opportunity to follow Jesus' example of caring for those who are sick and lonely, those who are marginalized and in poverty. We can do this every day in very small ways wherever we are. Compassion is the heart of the Christian life.
Christian identity	Sent
Christian character	Neighbour
Why I read Scripture	I am instructed by the Hebrew Scriptures about looking after those in economic and social need and I'm inspired by the parables and stories of Jesus' ministry of healing, inclusion and compassion. In the kindness people offer one another, I am reminded of God's love for this world, despite the distress some people endure every day.
Distinctive focus related to Sin and Grace	God is like Jesus. Jesus held back nothing for the sake of others. In this way, he showed us that we are for each other: to love our neighbour is to love God. It is sinful to turn away from God by turning away from others. Grace is experienced as compassion; God's compassionate forgiveness when we fail to love and God's compassionate love moving through every life that is turned toward another.
Key Biblical texts	Mtt 25:44-45 Luke 10:25-37
Strengths	Concrete Practical
Shadow	Naïveté
Antidote	Sophistication and systemic analysis of ecumenicals

Table 5: Missional

Chapter Seven Living Missional Faith

Notes

1. A widespread catchphrase of the *missio Dei* or missional movement made popular, in part, by the Methodist Church in Britain and the United Methodist Church, USA in the early 2000s.
2. While the goal of Fresh Expression or mission-shaped-ministries with respect to establishing Christian communities is still very much a topic of discussion in UK denominations, the missional movement as it has been adopted by evangelical churches in the USA *does* include the goal of creating churches from the missional experiments. This is not an expressed goal of the United Church's adoption of mission-shaped-ministries, nor was it of its community ministries. A thorough discussion of the ecclesiological agenda of mission-shaped-ministries in the UK is offered in Phil Wall's *Salvation and the School of Christ: A Theological-Ethnographic Exploration of the Relationship Between Soteriology, Missiology and Pedagogy in the Fresh Expressions of Church*. Doctoral dissertation, Kings College, London: 2014.
3. Shaun Loney and Will Braun, *An Army of Problem Solvers: Reconciliation and the Solutions Economy*, (Victoria, BC: Friesens, 2016).
4. Reference to theology of mission associated with Lesslie Newbigen (*The Gospel in a Pluralist Society*, 1989) and David Bosche (*Transforming Mission*, 1991).
5. Alan Roxburgh, *Missional: Joining God in the Neighbourhood* (Ada, MI: Baker, 2011) and Dwight Friesen et al, *The New Parish*, 2014.
6. Brad Morrison, *Already Missional: Congregations and Community Partners* (Eugene: Wipfandstock, 2016).
7. Sharon G. Thornton, *Broken Yet Beloved: A Pastoral Theology of the Cross* (St. Louis: Chalice Press, 2002).

The Ecumenical Banquet Table

Chapter Eight
Meeting Ecumenical Lived Faith

To seek justice and resist evil[1] —A New Creed, UCC

It took me a while to find my voice for justice and peace. It started to come in 1984, after my first marriage ended...because he realized...that he was gay. It was a beginning of a steep learning curve for me, and one of the things I learned was how terrified he was to come out...and I began to realize how much the church contributed to that fear. I became passionate about making sure that our church would be a place where people wouldn't be afraid to be who they are. I can't say I was out marching...but, I sure have found my voice to speak up...[and I] began to work more closely with the church's role in acknowledging what had happened in residential schools. When many of us marched to proclaim desire for right relations—that was living the gospel as I know it. —Janice Young[2]

JANICE TESTIFIES POWERFULLY TO THE ESSENCE OF THE FAITH OF AN ecumenical. She narrates a story of personal involvement in an issue wider than her own life, one that demanded something of her she had not anticipated or chosen. This is typical of the ecumenical. She is pulled into the world and into the gospel in one motion and the two cannot be separated thereafter. Janice testifies to the way in which timidity is set aside and confidence found in finding one's voice alongside biblical, ancient, and contemporary witnesses to God's promise of abundant life. There is nothing generic about this lived faith; it is manifest in the midst of particular, historic, contextual struggles for life. As Janice articulates, this lived faith often comes unbidden, collects you in a sense of a wrong that must be righted, a longing that feels as much like a longing for justice as a longing for God. For the ecumenical, these cannot be pulled apart.

Another testimony might sound like this:

> *If you google Sarah's name, your screen will fill with Facebook posts, open letters, speeches, and articles she has authored over the past eight years. Sarah is a Kairos Winds of Change facilitator and spokesperson on colonial violence. She sits around tables for hours, days, months of her life with others who together teach and learn how to work in a good way to push back the tide of the harm that is done on and to this and other lands in the name of economic prosperity and progress. The interconnection between colonialism, the health of old growth forests, Guatemalan human rights, and coal mining in China is plainly evident to Sarah; to join one struggle is to join them all. She believes that to work for justice is to follow Jesus. As a member of the United Church and a Heiltsuk First Nation Canadian, she is committed to processes of reconciliation from the vantage point of this intersectionality.*

And another:

> *Greg was raised in the United Church, child of two ministers. For six years Greg served on the Naramata summer staff as a youth leader. Greg graduated with a degree in Social and Ecological Sustainability and maintains a commitment to community activism through offering facilitation skills to community engagement projects related to local watersheds. Greg's deeply rooted faith sees no disjunction between Christianity and the protection of life forms. They insists that "this isn't about stewardship of what has been given to us; it's about cleaning up what we destroyed and learning to live differently." Seeing polystyrene cups and plastic water bottles in*

Chapter Eight Meeting Ecumenical Lived Faith

> *United Churches feels "sacrilegious, somehow. I know we don't all see it that way but it's hard to pray 'deliver us from evil' when we keep being part of it."*

If there is someone in your congregation providing you with resources on Indigenous rights, climate action, peace in Palestine, the needs of asylum seekers, or the status of food security, it will be an ecumenical. Behind them, are a network of organized researchers, educators, and activists who are working tirelessly together to turn the world around. Ecumenicals may appear distinctly more political than pious. On the contrary, the weight of the world on their shoulders can only be borne in faith. As in all our categories of lived faith, theirs too is shaped by their felt experience of life with God—in this case, in their felt desire for God's justice to reign. For the ecumenical, moral agency is not an autonomous human virtue but a gift of the Spirit enacted in the gestures of advocacy, resistance, solidarity, and compassion; through these actions, their life is thread to God's own.

Who are the Ecumenicals?

> "The creation God loves is sick unto death, and needs caretakers, lovers, gardeners, companions and partners who will work to preserve life rather than death, collective security rather than national security, rice in the mouth and a roof over the head rather than military and nuclear hardware."[3]
> —Lois Wilson

Who is voluntarily standing in that painful gap between the status quo and the flourishing of life? Whose lived faith stirs them in the direction of longing for what *could* be, for what *should* be? Who is animated by their faith both to see the social inequity and global suffering we swim in, and to seek elusive solutions to the terrible tangle of it all? Meet our ecumenicals, those whose way of being Christian, of being human, whose way of faith and of loving God, is to allow the world's pain to demand their attention and to keep it.

"Sign a petition; meet with your Member of Parliament; share this action on social media using this hashtag;" this is the language the ecumenical faith speaks. Flip open the pages of Broadview[4] or log onto the denominational website or

Facebook page and you will be addressed by an ecumenical's faith. They are baby-boomers who divested of personal use plastic before millennials were born, and they are Gen-Z climate activists. They are millennials writing blogs advocating for international gender-justice, and they are the inter-generational community of Indigenous educators. They are Korean, Nigerian, Jamaican, and Japanese church leaders whose understanding of the church, community, and communion is inextricably global and whose read of the gospel is narrative and contextual. In your congregation, they are the ones who make the announcements about the fair trade coffee for sale. In the national church offices, they are the researchers preparing the briefs about the impact of the government's latest budget cuts on the vulnerable sectors of society and drafting reports offered on our behalf at the World Council of Church's meeting on gender-based violence. In our theological schools, they teach decolonizing ministry practices[5] and Christian social ethics.[6] In the pulpit, they are the ones who are told their sermons are too political and that they fail to see "both sides." Ecumenicals include former moderators, denominational women's organization presidents, Indigenous leaders, mission partners, youth and young adults, along with innumerable lay and ordered committee members and delegates who advocate in countless local, national, and international fora for a vision of the future that in a material, this-worldly way is reflective of the peaceable kin-dom announced by the prophets—a peace inextricably linked to justice, reconciliation, well-being, health, and the integrity of all life on the planet. They are academics and activists, privileged and disadvantaged, professional and on the edges of the economy, bold and meek, all of them compassionate, courageous, and willing to be scrutinized by Jesus' version of the kin-dom.

Remember that the restlessness at the heart of the ecumenicals' lived faith is the question "why is this happening?" In light of what Christ inaugurated, why this suffering? Where missionals are drawn in compassion to ameliorate the suffering, ecumenicals are drawn to stop it. Pulling on the thread of inadequate minimum wages, or dying rivers, or systemic racism, the skein in which these realities are tangled is complex and global, thereby linking the ecumenical to an international web of sustained attention to the inner workings of economies, policies, practices, and habits world-wide. That web is characteristically inclusive of those with both lived experience and hard-earned expertise. The deliberate "working with" rather than "working for" collaboration of ecumenicals makes the circles in which they find themselves among the most ***diverse*** in the church. Here, the middleclass North American Christian nurse meets the Indigenous Guatemalan artisan; the Nigerian professor meets the LGBTQI2S+ youth activist; the BC Gulf Islanders meet the Senate Committee; the Jewish, Christian, Muslim, and Indigenous community leaders work together on lobbying against ecological disaster. The networks to which our ecumenicals belong may be hubs of denominational think-tanks guided by disciplines of Christian life, or small local advocacy groups grounded in first-hand experience. From Kairos (Canada) to the Joint Public Issues Team (UK) to the World Council of Churches public witness programs (global), ecumenicals are linked in networks and coalitions in both comprehensive and issue-focussed, justice-seeking agendas. They are also engaged in ground-up, experience-rich informal communities formed in real time around particular concerns. Ask an ecumenical where their church is and they may invoke a small group of people with whom they share a particular justice concern or reference the worldwide community of Christian or interfaith activists with whom they feel a defining affinity.

Ecumenicals hold themselves and their *communities* to a high standard of ethical living. This reflects their desire to align their personal lives with the goals of the kin-dom even as they work to do the same on a global scale. This is not so much a notion of "justice begins at home," but rather a question of integrity, an attempt to untangle their own actions from injustice and harm while they work to unravel the threads of social and political culpability in global suffering. For this reason, they will bear the insult of being called "politically correct" for choosing, for example, second-hand over fast-fashion, though this misunderstanding of their motives obscures their purpose. As for their personal lives, so too for their collective life: it matters to ecumenicals who is at the board table and who is missing from places of decision-making, which images of God dominate the liturgy, what policies are implemented that open leadership to all people, how accessible the building, governance, and activities are, where money is invested, and how much energy we use. These preoccupations may appear to others as if the desire for God's justice has turned inward and myopic, but for the ecumenicals it is reflective of the commitment to align one's life and activity, including one's faith community, with the one who is the Life of the world.

What's in a Name?

The Greek word "*oikoumenē*," from which the word "ecumenical" comes, is most often translated to mean the (whole inhabited) earth. The meaning of "oikos," translated as *eco-* in eco-nomy and eco-logy, is variously related to concepts of house or household. Traditionally in the church, *ecumenical* has come to refer to a collection or organization of Christian churches as in the World Council of Churches, an *ecumenical* organization. None of these associations is contrary to how we are using the term here but as with the other categories, using the term as a label rather than a definition means it has a particular focus. The label refers to those whose lived faith is expressed in care for the integrity of creation and who hold fast to the vision of the flourishing of all life, a world reflective of God's justice, peace and reconciliation. Seeing the term "ecumenical" may conjure an image of many churches, or even of a global church movement or coalition which is true of the community in which ecumenicals find themselves. Even though some ecumenicals may be involved in these communities, it is by virtue of their commitment to the whole inhabited earth, *not* their association with a coalition of churches, which gives them their name.

Here we are stressing commitment to the well-being of the "household of God," by which we mean, the whole world or universe. Concepts such as **pluralism, partnership** and the **common good** are characteristics not only of ecumenism or the ecumenical movement in the broad sense, but also of the way we are using "ecumenical" here as a nametag at the theological banquet. For us, an ecumenical lived faith is one concerned with the well-being of the whole inhabited earth and *collectively* and *inclusively* engaged in trying to bring that well-being about. This means our ecumenicals' network is vast and global. In terms of our focus on lived faith in this denomination and its communities of faith, we might think of the ecumenical label as one that refers not only that wide community but more to the point, to the wide *concern*: the vision they carry of abundant life for all, for the kin-dom[7] of God and the commitment they hold to journey from here to there.

Chapter Eight Meeting Ecumenical Lived Faith

Flashback

[After the 1960s, the United Church saw] a movement away from assimilationist policies toward First Nations peoples, the repudiation of supersessionist understandings of Judaism, a new openness to other religions, a movement toward partnership in mission with overseas churches, and increased recognition of the agency and autonomy of women, and the decision that in and of itself, sexual orientation was not a barrier to ordination."[8] —Don Schweitzer

The emergence of the ecumenical lived faith within our denomination can be understood in the context of a flashback to the history of evangelism and mission we visited in previous chapters. Historian, Phyllis Airhart calls the year 1964 "the end of an era" in the United Church, brought about by a new generation of leaders inspired by a vision of mission which

> ". . . rejected the traditional approach to evangelism. Instead of the church proclaiming the gospel to the world and calling Canada to Christ, they appealed to the church to 'listen to the world.'"[9]

This was not an impulse without ompany or precedent. A decade earlier, the World Council of Churches had articulated a theology of mission which set God in primary and direct relationship to the *world*, rather than to the *church* in service to the world.[10] Because the United Church had institutionalized the inextricable connection between evangelism and social service through the creation of a single board (Evangelism and Social Service) responsible for both aspects of the church's mission, the tension in the world church in the 1960s between the two objectives was felt deeply within our own denomination. Theologically and collectively, the United Church could hold 'sharing God's love' with 'social action,' but practically and individually, those with commitments to one or the other outnumbered those who held them together. Moreover, as we saw above, evangelism itself was under review as the impact of becoming Christian failed to produce the enthusiastic disciples the evangelists anticipated. When social services moved into the hands of the social welfare state, the church's role changed from hands-on deliverer of needed services to policy advocate or agitator, ironically just as any activity the church engaged mattered less and less to the population at large.[11]

By 1966, denominational leaders were turning up the call to political (even partisan) engagement. A network of concerned evangelicals within (United Church Renewal Fellowship) and beyond (Evangelical Christian Fellowship) the denomination resisted the trend to reframe evangelism as a call to join the post Vatican II ecumenical movement. Despite that resistance, over the decades that followed, the United Church's self-understanding as well as its collective lived faith and theologies, were shaped by our involvement in ecumenical inter-church councils and coalitions which addressed, on national and international fronts, the most pressing concerns of the day—peace, human rights, and economic justice.

What is helpful to remember, however, in situating current ecumenicals in our church's lineage of lived faith, is that while the United Church has consistently *understood itself* to be a faith community committed to social change and social justice, in truth, this commitment was likely disproportionately held by the denominational councils rather than by the congregational or regional ones. The local courts were far more engaged in pastoral (ecclesial) and local (missional) expressions of lived faith than with the global and planetary agendas emerging in the national offices inspired by liberationist movements in the worldwide church from the end of the wars in Europe (1940s) onward.

The denominational self-understanding as a church in and for the world, inspired by Jesus' kin-dom of love's justice and reconciliation, was widely shared for many decades in united and uniting churches. Within the context of the broad association of Protestant denominations, they shared a self-understanding as social reformers, agents of the common good. Latterly, that description slid into the more passive portrayal as "liberal" churches, pointing to our perceived worldview influenced by nineteenth century's faith in human ingenuity to bring about the kingdom of God, our tradition's moral influence atonement theology, and our on-going involvement in broad-based social movements.

Without the rigorous constructive soteriologies (understandings of Christ's saving life and work) they demand, the ecumenical lived faith can both seem from the outside and feel from the inside, somewhat lacking. A return to neo-orthodoxy's strong God and discipleship-focussed faith formation is appealing in this light. Who chooses wisps of hope for the world over certain victory in God? Apparently, ecumenicals do. For decades, this *realized eschatology,* by which we mean that God's future for which we wait emerges in the present to some degree, ran visibly through our denominational ethos in its official reports. By the early 2000s when Faith Talk[12] collected statements of faith from across the church, such commitment for the church to "be part of God's kingdom-building" was fully present even while neo-orthodoxy remained the dominant theology of pulpit and pew over these years. Arguably, an ecumenical lived faith belonged more to our collective self-image as a daring[13] church than to our local life blood, but its influence on the denomination's public face and work is significant.

It is possible in this brief flashback to trace an ecumenically lived pattern of attention to *being the change* while working and waiting for change. Indeed, this denomination is a learning institution: in the early years after union, some Western missionaries learned to become partners rather than managers of overseas projects, and in the 1980s, some men learned to collaborate rather than dominate women, and in the 2010s, some in the church learned to check their privilege and assumptions in order to redefine expertise. Ecumenicals have learned, practiced and modelled a justice-seeking lived faith. Not only the concerns that preoccupy them, but the *way* of working to address them collectively, collaboratively, inclusively, and respectfully incrementally charts a course toward systemic and social change. In other words, ecumenicals take on the struggle for a better way to live together by trying it out themselves. Looking back, it is fair to say that an ecumenical lived faith has shaped this denominational and its on-going work in very significant ways: our approach to mission, to women's leadership, to intercultural ministry, affirming policies and practices, inter-faith relationship, approach to dis/ability, reconciliation, and to racial justice.

One Line Credo

I believe God's unfolding justice and peace is redeeming the oikos—the whole inhabited earth—and the Spirit calls us to participate in realizing the promise of abundant life, the kin-dom/kingdom of which Jesus spoke.

Figure 8: Ecumenical symbol

The symbol which might capture the heart of the ecumenical lived faith is the dove of peace or the cross of barbed wire or of burnt trees, contextualizing the struggle for life in contemporary terms. Representations of people joining hands together around the globe are also used to communicate the desire for earth-tending and restoration of relationships.

The colour is blue, conjuring peace. Liturgically, it is the colour of Advent, the season of anticipation and hope.

Distinctive Features: Expertise and Hope

> To God, who through the prophets proclaimed a
> different age,
> We offer earth's indifference, its agony and rage:
> "When will the wronged by righted? When will the
> kingdom come?
> When will the world be generous to all instead of some?"[14]
> —John Bell and Graham Maule

Finding distinctive features in each of the categories of lived faith is always a matter of generalizing from a height of several meters above the more nuanced and blurred reality on the ground. We focus our distinction on the locus of faith: where God is met, felt, experienced, and by what means we feel closest to God or at-one with God. For the ecumenical, God is met and experienced in the world's hunger for the kin-dom, the longing for justice and peace. Longing for God *is* love of God for an ecumenical. They live in anticipation; their home is made of hope for what is yet to come and furnished by glimpses of God's reign erupting in the meantime.

Eyes shaped by **hopeful anticipation,** or in theological terms, *realized eschatology,* is a dominant feature of this lived faith. Mistaken for a thin or evidence-based faith, on the contrary, ecumenicals' confidence in God's reign outstretches their realistic grasp of the weight and complexity of this world's ills. They are faithful realists, believing that God is *for this world,* so we meet God in being *for this world* as well; this means learning it and understanding it.

A second distinctive feature of ecumenicals, therefore is their **expertise and rigour**, gained through experience, relationship, and study. Knowledgeable engagement is key to the ecumenicals' lived faith, leading them close to the heart of God through aligning their actions with what they believe God intends for the world. Where ecclesials live their faith among the gathered community of the church, and missionals enact their faith in care of others in their vicinity, the ecumenical lived faith lands in broad circles, international networks, and interfaith coalitions, both local and global, where complex and systemic injustice is faced head-on through actions as diverse as research, policy-making, solidarity, and resistance.

Thereby, in addition to a theology of hope[15] and a grounding in experience and expertise, a third distinguishing feature of the ecumenical lived faith is **the transformational influence** of company it keeps. They are committed to work together in a manner that reflects what they are working for: a place for all to flourish. Because of the scope of the ecumenicals' meeting place with God—the lived reality of God's people—their lived faith is situated in diverse contexts, global in breadth. In Christian terms, the circles in which ecumenicals find themselves are little *koinonias* (communities) of justice which foster and host the very *metanoia* (about-face) which the in-breaking of the kin-dom invites. In secular terms, these circles are incubators of new communities based on right relationship.

This transformative opportunity is made possible because of the willingness of the ecumenical to be **self-reflective.** This fourth distinctive feature arises because their commitment to inquire about the causes of suffering in the world leads to the development of a particular lens on human activity and relationships. The ecumenical does not escape that lens and is painfully aware of personal and social culpability. Moreover, because the ecumenical lived faith also hopes for the church to become an incarnation of the very kin-dom they seek in the world, ecumenicals contribute to the church practice of its own critical self-reflection.

Credo Unpacked

> Jesus announced the coming of God's reign—
>   a commonwealth not of domination
>   but of peace, justice, and reconciliation.[16]
> —A Song of Faith, UCC

We want to have an understanding of the anatomy of the faith of the ecumenical which forms their life in this particular justice-seeking, world-embracing shape. The ecumenicals' identity as a Christian is as one who shares God's longing for all life to flourish. In biblical terms, this is a faith spoken of in the language of the kin-dom/kingdom of God, the reign or manifestation of God's justice and peace, the promise of abundant life, the flourishing of creation. The images of God's intension or desire for the world in the Christian tradition are variously rooted in scripture through the call of the prophets in the Hebrew bible, the parables of Jesus and his resurrected life in the gospels, and the description of the goal of creation in the epistles. These speak of God's intention for the world in *eternal* terms which *transcend time and space* as well as in concrete *historical and immanent* terms.

For ecumenicals, to become at-one with God, to share God's life, is to meet God in *both* the promised and the historical manifestations of God's justice and peace. It is to experience the holy in the worldly intimations of what is *not yet* fully realized. We speak of the ecumenicals' lived faith as being expressive of seeking to be at-one with God in God's *desire for life in all its fullness*. This, in turn, shapes their faith in the mould of desire, anticipation, longing, and hope. Where we meet God, so too are we shaped. Ecumenicals are future-leaning, hope-seeking, change-making people of God. To look forward to God is to hope. Ecumenical faith then, aligns with theologies of hope which are often political theologies.

What is God doing?
    God is eternally healing, reconciling and restoring the world God desires to flourish.

How?

Through the in-breaking of the promised and longed for kin-dom/ kingdom of Abundant Life and aided by all who participate in making real the vision of God's anticipated commonwealth of justice, peace and the integrity of creation.

What does it mean to believe in Christ?

To believe in Christ is to live in, with and for his promise of life abundant, his kin-dom (Kingdom) on and of this earth.

What is the church for?

To be an agent of God's justice, peace, and reconciliation.

What is the Christian life?

It is to side with the all who share the struggle for fullness of life, as Christ did, by working for social change, and for transformation of our relationships to and on the earth.

Christian identity:

A creature of the Creator and partner with others and with God in the work of the kin-dom/kingdom of justice and peace.

Why I read Scripture:

The Hebrew bible reveals God's justice as a love that brings peace, right relations, and the flourishing of all life. The parables of Jesus reveal a world founded on a love that reorients the world toward God's justice. I am reminded in Scripture of God's love for the world, of the way the Spirit ignites our hearts with passion for aligning our lives with God's vision of abundant life.

Distinctive focus related to sin and grace:

Sin is participating in an oppressive social, ecological and economic system that undoes the life that God has created. Grace, in Christ, that God's justice is manifest in the love for which we too have been created (*imago Dei*). It is the assurance of hope in things seen and unseen.

Biblical texts:

Isaiah 2:4 Swords into ploughshares

John 10:10 Abundant Life

Gifts

> What does the Lord require of you but to do justice,
> love mercy and walk humbly with your God? (Micah 6:8)

Love needs reality.[17] The ecumenicals' heart loves God through, not around, the ways things are. "It doesn't have to be this way" is their weighty mantra, the language of their love of God. They offer the church this love through three particular strengths: expertise, relationships, and integrity.

When a Senate Commission is prepared to hear from citizens across the country on climate, reconciliation, poverty, migration, or arms control, our ecumenicals sit in front of the computer screen studying links to books and journals, SPIRI[18] data and testimonials. Ecumenicals deal in facts and figures and well as protests, plans, and programs. From theological scholars to lay activists, expertise is a feature of the ecumenical lived faith. They learn economics, climate science, human rights, international refugee and migration policy, moral and social ethics, about weapons of war, strategies for peace, environmental law; the list goes on. They learn it as an act of faith, as love of God in a world that longs to reflect the purposes of God. They learn these things because facts, figures, stories and photos represent the gap between the way things are and the way they could be, a gap the ecumenicals consent to occupy for the sake of those who suffer because the kin-dom of God is not yet fully realized among us. The church is indebted to their patient labour for being not only our eyes on the world but contributing to our critical understanding of it. What a gift.

Those who occupy the gap between what is and what could be are a diverse group, including many who have suffered the very injustices they work to end. The activist communities of which ecumenicals are often part, form a microcosm of the society they work towards. In such circles, participation is not earned through privilege but through experience and attention. Among ecumenicals, the experts on migration are migrants, on poverty are those who live in poverty, on identity are the LGBTQI2S+ community, on Indigenous rights are Indigenous people. Ecumenicals gift the church with these trusted relationships in the shared work of justice-seeking.

Finally, for the ecumenical, standing in the gap between what is and what could be means every attempt to close the gap will be made at every moment. The lived faith of the ecumenical demands integrity in every aspect of day to day life on the planet: how they vote, where they live, how they commute, what they eat, what they wear, even their contribution to congregational life. Famously unpopular as it is in most communities of faith, they will insist on fair trade coffee and plastic-free potlucks, not because they are "imposing their lifestyle on others," but because they love God through love of a hurting world that they do not wish to harm. Theologically, they are attempting to embody little pockets of the kin-dom, even while we wait for God's justice to roll down like mighty waters. They gift the church with an encouraging invitation into this holy, "minding the gap" integrity.

On the whole, their lens focussed on "what is going on here" is a systemic one and one through which they read not only the world but the church itself. In this way, it is ecumenicals who have bought the church's attention to the quest for equality for women, the call for racial justice and inter-racial understanding, attention to power and privilege, a focus on Indigenous rights and the path to reconciliation, and LGBTQI2S+ awareness and advocacy. This critical self-reflection shapes the church's approach to personnel policy, resource development and education, and to mission priorities, partnerships, and advocacy. The courageous gift of the ecumenical is this: lived faith that willingly situates itself in the gap between the realities of these times and that which, in Christ, has been promised and begun. We would not recognize ourselves without the mark of this expression of lived faith on our church.

Dangers and Shadows

In earlier chapters, we differentiated a danger from a shadow. Dangers are much more self-evident. In this stream, for example, there is an obvious danger of burn out resulting from the weight of worldly crises and concerns. Also a hazard, ecumenicals are susceptible to a sense of urgency and may become both impatient with others and demanding of themselves. A further danger is that the close community of companion activists may run the risk of being impenetrable from the perspective of an outsider, ironically even exclusive or elitist. This apparent exclusivity may be compounded with the tendency of ecumenicals to resent those who appear to them to contribute to the "problem with the way things are" by perpetuating habits which continue the very injustices they work so hard to undo. Even the missionals, whose implicit theology and lived faith makes them the closest siblings of the ecumenical, can feel *not good enough* in the face of the at times no-win analyses offered by ecumenicals. These dangers are self-evident. Every honest ecumenical is aware of them.

The shadow of the ecumenicals, as with all shadows, is less obvious even to the most honest and self-aware among them. Like other shadows, this is because it disguises itself as a strength. The first of two strands of the ecumenicals' strength are their conviction that God's promise of abundant life belongs in and to human history. The second is their willingness to be deployed in the divine unfolding of that promise. They meet God in their desire for the flourishing of life. What we, and they, do not always recognize is when those strands begin to fray. When the ecumenical has lost hope in God, their desire turns to desperation and their meeting place with God, their *faith* in God, erodes. This desperation wears the guise of proficiency and drive: an admirable cover-up for an atrophying hope. Lost hope can remain in place for a long time, disguised and commended as commitment to hard work.

At a certain point however, it becomes plain. Desperation turns to dogmatism. Ecumenicals caught in their shadows are rule-bound and uncompromising—bearing the sure signs of fear and desperation. They collapse into ideological battles amongst themselves and are equally unreasonable with others. If an ecumenical is insisting that without becoming vegan there is no hope of justice or without naming our pronouns there is no chance for peace, they are most certainly suffering. Generosity is lost along with perspective and they find fewer friends than foes. The unlikely shadow of the ecumenicals' insistence that God's justice must triumph turns out to be cynicism and despair. How does that happen? Despair is the absence or loss of hope. It is a serious undoing of the ecumenicals' collective life blood. Worse, when the weight of despair cannot be managed, it turns to cynicism, the easier burden to carry. Cynicism is the mockery of hope rather than the loss of it. Ecumenicals seek a replacement for lost hope in ideology. This is the ugly temptation suffered in this stream of lived faith, a shadow that makes it rigid, angry, and both faithless and uninviting.

Chapter Eight Meeting Ecumenical Lived Faith

Antidote

The shadow of the ecumenicals is cast by the bleak landscape of hopelessness, a loss of faith in who God is and what God can do. Ecumenicals in despair, in need of hope which comes from God, are surrounded instead by the reality that everything is "on fire"[19] and the fallacy that change is entirely up to them. From the outside, ecumenicals may appear angry. This is often a misinterpretation. There is a fight going on within them against despair. This despair most often drives the ecumenical harder but at times wears the inverse of itself by leaving them in a depressive malaise. The antidote for the ecumenical caught in its own Janus shadow is the reassurance of God's abiding presence and the ability to rejoice in the world even in its pain, a recovery of a lived faith based on love of the world rather than desperation to fix it or despair over its apparent demise. Ecumenicals needs to walk with those on an adjacent path into the heart of God, those who, like them, do not leave the broken world behind.

What lived theology is tethered to a faith in God's agency in the present, to God's constancy, proximity and immediacy? This is the antidote for the faltering faith of ecumenicals, the hopelessness that leads to desperation, impatience, despair, and resentment[20]. Lived and operative theologies which are radically incarnational, which stress the immanence of God, the world as the meeting place with God, provide solace to the ecumenicals' need to meet God in the world in every moment of every day. At our theological banquet, the spirituals provide the antidote to the ecumenicals' shadow. Moreover, the spirituals' commitment to inner work, their apophatic theology where few, if any, names for God are used, their openness to other faiths and no faith, and their connection to the natural world offer the ecumenicals a threshold to venture back and forth from their activist communities into a compatible arena of deeply lived spiritual life and faith, a place to be at home with God in the world.

Notes

1. A New Creed, The United Church Manual, 20.
2. Used with permission, this is an excerpt from Janice's testimony from the panel presentation (May 26 morning) at the BC Conference Annual Meeting, How Big is Our Tent? University of British Columbia, Vancouver, May 25-28, 2017.
3. Lois Wilson, Turning the World Upside Down: A Memoir, (Toronto: Doubleday, 1989), 252.

4. Formerly *The United Church Observer*, Broadview is an independent magazine affiliated with the United Church of Canada.
5. For example, the work of Hye-Ran Kim Craig, Interdependence: A Postcolonial Feminist Practical Theology, 2018.
6. For example, in the tradition of H. Richard Neibuhr and continued in our context through Marilyn Legge of Emmanuel College, University of Toronto (Victoria College).
7. Though the radical nature of the image of the kingdom of God over the kingdom of Roman imperialism is understood, the term 'kin-dom' in place of 'kingdom' nevertheless has been adopted intentionally by many Christians. First used by mujerista theologian, Ada Maria Isasi-Diaz, it replaces the political and hierarchical imagery associated with kingship with more familial and domestic imagery by which to imagine and anticipate the world Jesus enacted and announced. Used by feminist theologians for several decades now, those most likely to have adopted this language at the Theological Banquet are ecumenicals and spirituals.
8. Don Schweitzer, The UCC: A History, 292.
9. Phyllis Airhart, A Church with the Soul of a Nation, 226.
10. Airhart, 228.
11. Airhart, 232.
12. Faith Talk 2002, UCC archives.
13. Reference here to both the United Church Dare to Be anniversary video and to Alyson Huntly's earlier book by a similar title, Daring to Be United: Including Lesbians and Gays in the United Church of Canada (Toronto: United Church Publishing House, 1998). https://www.youtube.com/watch?v=66WctH5kE-M&ab_channel=TheUnitedChurchofCanada .
14. John Bell and Graham Maule, Inspired by Love and Anger, (Glasgow: Wild Goose Iona Community, 1987).
15. Examples of theologies of hope, sometimes called political theologies, include those in Luther's thin tradition of the cross: Jürgen Moltmann, Dorothee Sölle, and Douglas John Hall. Largely a western and male theological conversation initially, a second generation of feminist and eco-political theologians include Cynthia Moe-Lobeda, Kathryn Tanner, Catherine Keller, Elaine Graham (western) and Kwok Pui-Lan, and Chung Hyun Kyung (Asian).
16. A Song of Faith, UCC Manual.
17. Simone Weil, Gravity and Grace. First French edition 1947. Translated by Emma Crawford. English language edition 1963. Routledge and Kegan Paul, London.
18. Stockholm International Peace Research Institute (SPIRI).
19. Reference is to the title of Naomi Klein's book On Fire: The Burning Case for a Green New Deal (New York: Knopf, 2019).
20. Theologies which miss the mark of the ecumenicals' need for present and real hope include theologies which stress God's transcendence as some orthodoxies do, or theologies which stress the personal over the social agency and efficacy of salvation as some evangelical theologies do, and those which stress God's past or future over God's present, as even some liberationist theologies do.

Chapter Nine
Living Ecumenical Lived Faith

Congregational Snapshot

WITHIN MOST OF OUR LOCAL CONGREGATIONS, THERE MAY NOT BE MANY ecumenicals. Those who are there will find affinity with missionals as outward or world-oriented people of faith. The activities that fall under the banner of "social justice" in many congregations span both these categories of lived faith: a reconciliation group and a request for sock donations, for example. Despite the blurring of these two streams, the distinction between the missionals' commitment to practical support and the ecumencials' focus on root causes will be felt, sometimes as a tension.

Among youth and young adults in the church, however, the number of those with an ecumenical lived faith is disproportionally large. Young adults are on the forefront of climate action, Indigenous rights, and gender justice, both within and beyond the church. Though some world events or eras inspire and form lifelong activists (Vietnam in the 1960s, nuclear proliferation in the 1980s, the Oka crisis in the 1990s), we accurately associate activism with younger adults. These young and older adults have in common their arms' length connection to our congregations. They live their faith primarily among those with whom they share an urgent commitment to the alternative societies, economies, and futures their faith enables them envision.

For example, the seventy-year-old woman in the local Grandmothers-to-Grandmothers[1] campaign may be in your congregation, but her faith is nurtured, challenged, and lived out elsewhere among the circle of women with whom she meets to hold the reality of HIV/AIDS in their vigilant attention. So too, the young adult confirmed five years ago who strikes for the climate every Friday[2] on a university campus away from home. Often, the ecumenicals' lived faith brushes the life of the congregation from a distance. In this way, it doesn't often have chance to shape the lived faith of the congregation as a whole. In other words, one doesn't often meet an "ecumenical congregation," though for those with this lived faith, the local Kairos group, anti-poverty policy advocates, watershed disciples, sustainable farming community, or Reconciliation Circle are communities of the living spirit where their faith in a God of love, justice, and mercy is sustained and grown.

An obvious exception to the claim that an ecumenical congregation is difficult to imagine, is found in alternative communities of faith formed with ecumenical lived faith at the centre. These form off the grid of local congregations, sometimes unrelated (officially) to a denomination, and sometimes supported by one or more established communities of faith or ecclesial funding bodies. They are often not particularly easy to locate from outside the activist community. The Anglican community of Salal and Cedar[3] or other expressions of the Wild Church, like those associated with the United Church in BC's Okanagan Valley, or the Forest Church movement[4] throughout Britain have a very explicit reconciliation and justice focus, making them good examples of an ecumenical community. Drawn together by a lived faith that is nurtured and expressed in love of God *in* the world *on behalf* of the flourishing of the planet, many of these worshipping communities are deeply engaged in acts of solidarity and resistance to protect particular land or lands from exploitation. Their worship and activism is inseparable, so they pray, sing, and share the sacraments and scriptures on the very land they seek to protect, be it a representative piece of forest, agricultural land, an unceded territory, or a watershed destined for a pipeline. The spiritual and the ethical are inseparable among such ecumenicals. It is true that some of these alternative spiritual communities are more aesthetically than politically drawn to nature, in which case they belong in our schema as expressions of the "spiritual" lived faith rather than representing the ecumenical stream.

As we acknowledged above in their profiles, ecumenicals often take on the justice-seeking work of the church with or without the participation of their own communities of faith. For example, by pursuing relationships with local Indigenous communities and their leaders, ecumenicals will be the ones to take on the work of living the apology toward reconciliation. A congregation which follows their lead will take on the shape of an ecumenical lived faith, but this cannot happen second-hand by way of representation or out-sourcing that which must be born from and borne by genuine relationships. Most certainly, such ecumenicals populate local communities of faith to some extent. Moreover, it doesn't take much for the secondary or tertiary operative theology within a community (often ecumenical) to be ignited in larger numbers on such occasions as the Reconciliation Walk or the Women's March.

An organizational snapshot rather than a congregational one would better highlight the ecumenicals' communally lived faith. For example, we find ecumenicals at the helm of denominational groups gathered around specific initiatives (living the apologies, refugee and asylum seeker advocacy, peace initiatives in Israel and Palestine, climate action, gender justice, anti-racism), or in faith-based ecumenical organizations such as Kairos, The Canadian Council of Churches' Commission on Justice and Peace, Citizens for Public Justice, Project Ploughshares, and ACT Alliance, or in citizens' action groups like David Suzuki Foundation or Reconciliation Canada. Here, among like-minded and like-hearted people, ecumenicals are often formed in and for love, just as congregations endeavour to do. Their love may take the peculiar shape of learning to identify their connection to the land they occupy, their relative racial and gender privilege, their voice, as well as their faith and their hope. There is indeed no way to bring change without being changed: the way is made by walking it. Ecumenicals are walking.

Sacraments

God of the just weight
and the fair measure,
let us remember the hands
that harvested this food, this drink,
not only in our prayers
but in the marketplace.
Let me not seek a bargain
that leaves others hungry.[5]
—Janet Morley

THE IMAGE OF COMMUNION AS A FORETASTE OF THE MESSIANIC BANQUET, or the kin-dom/kingdom of God, is sacrament indeed for the ecumenical. A table where all are invited and everyone is fed is nothing short of the reign of Christ for which ecumenicals work and pray. To be reminded here that a world like this *is* possible not because it will happen in their lifetime through their efforts, but because it is the very nature of God to bring this vision to life, is a source of hope and sustenance for ecumenicals. Their worldly knowledge means that words of hope for the ecumenical are always words which begin by *naming reality*. If God's love is proclaimed in a vacuum, it misses the mark completely for those who consent to see the world as it is, to look it in the face and to learn the contours of its inequities.

For the ecumenical, the bread becomes life when the community's *double vision*[6] is invoked: an acknowledgement that these are the circumstances of our times and that God is both the reality we trust and the future in which we hope. The lived faith of the ecumenical is fed by a *shared* acknowledgement that daily in this world "Christ dies," and by a reminder that because of God's love "Christ rises" in ways we recognize when life is protected, land is restored and peoples are reconciled, and finally by singing together that the future is not finished, "Christ will come again." Here, at Christ's table, where the reality of suffering and the promise of new life meet, the ecumenicals' faith is fed hope.

"Water heals the body; water heals the soul. When I go down to the water, in the water we are whole."[7] So sang the circle of Kairos members at the closing ritual of their recent annual gathering. The small group of mostly senior Christian women included some younger members of other or no faith, and so, in keeping with the commitment to inclusivity, no exclusively Christian reference was given to the symbols or words prominently featured in the gathering. A bowl of water on a carpet-sized image of the earth was the centre-piece around which the group sat. For the ecumenical, the bowl served as a font-like symbol of the waters of creation, of liberation, and of baptism while simultaneously representing the water of wells, of watersheds, of dying oceans and of poisoned rivers, of typhoon and draught, of endangered fish and sea life, of the cycle of threatened life on the planet, and the ever-present hope and potential for cleansing, healing, transformation, and life. These symbols—religious, natural, and social—are not added together for the ecumenical; they are conflated as immanent and transcendent symbols of life, death, and new life, symbols of reality and of hope. The world is sacrament for the ecumenicals: it is the place we meet God in the divine solidarity of shared suffering and in the experience of risen life. For ecumenicals, life is transformed by sharing the reality of the broken body of the world with God and with one another.

Trends and Sources: What Else is Going on?

> I heard a few people say that the only thing we can do about racial injustice is pray. Don't get me wrong, I am a praying person, and deeply believe in the transformative power of prayer. So, while I may get down on my knees and pray to God, I also then need to get up and preach. I need to protest. I need our churches to not only pray on Sundays, but to also offer a prayer through a lifetime commitment to systemic change.[8] —Adelle Halliday

The face of an ecumenical lived faith has changed dramatically from the days when inter-church movements and their NGO partners enlisted denominations and congregations in organized campaigns. With the end of that era,[9] the ecumenicals' lived faith has not vanished but parts of it have disappeared from view: it is closer to the ground and closer to the bone. We'll look at both those trends and at the way this work continues to shape theologies from the ground-up.

Closer to the Ground

> Salvation is not a possession but a relationship.[10]
> —Andrew Park Sung

While some large and established local and international social justice organizations remain (Kairos or Amnesty International), the landscape has changed, and the culture of even those organizations along with it. Of all the changes, the most profound is in the notion of expertise. Most decidedly, the previous generation of Christian social activists followed the liberationist popular educators' emphasis on "education from below," or learning from those who bear the scars of history rather than those who write it. Nonetheless, a tendency remained to consolidate those testimonies into a single analysis or narrative which attempted to tell the truth about a particular context. In this way, there were experts whose interpretation of these voices and analysis of the systemic forces which contributed to their situation, who often served as intermediary or auxiliary witnesses to the realities of injustice which held our attention. The new incarnation of social and climate justice, reconciliation and rights work is more organic, inter-disciplinary, diverse, more Indigenous, more divested of institutional privilege, closer yet to the ground than even the previous generations' disciplines of listening allowed. In short, the intermediaries are largely gone. For the older ecumenicals on our pews, this means it is a much longer reach than it was thirty years ago from the sanctuary or board table to the climate action or reconciliation circle, or to the energy alternatives, fair wages, sustainable agriculture, or any number of concerns which we now understand are inextricably linked.

In part, it may have been as a result of the austerity measures which removed such intermediaries from our denominational and inter-church social justice desks in the late 1990s that we lost those expert witnesses. It may have been the result of a more deliberate shift, or a combination thereof. Whatever the cause or causes, the next generation went further than its predecessor in its intention and ability to learn "from the underside of history." Young ecumenicals are directly exposed, through experience, migration, and technology, to opportunities to speak and listen without an intermediary. They sit physically and virtually in far more proximity to the people and issues of concern to them. To organize in support of women's rights in India, they sit at a virtual table with those women, governed by the norms of just and participatory conversation which emerge organically from those gathered. What once took an international delegation of prepared panellists is daily available on *WhatsApp*. Moreover, these are more radically diverse and democratic circles than previously imagined.

It must be said that when these young ecumenicals move from those circles into the church and back, there is a challenging cultural shift for them to negotiate. In truth, we don't see many of them remain in congregational communities of faith. This should lead to inspiration more than to disappointment on the part of the church. The fundamentally diverse circles in which they sit, the proximity to the struggles they engage, and the high bar of authenticity and norms for inter-cultural engagement in those conversations, are forming a generation of ecumenical leaders to embody this beautiful expression of lived and living faith.

Chapter Nine Living Ecumenical Lived Faith

As we have seen, genuine ecumenicals find their way to those on-the-ground real-time convergences of activists. There, their faith is fed through the challenge and joy felt in the holy conflation of working and waiting for the kin-dom of God. It is in these communities of people drawn to specific concerns that they continue to learn in circles of mutual respect: religious, non-religious, a-religious, colonized, colonizer, and migrant, learning at thresholds and intersections of social and personal identities even while campaigning or organizing resistance to the forces that diminish the flourishing of life.

It is unfair to characterize this as a good news story. The shape and make-up of movements for social justice, advocacy, resistance, and reconciliation have changed in positive ways over the past decades, but only in response to increasingly devastating circumstances and unimaginable threats. That faith continues to grow in the shape of an ecumenical lived faith is testimony to God's nearness despite what they and others are tempted to view as evidence to the contrary.

For those outside these circles, the forces poised to push against mounting threats to civil society, food security, and planetary sustainability seem sporadic and weak. They are not.[11] There are a growing number of spiritually rooted, disciplined, sustained, and inter-generational groups in which ecumenicals find themselves, not as "delegates" of the church but by virtue of their own relationships, commitments, and circumstances. This is, in many respects, where the heart of the ecumenicals' faith has long lived: in an experience of participation in the divine life through shared sorrow over the world's wounds and shared joy in solidarity with all who desire to see life on this shared planet flourish. There is, for them, a taste of the world for which they long in the very work itself.

Closer to the Bone

> "Righteous anger does not lead to transformation, but the spiritual path does, because the story that is damaging the planet is carried in each of us. The work of transformation must begin within."[12]—anonymous participant, Kairos local event

This quote from a participant in a recent Kairos event in BC echoes of ancient wisdom in every spiritual tradition. In religious and non-religious activist communities and networks, this wisdom is taken increasingly seriously. Asking the question, "why is this happening?" in the face of the world's most knotted and pernicious ills, ecumenicals, within the church and beyond it, are led toward exploration of root causes. In this, there is no way to avoid oneself in this inquiry. Whoever we are, not only are we politically implicated by virtue of playing some part in the global economy, we are personally implicated by virtue of being human in a world where humans do harm. This particular framing of the ecumenicals' commitment to social transformation typically leads to two domains of exploration: sociological and spiritual. This is not new. For example, several decades ago, the anti-war movements critiqued the military industrial complex *and* raised concerns about the effects of war toys on children. These branches of inquiry, about how humans self-organize and what makes us the way we are, are typical of movements for social justice and social change.

While this has always be typical of the wisest elders among the ecumenicals, attention to the spiritual life of the ecumenical is a growing trend. Those we assume are all about "issues" turn out to be more complex and self-reflective than their slogans betray. They are fully aware that patterns of human behaviour at the root of social, political, and planetary crises are as good as bred in the bone. Unlike earlier generations, it would be difficult to find an activist under forty who didn't concur with some aspect of the notion that while social transformation doesn't *depend* on personal transformation, it does *involve* a level of commitment to spiritual awakening. An example of this within the regional church was a reframing of the "justice network" to take the approach of "contemplative justice," a deliberate acknowledgement of the relationship between personal and political transformation.

While Indigenous and Eastern ways of knowing have not separated life into these inner and outer, personal and social, human and planetary spheres, the Western mind has. For this reason, non-Western traditions are mentors for ecumenicals who embrace this closer-to-the-bone approach to activism. For most Westerners, this means the retrieval of ancient religious wisdom, including biblical wisdom, or learning new practices and epistemologies. It might also have a more politically pragmatic frame, including unlearning colonial identities. Activist ecumenicals draw on art, music, and street theatre to both *do* the spiritual work of integration and to *express* resistance, hope and a vision for life transformed, Life in Abundance. Going by a variety of names associated with theories of integration, leadership, and systems,[13] ecumenicals are drawing on inter-disciplinary sources to aid this integrative inner and outer work. For example, the work of wisdom elders like Richard Wagamese[14] and Joanna Macy,[15] guide groups and individuals in paths of awakening, gratitude, connection, attention, and self-giving, all of which we will encounter in the next chapter on the "spiritual" lived faith. Indeed, having navigated their way into their own antidote for the shadow of despair which tempts them, here the ecumenicals' movements and communities blur with the spirituals'. For non-theists, hope is found in a worldview which highlights interconnection, community, inner peace, and self-healing. For the Christian ecumenical, the source of hope is always in God's life, the Life of the World, both present and promised and revealed in these same manifestation of divine healing, peace and the integrity of creation.

Theologies of Hope, Again

Though passed over by a generation of church leaders who pushed back on perceived capitulation to liberal cultural values, contemporary liberationist theologies are being embraced again by a new generation of faith leaders who, in addition to its commitment to transformation, are drawn to its diversity of voices, to its openness to other faiths and no faiths, its rootedness in social movements for liberation, and its commitment to be informed by and accountable to the socio-political context, global economy, and planetary concerns. There is no single approach to the theologies which ecumenical lived faith births and draws upon, but these pluralistic, global, democratizing characteristics of it are consistent. By starting first with faith in God's future and working backwards toward the present, focussing particularly on what we *do* over what we *believe*, many of these theologies are characterized by an enacted eschatological hope, committed to speaking of God's engagement with the world in terms of both social and ecological history[16]. They are contextual constructive theologies[17] which take seriously post-colonialism, diversity, inter-dependence, and the themes of convergence and disruption. Practical ecumenicals will also be drawn to Christian ethicists and activists' work like Ched Meyers' "Watershed Discipleship," for example, and other theological work that addresses particular contexts and concerns.

The biblical image of the end of the world (apocalypse) or the "end times" (the eschaton) is increasingly invoked in our time in both religion (the forecast of the end of the world) and culture (dystopian themes). The climate crisis, nuclear instability, racial violence, and political chaos contribute to a sense of dread and doom. Classical Christian doctrine is very human-focussed whereas the ecumenical lived faith keeps the *oikos* (the whole created world, human and nonhuman) in view. As more and more people of any faith or no faith take in the images and are haunted by hints of "end times," the faith of ecumenicals in our midst will be instructive. For them, the in-breaking of God's future is a constant reality, even in our terrifying present. Their faith is tethered to a promise of a new heaven and a new earth, not *instead* of this one *someday*, but *for* this one *now*. They are our practical theologians of hope, not merely because of what they do and say about how the world *could be*, but because of the hope they have within them borne of their experiences of it in the present struggles for life in which they are engaged.

From the globalization of economies to the devastating impact of human life on the climate (and *vice versa*), ecumenicals takes seriously that interdependence is the lens through which the world must now be viewed and understood. Contrary to its critics' assessment, ecumenical lived faith is not about doing God's kin-dom-building work for *lack* of faith in God's future, but in anticipation of it and by way of beckoning it forward, borrowing it from the future. To "partner" in the work of healing the world or to "participate" in the present intimations of the kin-dom of God is not a delusionary gesture of presumed equality with God. Nor is it functional atheism: acting as if there were no God because God appears absent. Rather, it is the lived faith of one who meets Christ, communes with the Spirit, is at-one with and within God, through doing what God is doing: siding with life.

Lived Faith	Work for Social Change
What is God doing?	God is eternally healing, reconciling and restoring the world which God created and desires to flourish.
How?	Through the in-breaking of the promised and longed for kin-dom/kingdom of Abundant Life and aided by all who participate in making real the vision of God's anticipated commonwealth of justice, peace and the integrity of creation.

Chapter Nine Living Ecumenical Lived Faith

What does it mean to believe in Christ?	To believe in Christ is to live in, with and for his promises of life abundant, God's kin-dom on and of this earth.
What is the church for?	To be an agent of God's justice, peace and reconcilliation.
What is the Christian life?	It is to side with the all who share the struggle for fullness of life, as Christ did, by working for social change, and for transformation of our relationships to and on the earth.
Christian identity	Partner
Christian character	Prophet
Why I read Scripture	The Hebrew bible reveals God's justice as a love that brings peace, right relations, and the flourishing of all life. The parables of Jesus reveal a world founded on a love that reorients the world toward God's justice. I am reminded in Scripture of God's love for the world, of the way the Spirit ignites our hearts with passion for aligning our lives with God's vision of all life flourishing.
Distinctive focus related to Sin and Grace	Sin is participating in an oppressive social, ecological and economic system that undoes the life that God has created. Grace is the assurance of hope in things seen and unseen, in Christ that God's justice is manifest in the love for which we too have been created (imagoDei).
Key Biblical texts	Isaiah 2:4 John 10:10
Strengths	Expertise, Scope, Analysis
Shadow	Ideology, Cynasism, Dispair
Antidote	Spiritual grounding, restored faith

Table 6: Ecumenical

Notes

1. GreaterVan gogo Grandmothers is a chapter of the GoGoGrandmother's campaign, a project of the Sub-Saharan Africa Family Enrichment, a faith-based NGO established in Malawi in 1993 to address the HIV/AIDS pandemic.
2. Fridays for Future Canada is part of the international movement that began in August 2018 in response to Greta Thunberg's climate crisis actions.

3. Salal and Cedar Watershed Discipleship is a ministry of the Anglican Diocese of New Westminster in BC centred on eco-justice and land-based reconciliation in the form of a worshipping community of faith. http://salalandcedar.com.
4. The Forest Church movement is a British Fresh Expression church movement aware of the natural world as a threshold to God and may include commitment to protection and conservation of forests and woodlands. Similarly, the North American Wild Church movement is deeply rooted in relationship with the earth, spiritually and ethically. http://www.mysticchrist.co.uk/forest_church and https://www.wildchurchnetwork.com/.
5. Janet Morley, "God of the just weight," in *Blessed Be Our Table: Graces for Mealtimes and Reflections on Food* by Neil Paynter (ed), (Glasgow: Wild Goose, 2002), 26.
6. Reference to Northrop Frye, *The Double Vision: Language and Meaning in Religion* (Toronto: University of Toronto Press, 1991).
7. Coco Love Alcorn, "River," (adpt) *Wonderland*, Speak Music, 2016.
8. Adelle Halliday, "What I Need From White People" *Broadview: Justice/Opinion* https://broadview.org June 3, 2020.
9. Gregory Baum, "Goodbye to the Ecumenist," *The Ecumenist* 29, no. 2:2, 1991.
10. Andrew Park Sung, *Triune Atonement: Christ's Healing for Sinners, Victims, and the Whole Creation*, (Louisville: Westminster John Knox, 2009) p 92.
11. See for example, Bill Phipps' commentary on David Korten's *The Great Turning: From Empire to Earth Community* (San Francisco: Barrett-Koehler, 2006), entitled *Cause for Hope: Humanity at the Crossroads* (Kelowna, BC: Copperhouse Woodlake, 2007).
12. Anonymous participant, Kairos Regional Gathering, July 2019, Vancouver, BC.
13. These vary widely and are pulled from fields of leadership and systems theory (Margaret Wheatley), futures (Otto Scharmer), psycho-social analysis (Ken Wilbur) ecology (Brian Swimm, Thomas Berry) and spirituality (Richard Rohr), to name only a few.
14. Richard Wagamese, *Embers: One Ojibway's Meditations*, (Madeira Park, BC: Douglas and McIntyre, 2016).
15. Joanna Macy is an educator and author connected to movements for social and personal transformation. https://workthatreconnects.org/network/.
16. This generation of ecumenical theologies and theologies of hope includes process theologies along with Latin American, Asian *minjung* (suffering), Black, womanist, queer, feminist, indigenous, and political theologies of embodiment.
17. Additional examples of such theologies include the work of post-colonial, eco-, queer, and liberationist theologies: Hye-Ran Kim-Cragg, David Hallman, Marcella Althaus-Reid, Sallie McFague, Rita Nakashima Brock, Kwok Pui-Lan, Andrew Sung Park, Joerg Rieger, John Thatamanil, R.S. Sugirtharajah. We would add to these, theologies of hope, radical theologies (21st century) and other western incarnational and ethical theologies which match the implicit theology of the ecumenical whose understanding of God's agency is inextricably linked to human participation in movements of life-affirming love and justice (Paul Tillich, John Caputo, Peter Rollins, Catherine Keller).

The Spiritual Banquet Table

Chapter Ten
Meeting Spiritual Lived Faith

To live with respect in creation[1] —A New Creed, UCC

Reality sat between fields of green and fields of stars. . .the wonder and presence of that natural world—the forces of earth and sky. . .I think first set in motion. . .a quest to discern a relationship between the immanent and the transcendent. [This path] is trod by those of us with a determined trust that God can bring creation out of chaos, [and] that chaos is the precondition from which God draws new meaning and new life. So, I am a pilgrim.[2] —Murray Groom

MURRAY'S TESTIMONY TO THE QUEST AND DEPTH OF WHAT WE ARE calling a *spiritual* is extraordinary. He is, quite typically, poetic. His words reveal an awakened sensitivity to the whole of things born of an inward journey. This mystical sensibility is worldly and raw, thread with his human journey of loss, struggle, failure, and rebirth. The natural world is inextricably linked to his sense of belonging in the world and in God. Murray is a spiritual director with Pacific Jubilee and a retired minister.

Another testimony to spiritual lived faith might look like this:

> *Erin went to Catholic school, but she did not consider herself Christian however, until she came back to church by way of attending a memorial service. She is a professional musician and music therapist. The service at a United Church moved her*

> to return to weekly worship where she discovered that what she had considered an amalgamation of "personal beliefs" gathered throughout her life were indeed deeply Christian. The day she joined the church, she felt a profound "home-coming of her soul." Erin says her work in music therapy has always been anchored in a belief in the power of healing that comes from the same place music does, an intimate "beyondness" she now recognizes as what this community calls "God," the Spirit of life. Erin attends worship regularly and enjoys serving communion. Many of her peers remain "spiritual but not religious," but she is happy to be both.

And another:

> Paulus is a botanist, "hobby-cosmologist" and nature photographer. He was raised at an intentional distance from religion, but met the United Church minister at his coffee shop "office." Paulus contributes to the congregation's Facebook page, often sharing quotes from authors of religion and science he is reading, photos, and notes about his field work where he is reminded daily that "everything is contingent and inter-connected." Paulus insists that "the living universe is enough to believe in" and "all the rest of it [Christianity, Buddhism, and Indigenous teaching] helps me figure out how to live in it."

This theological world covers the widest territory at our theological banquet. The lived faith practiced here includes both the most ancient and the most new. This is the stream connected to the deep and ancient roots of the Christian tradition and at the same time props wide open its door to the spiritual seeker. On one hand, the wisdom of the Christian mystic is rooted in this soil. On the other hand, those with no church experience whatsoever are most often introduced to the Christian spiritual life and community across this threshold. In some respects, the breadth of this landscape means people at this table may not recognize one another. The physicist and the poet, the jazz musician and the psychologist, the inter-religious scholar and the ornithologist, the former Benedictine and the practicing Buddhist all potentially find their faith home here. Whether a contemplative, intellectual, adventurer, or performer, the spirituals' faith is lived in reverence, wonder, a profound trust in the scared nature of reality, and a sense of intimate connection with the creative heart of the divine life.

Who are the Spirituals?

> Blessed the universe, long unbroken story, spirit in all things[3]
> —Carolyn McDade

Spirituals in our schema are implicitly or explicitly attuned to encountering the spirit in all things. They may have been raised in a sacramental tradition among Catholics or Anglicans, but most simply have an innate sensibility to experience and view the world as holy ground. With or without such language for this experience, spirituals share a profound reverence which might be expressed as inquiry, curiosity, creativity, or silence. They are our scientists, explorers, artists, and contemplatives. Their connection with God is through experience of the holiness in and through all things. Because this stream sits across a number of disciplinary intersections, the language of spirituals is often cosmopolitan and pluralistic. It may sound to others at the theological banquet as if this group is stepping away from the church as opposed to bringing other disciplines and perspectives into it with them.

What do the spirituals look like among us? The first thing to say is that many spirituals are not among us. Like Erin before the memorial service or Paulus before the coffee shop conversation, many spirituals have not found their way to communities of faith. While we could spend a good deal of time describing *them* and where their path might encounter or cross thresholds of exploration or entry into our communities, our focus here is on those with a spiritual lived faith who *do* move among us. And there are plenty! How do we know them by their lived faith?

Somewhere in our congregations there is a young adult who is moved during the final hymn to rise from the pew and practice her dervish dance, and there is a scholar of the mystic, Thomas Merton[4]. These may also be the people more likely to want to read the bible as *lectio divina*[5] or poetry than through a historical-critical lens. Their list of spiritual mentors will span and transcend Christianity. It will include those who express, in a variety of ways, both implicitly and explicitly, experience of the inner and outer world as revelatory of the divine life within and beyond it. We might imagine them at a book table by-passing the literature related to church growth and instead picking up a volume on poetry, jazz, cosmology, Celtic prayer, process thought, or mysticism.[6] A person in this stream may not recognize themselves at the cross-roads of any of these particular intersections related to arts, science, and religion, but to understand how this diverse group ends up at the same table at the theological banquet, we use a wide-angle lens on this group's various ways of engaging the Spirit of life at the heart of their faith: the arts, the natural world, science, and religions. Here again, though mindful that there are spirituals on the edges of our communities of faith, we are describing those who are firmly planted within them.

The Arts

> [A]s artists and art-lovers, we experience art as one of the great ways to spiritual insight. In a culture that has been so word-heavy and overly cerebral, and where almost everything has been turned into a commodity for sale and purchase, art and the spiritual impulse are a vital counterbalance. When we open ourselves to the intrinsic value of art—in its vast array of styles and techniques—we open ourselves to being met by the Holy One who speaks in unexpected ways.[7] —Lois Huey Heck

The spiritual is often an aesthetically oriented soul. For them, the creative arts both reveal and express the presence of the One who *has created and is creating.*[8] Whether as vocation, profession, or avocation, for some on this path, faith and the creative arts are inseparable, because the arts are their *primary* way to experience the holy, the reality of God. Perhaps the comment "I go to this church for the music" is less a disparaging remark about the preaching or community and more a testimony to the lived faith of the spiritual!

For the spiritual, poetry, art, and music are not merely decoration on tradition. These artistic renderings of union with the divine life are part of liturgy for a reason: they are a path to God, a portal to the transcendent, food for the soul. Artistic and contemplative spirituals find prose-heavy worship distracting. It clutters, if not obscures the ineffable "rumours of the glory"[9] which surround us.

For every spiritual on a pew, there are countless whom we rarely, if ever, meet who are anonymously deepening their spiritual life by way of the community orchestra, the potter's studio, the bread kitchen, the art gallery. This is hardly a new phenomenon. The seventh century monks at Lindesfarne communed with God as much through *creating* the art which accompanied the scriptures as they did by their *studied* devotion to the text. Protestantism's unfortunate chapter of asceticism aside, Christian devotion and spiritual life has been aided by beauty. Like missionals whose professional lives are obscured on the pews, we may not know that the spiritual life of the lay reader is sustained by her oil painting or photography.

The Natural World

> *Earth is so thick with divine possibility that it is a wonder we can walk anywhere without cracking our shins on altars.*[10]
> —B. B. Taylor

Perhaps because we miss them in our congregations, we have disparaged the Sunday morning hiker, kayaker, and bird watcher for at least a generation in the church. Many such church sanctuary exiles are our siblings on the road of reverence. These nature-oriented spirituals walk this road with all those of faith or no faith whose spirits are awakened by wonder. For these spirituals, there is no need to create art when we live in it! The more wondrous the manifestation of creation, the more revelatory of the Holy: the snowy trail, the greening firs, the lakeside loon call, the return of the salmon, the migration of the monarch, the expanding universe. This does not mean that Christianity is the equivalent to love of nature. Rather, it means that on the spiritual path of reverence is a wisdom, a perception that is about far more than the wooded trail it took to get there. Reverence of the earth, wonder, and beauty are modes of awakening to the deep knowledge of union and communion where boundaries of subject/object, spirit/matter, faith/no faith, God/no God are transcended.

For the nature-oriented spiritual, the reality of the Spirit of God resides in the world and can be met in the world. Outsiders frequently accuse these spirituals of romanticism, paganism, or pantheism. In truth, the spirituals' ancient path echoes the psalmist's praise of God in the glory of God's on-going creation and has survived all the distractions, destruction, and devastation centuries of excessively human-focussed religious life have brought.

The Sciences

Dr. Charles Townes, Nobel prize laureate and inventor of the laser, worshipped regularly at the First Congregational Church of Berkeley (United Church of Christ, USA). His faith was lived as an adventure in reverent inquiry into the mechanics of the universe, a way of pondering the mind of God:

> *"Science tries to understand what our universe is like and how it works, including us humans,"* he wrote. *"Religion is aimed at understanding the purpose and meaning of our universe, including our own lives. If the universe has a purpose or meaning, this must be reflected in its structure and functioning, and hence in science."*[11] —R. Sanders

In our schema, the spiritual table hosts those who ask science to help them interpret the seen and unseen worlds to which these explorers pay such acute attention. For them, devotion and inquiry are one. It is this expression of lived faith that wades into the water of astronomical physics, psychology, biology and life sciences. For some on this path, "the more I give myself to the earth, the more I belong to God,"[12] as twentieth century theologian and scientist Teilhard de Chardin expressed it. Quarks and biomes become icons. The story of God is written across the face of all that 'came into being.' (John 1). This is *not* scientism, a worldview that considers real only that for which there is empirical evidence. Nor is it an argument for intelligent design. Rather, this is a way of interpreting reality in which science, as a discipline of attentiveness and curiosity, is a form of devotion to the unknowable and the knowable.

> *There is a preference for oneness in the universe, from the atomic level upward, but it is not predetermined or fixed... Everything in theology, in fact, looks different once we become fully aware that the universe is still emerging*[13] —John Haught

Cosmology, astronomy, "big history," and evolutionary science are connected to the lived faith of some spirituals. These include those who experience the divine in the emergence of the universe. The inseparability of the unfolding of God's story or the revelation of divine life in the material of the physical world, in some cases informs this stream's understanding of prayer as well. Healing touch and healing prayer are practices related to this stream's embrace of the mysterious connection of the body-mind-spirit, a connection that is the preoccupation of science as much as it is of religion. In fact, it is another threshold of encounter between the two.

Psychology is perhaps the social science that comes most readily to mind in considering those in this stream. Spiritual directors, counsellors, or other professionals frequently accompany spirituals across the psycho-spiritual landscape on which their journey in and with God takes them. Self-knowledge guards against the self-deception which our tradition, among others, recognizes as the root of harm (sin/evil). For spirituals, this self-knowledge and self-understanding becomes foundational and integral to their lived faith. The popularity of everything from the enneagram spiritual typology to spiral dynamics and integral spirituality reflects the pull of the spiritual life toward self-understanding for transformation.

The Life, Practice and Teaching of (Inter-faith) Mystics

Guides are needed to traverse the inner landscape of the self/soul and to enter more deeply into the divine life. We are not surprised to see on the bookshelf of the spiritual, Saint Teresa of Avila's *Interior Castle*[14] or the poetry of Sufi mystic, Rumi.[15] Here is where East and West, Indigenous, ancient, and medieval wisdom meet in the heart and mind of the spiritual pursuing a path toward transformation, enlightenment, at-oneness (mystical union), Christ-consciousness, or love.

Because the medium for wisdom teaching is practice, spirituals inspired by the wisdom traditions are engaged in practices from our own and other traditions associated with the contemplative or awakened life. They may adopt these in their ancient forms as in, for example, forty days of silence in an Ignatian retreat or three days of fasting and prayer in a secluded hermitage on a Gulf Island. While guarding against appropriation, these spirituals may be just as likely to adapt practices from other religious traditions: the way Zen meditation informs centring prayer and enneagram shapes the form of daily examen. Practices may include daily orders, *lectio divina*,[16] silence, meditation, breath prayer, centring prayer, chanting, movement, journal-keeping, fasting, pilgrimage, and praying the labyrinth. For those whose spiritual lived faith is connected to Indigenous life and communities, contextual Indigenous practices will be taught and employed appropriately for the benefit of the inner journey, healing, and vision. The ancient tradition of spiritual mentorship, master, teacher, elder, or director is anchored in these ancient ways of spiritual awakening to wisdom, vision, oneness, and love.

At the Theological Banquet workshops, spirituals aggregately and frequently make up the largest group. People seated at this table are shocked to discover this. They expect to find themselves alone. Immediately, they begin to share with one another the sense of insecurity they have about their belonging: Does the fact that they read Jewish mystics or practice Buddhist meditation or Yoga mean they are only quasi-Christian? Does using terms like *Beloved* or *Holy One* instead of *God* or *Almighty* make them heretics? They are conflicted about their connection to the church. They confess to one another that they feel more connected to the holy by watching the morning light than by reciting the Apostle's Creed, or might be more dependent on their spiritual director than the bible study group to guide their deepening journey of faith, or question the Christian anthropology of human as caretaker rather than equal creature within creation. Moreover, they discuss with one another whether these convictions will edge them deeper into the church or coax them into leaving it behind.

What's in a Name?

> Most hidden; most near[17]
> —St. Augustine of Hippo

What we are attempting to capture under this heading is the expression of lived faith that is most connected to the interior life, other disciplines, religious traditions, and practices, and to creation or the cosmos. People who seat themselves at this table choose to sit under this heading because they use the word 'spiritual' to describe themselves: "a spiritual person," having a "spiritual life," being on a "spiritual journey," looking for a "spiritual home," living their life "in the Spirit." While the lived faith of an evangelical may be deeply rooted in the power of the Holy Spirit, they will not likely find consonance with the more cosmological and universal orientation at this table. We might have given this group the label "mystery," "mystic," or "wisdom," terms which other tables do not readily claim. We have selected *spiritual* however, because it resonates with those who choose the name and because, like other labels we are using, this term could also stand to redeem its reputation, or at least to explain itself.

Here again, our label "spiritual" misses the mark as much as it makes it. Just as each of our labels could apply to any category in the schema, so too does the term "spiritual" apply across the board. A life of faith *is* a spiritual life, a life inspired (in-spirited) by God's very breath. In classic Trinitarian terms and in the lived experience of people of faith, the Holy Spirit—whether conceived as Advocate, Breath, Life, or Wisdom—constitutes, guides, companions, enlightens, unifies, minds, and draws all life into fullness. We acknowledge that no category has a greater claim to the Holy Spirit than any other. Obviously, we leave the Trinity intact in every category, no matter what language dominates the lived faith of those who find themselves there.

Though one might expect the spiritual but not religious (SBNR) to populate this table, welcome as they are, it is important to remember that most SBNRs very deliberately situate themselves at a distance from the *very* church our theological banquet seeks to explore. It is a disservice to them to photo-shop them into our portrait! It might be more accurate to name a sub-group of the SBNRs we might call the "spiritual and curious about faith" (SCAF) who most certainly are seated at the theological banquet, likely but not exclusively, at this table.

There is also a perception that what we are calling the 'spirituals' snuck into the denomination's big tent because we opened a flap too wide and do not maintain high enough standards of membership in Christian community. Setting those prejudices aside, we acknowledge that when the SBNR or SCAF *do* enter Christian community through this door, they are no longer "not religious" and may find themselves at home at any of the tables at the banquet. Contrary to the "Christian lite" preconception about this lived faith, the spiritual table at the theological banquet hosts a significantly large number of pilgrim people whose spiritual discipline and depth of faith exceeds rather than misses the bar.

We refer to the spirituals at the banquet as 'pilgrims' because their spiritual posture is one of journeying, openness to the unknown, exploration, self-emptying, and wisdom-seeking. Though a pilgrim is a primarily a solitary traveller, their sense of belonging to the whole of things could not be more profound. The spiritual journey is always to loosen the grip on "I" and to become at-one with all things at the heart of the Divine reality.

Flashback

The assumption about spirituals is that they are the centre of their own reality and the autonomous authority on their own religious life. While the turn in the 1960s away from institutionalized religious authority meant that by choice or by inheritance many Canadians for some time now have been navigating spiritual life as freelancers, we are not conceiving of people in this stream as those who deliberately reject the church in favour of other authorities and communities. Rather, our spirituals are people who pursue paths and practices, teachers and traditions, including but not exclusively Christian ones. Through broadening their affiliations with those who have similar experience of sacramentality, spirituals deepen their faith; they do not make it up.

What we discover in reading our own denominational history is that far from being the ones to blame for rejecting traditional church life and heading off to "find themselves," the spirituals in our midst are the resilient few who despite the profanely commercialized landscape, sought and found a spiritual path. Phyllis Airhart's history of the United Church[18] reminds us that though we have interpreted the turn in the 1970s from "clergy" to "counsellor" negatively, as an abandonment of the role of teaching the faith in favour of exploring the self, it reflected a shift, not a rejection. In some cases, this cultural recovery of the role of the "priest" in accompanying the human soul at work was a response of a generation seeking someone with training to guide them on an authentic spiritual path of awakening and deepening. If anything, the rejection was of the community and its norms, not of the quest or its guide.

We recognize too, that the rapprochement between the Catholic and Protestant church in the post-Vatican II era in the 1960s had the long-term effect of Protestant denominations like ours recovering liturgical practices, sacramental theologies and ministries, contemplative prayer and spiritual direction, mystical writings, arts, and Eastern Christian theologies, all of which inform and appeal to the lived faith of spirituals.

Chapter Ten Meeting Spiritual Lived Faith

One Line Credo

I believe that reality is an on-going creation of the Divine life. Christ's truth is God at-one with the world.

Figure 9: Spiritual symbol

Symbols or images most likely to connect to the implicit theology of the spiritual lived faith are related to light for truth or wisdom, such as a candle, or depictions of eternity such as a spiral or triskelion, or those related to journeying, such as a labyrinth, staff, or path of stones, or related to the earth, such as water, sand, or foliage. The Celtic cross and the Indigenous cross or four directions are deeply symbolic, earth-encompassing, circular symbols of faith common among spirituals.

The colour is green, conjuring living things. Liturgically, it is the colour ushered in by the epiphany of the sacred in the everyday, and the holiness of ordinary time.

Distinctive Features: Discipline

> Divine creation does not cease
> until all things have found wholeness, union, and integration
> with the common ground of all being.
> …we witness to Holy Mystery who is Wholly Love.[19]
> —A Song of Faith, UCC

Every religious tradition offers the world a path to becoming human—whether we call that the path of awakening, illumination, oneness, compassion, sanctification, or salvation. Though most religious traditions focus a good deal of energy on the means by which the traditions of the faith are learned and practiced, they also acknowledge spiritual experiences that do not come "second hand," through books or sermons, but "first hand" in the ordinary and extraordinary experiences of human life.

For someone with what we are calling a *spiritual* lived faith, these "first hand" experiences are primary. The migration of birds and the pattern of molecules, the Vedanta meditation and the augmented seventh on the cello may be for them as worship and service are for others. The lived faith of the spiritual is imbued with a sacramentality which permeates their person and their walk in the world; there is nothing outside of God. In this way, they are alive in the spirit, centred and grounded in the immediacy of the holy, and attuned to the presence of God. They have rethought God,[20] through the lens of their experiences of God's given-ness and are less concerned with how to be a church-going Christian than with how to be human at-one with the Spirit in love.

The authentic Christian spiritual journey is always a journey toward the fullness of our humanity in Christ. A distinctive feature of the spiritual is their deliberate attention to that journey, to the centrality of spiritual *experience* of the inner Christ over what is taught and learned by other means. Here, spirituals may sound indistinct from evangelicals who also value personal experience of Jesus. The distinction is in the deliberately universal breadth of sources by which spirituals encounter Christ as sacrament of the Divine life in the world. A characteristic of this broad and varied expression of lived faith then, is its relationship to a number of intersections. Among these are the natural world, the imagination and the arts (music, visual, culinary, movement, poetry), the sciences including psychology (understanding the self), physiology (body/soul connection), cosmology and the new science (quantum physics), the saints and mystics from our own and other traditions.

A further distinctive feature can be discerned by way of the larger context in which the spirituals among us are situated. Not only in Christianity and other world religions, but in multiple fields and their inter-disciplinary convergences, a growing quest for recovering the path to life against a backdrop of insecurity, violence, dislocation, and materialism has emerged. This widespread and somewhat amorphous phenomenon, a movement of the Spirit or emergent quest for upholding the dignity, integrity, and sanctity of life, has variously been named the "great emergence," the "Age of the Spirit"[21] or the "great transformation,"[22] the Universe Story,[23] the "Great Work,"[24] or a rise in cosmic consciousness.

The features of this larger spiritual *movement* or *moment* are articulated differently across disciplines and traditions. In very general terms, these features have to do with ways of seeing and ways of being which acknowledge the realities of continuous creativity, relatedness and a Oneness which collects and safeguards particularity. Such Oneness goes by many names and no name. For many spirituals at the theological banquet, this Oneness goes by the name Spirit.

Credo Unpacked

What is God doing?
>God permeates all creation and beckons all that exists into life.

How?
>Through creation and its unfolding. God is revealed in and uses all of creation in God's salvific agency.

What does it mean to believe in Christ?
>To believe in Christ is to see truth in him.

What is the church for?
>To serve people awakening to holy wisdom on the spiritual path to union with all life in God.

What is the Christian life?
>The Christian life is the path of awakening.

Christian identity:
>A pilgrim on the lifelong journey of rebirth

Why I read Scripture:
>Scripture contains truths about humanity and about the nature of God, and illumines a path to the Christ.

Distinctive focus related to sin and grace:

Sin is the disintegration of what has been created as oneness. Grace is the intimation and assurance of the eternal reality of God in all things.

Key biblical texts:
Genesis 32:22-31 Jacob wrestles the angel
Philippeans 2:7 the kenotic hymn

Gifts

In any religious tradition, the steps in the spiritual journey are rigorous and deliberate. This is true for the Christian path our spirituals follow. The journey is not so much a quest, even for enlightenment, but a practiced non-attachment, a way of surrendering an ego-driven life. Whether by way of the expanse of space or the mystery of the soul, spirituals consent to be "on the way" to union and communion on the earth by letting go of exceptionalism and finding themselves a humble part of a universal web of life. Whether as disciplined contemplatives or modest gardeners, this does not happen without work. Their work becomes instructive for people of faith and no faith who are searching for the purpose and practice of being human in the image of love, the image of God. Through them, we are inspired to discipline, non-judgement, curiosity, open-mindedness, self-awareness, attentiveness, and concern for the common good.

While this describes how spirituals approach the life of faith, it does not give us a sense of how they live it. If evangelicals are sharing Jesus, ecclesials are being the church, missionals are helping neighbours, and ecumenicals are mending the world, what are spirituals actually *doing*? Perhaps the greatest gift of the spiritual is not *what* they are doing but *how*. In fact, they may be doing any and all of those things, but they are doing them from a place within themselves of profound equanimity born of the fruit of their labour of deepening awareness of self and other, of the interdependence of all things in and with God, and the unfolding potentiality of greater and greater love within and outside the self.

In this respect, spirituals bring enormous gifts to the theological banquet. Attentive and sensitive, they are among us as poets and artists. They are open, creative, and capable of seeing and navigating connections between apparently disparate paths, whether across cultures, faiths, disciplines, or media. They are self-aware and disciplined, often contributing leadership to the church in the form of offering spiritual formation and direction. In relationship to other faiths and no faith, they demonstrate curiosity and suspension of judgement, and often find connections between wisdom traditions. Their path leads them to self-effacing generosity, acceptance, and joy.

Dangers and Shadows

Every shadow is hidden first and foremost from the one who casts it. It is thereby the last thing we are able to see without help. When does the pursuit of self-awareness for the sake of harmonious relationships and spiritual insight become self-infatuation or self-aggrandizement? There is no turnstile; it is far more slippery and subtle than that. To be curved in on oneself is a danger we have known about at least for as long as the church can remember.[25] In the case of the lived faith of spirituals, it is an innocent slip: a good gone bad.

Consumerism has bred individualism, and individualism drives consumerism: a perfectly closed circle in which to become trapped, particularly when the product being pedalled is "a better or happier YOU." The commodification of the self is a fact of late stage capitalism in the West. Its huge engine drives everything from basic needs (food, shelter, clothing, companionship) to algorithms (ads, fads, "likes," trends) toward narcissism and greed. The human spirit is equipped to resist this debasement. Ironically, it is the pursuit of that very resistance through deliberate attention to recovering the purpose, meaning, dignity, and integrity of human life that one might become caught in the trap of self-absorption: indeed the inverse of the goal.

What we see is that the shadow of the disciplined spiritual, like other shadows, emerges when the strength is over-played. It is experienced when the journey of the self becomes the journey to the self. It happens when the journey's destination is no longer a widening sense of belonging and union, but instead is a narrower focus on personal advancement. This can lead to elitism and egotism equally. This shadow, like all the rest, is the spirituals' core come undone, its opposite: it becomes attachment to self rather than transcendence or kenosis of self.

Antidote

One Sunday morning on my way into First Congregational Church of Berkeley (United Church of Christ), I caught sight of a tall man with a familiar gait crossing Durant Avenue on his way to the service at Trinity United Methodist. A regular church-goer, Huston Smith[26] strode purposefully along the sidewalk and disappeared into the sanctuary. Professor Emeritus, Dr. Smith was in his eighties at this time, a long recognized and world renowned scholar, author, and practitioner of religious wisdom traditions, a mystic and philosopher. The image of Huston going to church on Sunday morning guards against the temptation to imagine anyone "moving beyond" the Christian practice of communal worship or community life.

Much of Protestantism is suspicious of individuals' "spiritual experiences." There are good reasons to be suspect of certain claims of mystical union of any kind. Harm has been done in the name of so-called direct knowledge of God, just as certain interpretations of Scripture, tradition, and community norms have done damage over the centuries. This is precisely why the world religions insist on the interplay of the scholarly, the communal, and the mystical. In the best case scenario, these paths inform and correct one another. For the spiritual, this means anchoring oneself in the community of faith, whether or not it appears to offer spiritual companions. Contrary to the temptation to elitism, the deeper one descends into the heart of faith, the more, not fewer, friends one finds.

Life in community pulls from the spiritual all the gifts of compassion, non-judgement, healthy detachment, and other-centredness which the disciplines of prayer, contemplation, solitude, and self-awareness bring. Community orients these gifts toward the healing of the world and away from any pursuit of perfecting the self. Moreover, the features of a community and the exigencies of the world are the refining fire for the soul at work. Wisdom traditions share an insistence on the outward turn, the unity of contemplation and action. Wisdom, equated with love, may be grown within but is spent and refined without. Like manna, love spoils if it is horded. It is destined for self-offering. At every level, both the community and world are essential for the lived faith of the spiritual to flourish. Engagement with others keeps spirituals away from the reclusive danger of its own self-turned shadow. At our theological banquet, the ecclesials' shared body is the antidote to the spirituals' shadow.

Chapter Ten Meeting Spiritual Lived Faith

Notes

1. A New Creed, The United Church Manual, 20.
2. Used with permission, this is an excerpt from Murray's testimony from the panel presentation (May 26 morning) at the BC Conference Annual Meeting, How Big is Our Tent? University of British Columbia, Vancouver, May 25-28, 2017.
3. Carolyn McDade and Mary Casey, *Blessed: A Litany,* 1996. (USA: Surtsey Publishing, 1982).
4. Thomas Merton was a highly influential 20th century Catholic monk, theologian, philosopher and poet, a prolific writer who popularized the relationship between spiritual (mystical) wisdom traditions and social action in the west.
5. Rooted in medieval Christianity, this meditative reading of Scripture has been popularized in both Catholic and Protestant communities of faith in the retrieval of ancient practices for contemporary spiritual life. It is sometimes appropriated for small group sharing, or as replacement for bible study or preaching though these are not connected to its contemplative origins.
6. Asked who their spiritual mentors are, "spirituals" at the Theological Banquet have the most diverse list: Thomas Berry, J.S. Bach, John Polkinghorne, Duke Ellington, Julian of Norwich, Annie Dillard, along with the popular Richard Rohr, Joan Chittister, Richard Wagamase and Ken Wilbur, and theologians like Teilhard de Chardin, John Cobb, and Catherine Keller.
7. Lois Huey-Heck and Jim Kalnin, *The Spirituality of Art* (Kelowna: Northstone, 2006).
8. A New Creed, UCC.
9. Bruce Cockburn, "Rumours of Glory," original recording on *Humans,* True North Productions, 1980.
10. Barbara Brown Taylor, *An Altar in the World: A Geography of Faith* (New York: Harper Collins, 2009) p. 15.
11. Robert Sanders, "Nobel Laureate and laser inventor Charles Townes dies at 99," *Berkeley News,* January 27, 2015. https://news.berkeley.edu/2015/01/27/nobel-laureate-and-laser-inventor-charles-townes-dies-at-99.
12. Pierre Teilhard de Chardin, *The Prayer of the Universe,* translated by R. Hague (London: Collins, 1977), 89.
13. John Haught, "Theology, Cosmos and Hope" in *Turning to the Heaven,* p 171.
14. Teresa of Ávila is a 16th century Carmelite nun, theologian and Spanish mystic. Among her works is the *Interior Castle*, a guide to spiritual faith development.
15. Rumi (Jalāl ad-Dīn Muhammad Rūmī) is a 13th century mystical poet of the Sufi tradition from modern-day Iran. His spiritual writing features largely in the interfaith spiritual canon.
16. See note 5.
17. Augustine of Hippo in his *Confessions* uses numerous intentionally contradictory descriptive names for God.
18. Phyllis Airhart, *Church with a Soul of a Nation,* 255-291.
19. Song of Faith UCC 2006.

20. John Phillip Newell, *Christianity's Struggle for New Beginnings: The Rebirthing of God, Christian Journeys* (Woodstock VT: Skylight Paths, 2015).
21. Phyllis Tickle, *The Great Emergence: How Christianity Is Changing and Why* (Grand Rapids: Baker Books), 2008.
22. Karen Armstrong, *The Great Transformation: The Beginning of Our Religious Traditions* (New York: Anchor, 2007).
23. Swimme, Brian, and Thomas Berry, *The Universe Story: From the Primordial Flaring Forth to the Ecozoic Era-a Celebration of the Unfolding of the Cosmos.* (San Francisco: HarperSanFrancisco, 1994). This theme is central, for example, to United Church author, Bruce Sanguin's *Darwin, Divinity and the Dance of the Cosmos: An Ecological Christianity* (Kelowna: Copperhouse Woodlake, 2007).
24. Thomas Berry, *The Great Work: Our Way into the Future,* (New York: Bell Tower, 1999).
25. The early church, followed by Luther who referenced Romans, used this term: *incurvatus in se* to refer to being "curved in on oneself."
26. Huston Smith was a scholar, teacher and prolific writer on world religions, including *The World's Religions: Our Great Wisdom Traditions* in several editions beginning in 1958.

Chapter Eleven
Living Spiritual Faith

Congregational Snapshot

WHILE UNITED AND UNITING DENOMINATIONS, AMONG OTHERS, ARE experiencing a decline in participation in inherited forms of congregational life relative to population growth, the number of people of all ages who identify as "spiritual" is on the rise. Of these, there are those who have been exposed to institutionalized religion and have left or rejected it. Some call these the DONES; they appear on the census data as having NO religious affiliation. This same category of "NO religious affiliation" includes people with no experience of institutionalized religion to speak of. Frequently contrasted with DONES, some literature refers to this latter group as NONES. The group referred to as spiritual but not religious (SNRB) spans both the DONES and the NONES groups. In the case of Christianity, the phenomena of people open to *a spiritual life* while maintaining distance from the church-as-we-know-it, is of endless, even desperate, interest. Some church leaders are irritated by this group, because they appear to have no need for the church, and others are intrigued by them for the same reason! Fortunately, the bourgeoning literature based on study of this population is increasingly nuanced and can be useful to church leaders wishing to understand or to serve this group.

It is important, however, to acknowledge that among the spirituals at our theological banquet, a number are only one step away from standing altogether outside the frame of our congregational snapshot. They have either *just* stepped in

(NONES), or are *about* to step out (DONES). Church decline bleeds across the theological spectrum to be sure, but our spiritual category has perhaps the most fluid border in and out of the church. Why? Some of what spirituals in our schema seek in the church is available elsewhere: a celebration or acknowledgement of the sacramentality of life and all living thing; a path and leader to follow deeper into life in God; apophatic or poetic theologies; beauty. Indeed, there *is* an altar in the world, as Barbara Brown Taylor[1] has observed.

Moreover, some of what our spirituals *reject* is alive and well in our churches and detracts from the flourishing of their life in God: anthropomorphic, domesticated or hierarchical images of God, human-centred worldview, self-satisfaction, inattentiveness to aesthetics, absence of the mystical, and lack of attention to a path of spiritual deepening or awakening. As we observed earlier, in taking a snapshot of our congregational life and faith, out of respect for those who have stepped away from the church (DONES), we will not photo-shop them in. Our focus is on the lived faith of those whose faces still appear in the congregational portrait. For this reason, though we could focus on a number of destinations along the path of the SBNR seeker, as many have,[2] it is not their path we are examining here but the implications for the church of their particular route or search.

Picture this fictional community of faith:

> *The place where this faith community gathers pays attention to beauty, both natural and created. The service of worship is uncluttered and reverent. The reflection is likely intellectual or artistic in orientation. Perhaps the preacher is a trained spiritual director or has an undergraduate degree in earth sciences or wrote a master's thesis on the Upanishads. There is local art in the building. There is a labyrinth on the floor of the sanctuary. Every Tuesday, a walkers group gathers to "meet the holy in the hills," and every Wednesday night there is centering prayer. Bursaries are offered for people to attend silent retreats. There is a marker of a scallop shell on the exterior door, brought back by someone who walked the camino de Santiago. During Lent there are readings from the Christian mystics read in worship in addition to scripture. The four weeks of Advent fuse images of earth, wind, fire, and water with hope peace, joy, and love. The*

book study is Richard Rohr's The Naked Now. *Last spring's public lecture series was on Suffering, Surrender, and the Spiritual Path featuring speakers schooled in Islam, Judiasm, Buddhism, and Christianity.*

Of course, finding this under one roof is an imagined scenario, but it may resemble pieces of several congregations on the West Coast of Canada, Cascadia, and beyond. Many congregations are responding to the hunger for spiritual nourishment from both seekers and followers of the Christian path. They are paying particular attention to the intersections at which those with a spiritual lived faith may live: the arts, the natural world, science, contemplative life and practice, and mysticism, including inter-faith expressions thereof.

Not unlike the ecumenical lived faith however, the spiritual will live their faith as much outside the congregation's reach as within it. They will find their spiritual lived faith companions more readily at the retreat centres, studios, hiking trails, and pilgrim paths as they will on the pews. Indeed, just as missionals are in their neighbourhoods and ecumenicals are focussed on the planetary emergency, our spirituals' faith is fed where their faith is lived.

If we look at the lived faith of our spirituals, what do we find them *doing* with their faith both in and out of the church? They are doing what people who experience life as sacred do: they are walking gently and attentively on the earth, seeking and practicing harmony with all living things, gathering to celebrate, to mourn, to support, and to befriend one another, seeking and sharing wisdom, allowing art and creativity to meet and express the ineffable, praising the great mystery at the heart of the universe. They are looking suspiciously like ecclesials. This might be the reason Richard Rohr refers to his Living School[3] as "the monastery without walls;" it looks like Christianity because it is. However, we remember that for the spiritual lived faith, the connection to God is not first through the *community* but via the *path or journey* toward the holy in and through the ordinary and extraordinary things of life—from the laundry on the line to the pattern of the planets. So even those who still have at least one toe in the congregation, their home base of faith is often elsewhere among para-church/para-religious gatherings, alternative spiritual communities, in nature, in study, or in art.

Sacraments

Christ the source and ending, he
of the things that are and have been,
and that future years shall see,
evermore and evermore.[4]

Encountering the sacred in the ordinary is commonplace for the spiritual lived faith. For spirituals then, church sacraments are a way of celebrating mystical union—the holy fused with the ordinary. Sacraments, by their nature, invoke this union: the reality of God coming to us through matter, including through the incarnate life of Christ. In the operative theologies of the spiritual lived faith, the sacraments also invoke transformation as part of the divine life. The juice and bread are transformations of vine and wheat; they illuminate the transformation which takes place in the open cycle of life, death and self-giving present in all living things and in the eternal divine self-giving within the Trinity.

We can anticipate a variety of communion celebrations among the diversity of spirituals—meditative, artistic, cosmological, corporeal, or earthy—employing liturgies which may be ancient, sung, and poetic. Those whose roots are in Catholic or other highly sacramental traditions favour ancient and sung liturgies, as do new Christians who are drawn to the ancient/new forms of liturgical life and orders. Creation-centred sacramental and worship life may employ Celtic liturgies, Indigenous (when Indigenously led) symbol and ritual, or be informed by the emerging Forest Church (UK) or Wild Church (Canada and USA) movement.[5]

Trends and Sources: What Else is Going on?

If we are part of a shrinking church membership, at some point we will get booted out into the world. So, from one point of view, why wait for the doors to hit you on the way out? Why not reinvent the church in the very centres of our communities? At least we will get to meet a lot of new people who are not going to darken our church doors. However, such a shift requires a new theological frame for ministry, a sense of adventure, and

support and training for adventure travel. We could think of it as Christ leading us in a new dance for becoming fully alive.
[6] —George Meier

Though we are not speaking here of "new age spirituality," the spirituality of our age is characterized by a genuinely global, burgeoning renaissance of the quest for life's deeper path and purpose, a path toward the personal and planetary healing so many people are seeking, including those who find themselves in the spiritual category in our schema. This path leads through traditional religious belief and practice, culture, therapeutic practices, ecology, activism, to name only a few. There are hallmarks of this quest, ways of both seeing and seeking that make the quest a *spiritual* and not an idolatrous, frivolous, or *commercial* one. These hermeneutical or interpretative commitments insist on reading the world a particular way, namely through the lens of the interconnection and interdependence of all things, immanent and transcendent. We see this same commitment in our spirituals' orientation toward unity or interdependence (at-one-ment, mystical union), making their worldview sacramental (the world reveals the holy), their beliefs panentheistic (everything is held in God), and their practices aimed at sanctification (carrying the holy within).

This integrative worldview, ethic, spirituality, and practice is at the heart of the spirituals' lived faith. Google anything from "biodynamic farming," to "open and relational theology," from "chakras" to "camino" and you will be led into the web of life-affirming communities of practice and inquiry which populate this swelling wave of spiritual and ethical vitality of which our denomination's spiritual stream is but a small part. For this reason, placing the trends listed below under separate headings is an exercise in contradiction. In truth, from the spirituals' vantage point, emerging forms of spiritual community, their activities, commitments, and theologies cannot be separated, and this is entirely the point. Nevertheless, we have highlighted four areas of interest to church leaders looking to nurture the lived faith of the growing number of spirituals among us: new ecclesiologies, a focus on faith and the arts, interest in process, radical and eco-theologies, and a convergence of contemplation and action.

New Ecclesiologies

> *For the moment...community is emerging in two incomplete forms: Meaningful secular communities grow rapidly but struggle to engage with life's ultimate questions. Imaginative religious communities pull from deep wells of wisdom but struggle to appeal to a rising generation.*[7] —Casper Ter Kuile

By way of the Fresh Expressions movement and beyond, united and uniting denominations are in a particularly creative time with respect to forms of worship and congregational or communal Christian life. We noted earlier, for example, how mission-shaped ministries reform communities of faith, shifting the locus of energy from Sunday morning corporate worship in the building to other ways of, and spaces for, gathering. More interesting yet than re-shaping existing communities of faith, is watching how religious life forms on a blank canvas. We have already observed that spirituals in our schema include those people of faith who have not yet found, or have slipped away from, congregational life. Though not community-oriented or institutionally focused first and foremost, by doing the "soul work" that is most natural and life-giving to them, spirituals will experience the way community forms around practice.

> *Among these people, on the creek delta of this mountain valley above Slocan Lake, in relationship with this land and the beings that inhabit it, creation becomes a catalytic container for alchemical transformation of the heart.*[8] —Therese Descamp

This description of intent has the hallmarks of the spiritual conception of community life—an integration of place, relationships, and intentional practice. *Heart's Rest* is an example of a new ecclesiology that is not about congregating people as much as it is about hosting people—offering nourishment to spiritual pilgrims in a place of physical beauty, in relationship with a living system, in a spirit of trust, of faith, in creation's unfolding in the direction of love. The adoption of the nomenclature "community of faith" to include but exceed our current conception of congregations, allows us to imagine even the pilgrims who pass through *Heart's Rest* as one such moment-in-time community, made and remade with each gathering.

Chapter Eleven Living Spiritual Faith

Observers of trends in religious life[9] uncover the widespread hunger for ways of wisdom by tracing the burgeoning growth not only in individual pursuits of ways of wisdom, but of new forms of communal life centred on these pursuits. These gatherings range from pop-up events to long-term circles of practice but have at their root a commitment to an integrated inward and outward journey as a way to living one's faith. These forms of lived faith have long been emerging within and around the edges of the Christian church and elsewhere. Under the umbrella, "emergent," they represent *transformation-centred Christianity* as opposed to *belief-centred Christianity*.[10] They have the characteristics noted above, including a convergence across traditions and disciplines. These forms of lived faith reflect and lean toward a oneness which safeguards and deepens particularity, thereby allowing life-in-diversity to flourish.

Obviously, it is not possible or desirable to fence the religious life as if it were in some way categorically different from the reverent and life-affirming ways of being which those with no religious affiliation also practice. For this reason, these new ecologies of spirit are often diverse in and of themselves. Rather than exclusively Christian, they may include gatherings and communities in which multi-faith (including no faith), Indigenous spirituality, and other earth-based spiritualties are also present. These communities may lean in the direction of particular practices (contemplation) or philosophies (process) or commitments (ecological). A congregation or its worship leader may embrace and respond to this moment of spiritual questing in a variety of ways. For example, a community of faith in Vancouver made a deliberate choice to embrace an evolutionary frame in its theology, another deliberately uses an apophatic approach to God-language in worship, another offers Pete Rollins' *Omega* course,[11] still another commits to process-informed preaching,[12] and many offer arts-based worship. All of these are examples of what congregations in united and uniting denominations have offered in order to nurture the faith of spirituals among them. These interdisciplinary convergences make such communities of faith places of constructive theologies as well as transformative practice.

Faith and the Arts

Figure 10: Dancer: This is my prayer

By drawing the connection between faith and the arts through events, programs, and centres, congregations, and faith communities are affirming two things: that the creative and performing arts are a means to experience God and practice faith, **and** that beauty itself is a threshold both for those who have and have not yet have stepped on a path toward faith.

While many manifestations of the relationship between faith and the arts on congregational websites appear to be commercially motivated, such as providing rehearsal, recording, and concert space for local musicians, this doesn't preclude something more substantive being sought after in these relationships. There is a sense in which the human spirit seeks beauty as the face of God. The spiritual deprivation many people experience in these times would naturally lead them to the arts. In this way, congregations have an opportunity to collaborate with artists in a genuine ministry of nurturing the faith of the congregation and the community beyond.

There is more to the connection between faith and the arts, however. This commercial or performance model suggests that artists and what they produce are objects of someone else's spiritual life rather than subjects of their own. To minister to and among artists by provision of studio space with no commercial end is an entirely different commitment. This is based on an appreciation of the artist's own spiritual path. In the same way one would not charge people for a chance to pray in the sanctuary, one would not charge rent to dancers who use their bodies to commune with God, or to a poet in residence for the inspiration of their compositions. This relationship with artists is less common among current congregational settings but is at the heart of both ancient monastic and some emerging models of arts-based faith communities.

An interesting threshold created within communities of faith who lean into the arts for spiritual practice and expression is the unusual common ground where both the evangelicals and spirituals in our schema meet. In the domain of the arts, certain modes of spiritual practice are shared across this otherwise less congenial or obvious pairing. An evangelical may speak of becoming lost in praise where a spiritual may articulate self-transcendence and unity, but both arrive at that place through an experience of the relationship of the arts to a prayer-centred life. This same cross-over between the evangelical and spiritual streams is true of the contemplative life and practice more broadly, including its connection to social justice.

Process, Radical and Eco-Theologies

Certainly, the relationship of science to theology is far from new but in our quick glance at the landscape influencing those who fall in our schema into the spiritual stream, it is worth noting that ways of conceiving and speaking of God arising from the conversation between theology and physical and natural sciences, have a particular appeal to spirituals. These include evolutionary and process theologies, eco-theologies, and open or radical theologies. It is important to say that there is tremendous variety in each of these schools of thought, producing a multitude of theological, Christological, and eschatological commitments or understandings of God's nature, agency, and future. The appeal for our spirituals possibly lies in the characteristic openness or open-endedness typical of these theologies and consonant with such scientific frames of reference as chaos, indeterminacy, reciprocity, and mutation. These concepts contrast with traditional theological notions such as immutability and impassivity related to God's nature (unchanged and unaffected by change). While not all spirituals conceive of God along these lines, many will gravitate in this direction as it makes sense of their own experience and lived faith as people committed to the ever-emerging possibilities of transformation of self and world.

By 'eco-theologies,' we are referring not simply to ethical commitments to "greening" churches or living more responsibly on the planet. These more closely reflect the ecumenical faith in our schema. Though most definitely related to these commitments, eco-theologies more specifically refer to those based on an ecological anthropology, by which we mean theologies that understand the person as a constituent part of a global eco-system and not somehow above, beyond, in charge or beholden to it. We remember that the nature-oriented spiritual expresses love and praise of God, the author and invigorator of all that is, through an experience of at-onement with all living things, an awareness of relatedness and inter-subjectivity. It is not surprising that those whose faith is nourished by their relationship to the natural world are drawn to traditions that uphold the worldview (epistemologies and theologies) of the creature-Creator relationship. Understanding oneself as sibling to the elements, offspring of the earth, creature of the Creator, are especially typical of Indigenous and Celtic spiritual traditions. These wisdom traditions shape many in our spiritual category whose lived faith keeps them intimately connected to the natural world. Moreover, a rising awareness of the precarious position in which humans have placed the natural world has fuelled both recovery and construction of theologies and practices of faith that are grounded in, and attentive to, the relationship of human and divine life to all created beings. Some such theologies take as a starting place an understanding of 'love of neighbour' that includes all created beings, indeed the planet, even universe itself, as the 'fellow subject' or 'neighbour' we are called to love as an end in itself, rather than an 'object' for use at our disposal.[13] Others, like the critically important papal encyclical *Laudato Si*[14] are ethically formulated with respect to building an economy which protects the planet.

By "open" theology, we do not mean "anything goes." Rather, "open" is a reference to the unfinished nature of creation, to its undetermined future. Open, relational, process, and evolutionary theologies share a view of God's activity as on-going, unfolding, ever-creating, and responsive rather than timeless, unchanging, or complete. Radical or negative theologies are *apophatic* (naming what God is *not*, rather than who God is) approaches which maintain God's unknowability. These also appeal to spirituals' mystical experience and their conversation with aspects of Buddhist and Hindu thought. Spirituals will often be drawn in our own tradition to disciples of Meister Eckhart,[15] Teresa of Ávila or John of the Cross,[16] all of whom are experiencing renewed popularity. Much of what is known as radical theology[17] is tied to postmodern philosophies and not particularly accessible, but it serves as an intellectual partner to mysticism. Radical theologies are strongly immanent rather than transcendent, appealing to the spirituals' orientation to the sacred in the ordinary. They also cohere with spirituals' lived faith by radically rethinking the nature of the human being as species among species, including the political implications of this worldview. In this way, these radical theologies are a good match for the spirituals' rejection of anthropocentrism and their interest in planetary ethics.

These theologies are largely panentheistic, in other words conceive of reality as taking place within God and not somehow below or beside or otherwise outside God. There are many variations of these theologies in conversation with one another and with science and philosophy. Overall, they appeal to the spiritual sensibility insofar as they stress God's *creativity* above God's *control*. This fits the spirituals' own proclivity to creative arts, to the natural world, and to the mystery of divine immanence.

Contemplation and Action

> *To claim to be aware of the oneness of life and not to regard all of it as sacred trust is a violation of the very purpose of contemplation, which is an immersion in the God of life. To talk about the oneness of life and not to know oneness with all of life. . .is not contemplation. . . .Transformed from within then, the contemplative becomes a new kind of presence in the world who signals another way of being. . . .The contemplative can never again be a complacent, non-participant in an oppressive system. . . .From contemplation comes not only the consciousness of the universal connectedness of life, but the courage to model it as well.*[18] —Sister Joan Chittister

Far from a retreat from the world, the path inward is a path of self-offering to the world. Sister Joan Chittister beautifully articulates the relationship between contemplation and action at the heart of Christian faith. She is not alone in creating greater awareness about this relationship. Both activists and contemplatives are walking toward each other. For example, groups such as Kairos, which is focussed on action for social change, justice, and reconciliation, routinely take time for silence in their gatherings and offer spiritual retreat for their members. At the same time, spirituals whose lived faith is anchored in contemplative practice are finding themselves more and more drawn to engage movements which resist damage to life and living systems. A perfect example of this relationship of the spiritual and the ethical happened several years ago when, for example, the social action arm of the denomination's coastal region reframed its agenda to be one of "Contemplative Justice," offering a program with all the hallmarks of the spiritual stream, including openness to other faiths and incorporation of interfaith spiritual practices as foundations on which to build competencies for leading social transformation.

Indigenous and other land-based spiritualties, including ancient Celtic spirituality and some contextually adapted Catholic spiritualties, offer a depth of integration which highlight the inseparability of ecological, social, and personal living systems. The closer the relationship between communities of faith and communities whose religious practice is informed by Indigenous wisdom and land-based spiritualties, the more models for integration of soul work and justice work will come to light. From both the active entry point and the contemplative entry point, efforts to support the flourishing of life are increasingly approached more holistically. A manifestation of the spiritual antidote to the ecumenicals' despair, this beautiful alchemy of the spiritual and the ecumenical appears to be a manifestation of the spirit of our time and one that hovers around, more than within, our communities of faith. Those who have been inspired by this spirit however, are populating our pews in numbers larger than they, or the rest of us, had imagined.

Lived Faith	Walk the path of wisdom
What is God doing?	God permeates all creation and beckons all that exists into life.
How?	Through creation and its unfolding. God is revealed in and uses all of creation in God's salvific agency.
What does it mean to believe in Christ?	To believe in Christ is to see truth in him.
What is the church for?	To serve people by uncovering holy wisdom on the spirtual path to union with all life in God.

Chapter Eleven Living Spiritual Faith

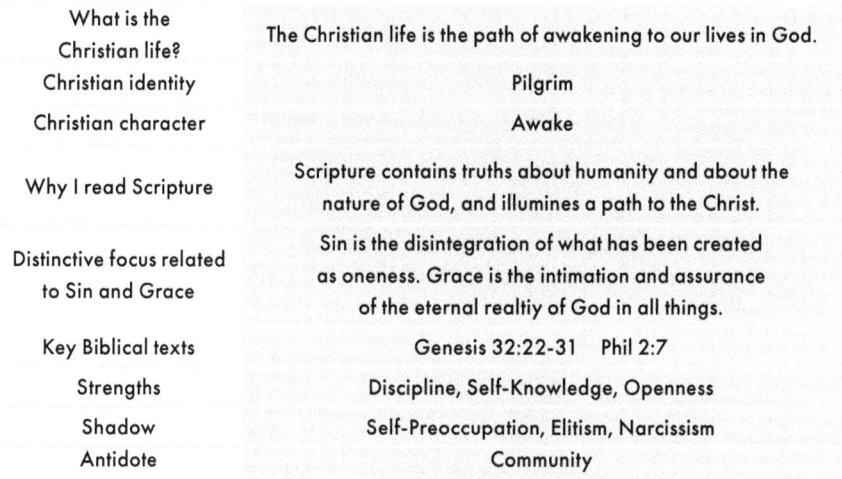

Table 7: Spiritual

Notes

1. Barbara Brown Taylor, An Altar in the World.
2. The path of the SBNR has been followed by United Church Observer/Broadview journalist, Anne Bokma in her book, My Year of Living Spiritually: From Woo-Woo to Wonderful – One Woman's Secular Quest for a More Soulful Life (Madiera Park, BC: Douglas and McIntyre, 2019).
3. The Centre for Action and Contemplation's Living School teaches the Christian spiritual path of prayerful engagement in the world. https://cac.org/living-school/living-school-welcome/.
4. John Mason Neale (trans), "Of the Father's Love Begotten" in Voices United, 61.
5. The Forest Church movement is a British Fresh Expression church movement aware of the natural world as a threshold to God and may include commitment to protection and conservation of forests and woodlands. Similarly, the North American Wild Church movement is deeply rooted in relationship with the earth, spiritually and ethically. http://www.mysticchrist.co.uk/forest_church and https://www.wildchurchnetwork.com/.
6. Heart's Rest is a retreat and resource centre for spiritual life and community engagement located in the Slocan Valley in B.C. https://www.heartsrest.com/.
7. Casper Ter Kuile and Angie Thurston, Something More, https://sacred.design/insights. Harvard Divinity, 2016.
8. See note 5.
9. Examples of purveyors of these trends include Beth Ann Estock and Nixon, Paul. Weird Church: Welcome to the Twenty-First Century (Cleveland: Pilgrim Press, 2016), Krista Tippet in her podcast, On Being https://onbeing.org/, and George

10. Meier who has reported on trends for the United Church in Transforming Church for North America's Evolving Spiritual Ecosystem http://www.heartsrest.com/wp-content/uploads/2014/12/Spiritual-Ecosystem.pdf.
11. These terms are credited to Marcus Borg, introduced in his The Heart of Christianity (San Francisco: Harper, 2003) and explored by various authors in The Emerging Christian Way, Michael Schwartzentruber (ed.) (Kelowna: Copperhouse, 2006).
12. Peter Rollins is a contemporary philosopher and theologian. His Omega course is a deliberate counterpoint to the Alpha course. https://peterrollins.com/new-page-1?rq=omega.
13. An example of process-informed preaching is that of United Church minister, George Hermanson on David Ewart's dedicated webpage, May the Lure Be With You, https://www.georgehermanson.com/.
14. Sallie McFague's panentheistic theology contributes significantly to an understanding of the world and all living things, indeed the planet and cosmos, as subjects in their own right. See, for example: Blessed are the Consumers (2013); Life Abundant: Rethinking Theology and Economy for a Planet in Peril (2000); Super, Natural Christians: How We Should Love Nature (1997).
15. Pope Francis, Laudato Si': O Care for Our Common Home, 2015.
16. Dominican philosopher and theologian, Meister Eckhart's (late 13th – early 14th century) mystical, non-dualistic thought has again been popularized recently by John Caputo, via Jacques Derrida, earlier by Matthew Fox, and also in the psycho-spiritual work of Carl Jung.
17. Saints Teresa of Ávila (see note #16) and Saint John of the Cross were 16th century Spanish Christian mystics. Like Teresa's writing, John's poem, The Dark Night of the Soul and commentaries are seminal texts of the Christian mystical tradition.
18. Radical theology is the field of philosophical and theological, inter-disciplinary conversation characterized by keeping the term "god" open to interpretation, rather than defined by doctrine (post-theism). Radical theologians of this generation include Catherine Keller, John Caputo, and Peter Rollins.
19. Joan Chittister, "Consumed with Love," the Daily Meditation for Friday, July 5, 2019. Centre for Contemplation and Action. https://cac.org/consumed-with-love-2019-07-05.

Chapter Twelve
Read to Lead

Today, the Church and the institutions that make up the Church are in a liminal state. An era...has come to an end, and a new way of being is not yet clear.[1] —Susan Beaumont

Gifts of God for the People of God

The purpose of reading our communities of faith is to lead our communities of faith, **pastorally** and **strategically**, perhaps more specifically, in the intersection between these two mandates in ministerial leadership. By leading pastorally, we mean with attention to the spiritual well-being of the community of faith, the individuals within it, and those passing through or hovering around it. By leading strategically, we mean with respect to guiding the decisions which lead to deliberate action. In most uniting and united denominations, this responsibility is shared by elected lay people and called or appointed ministry personnel. We are speaking here of the governing committees, councils, boards, and working groups of a community of faith—those who make decisions about everything from calling a minister to choosing an anthem, from the five year strategic plan to the whether to replace the floor in the lower hall.

We can think of the *faith* of the community as the leaders' two-fold charge. Their double duty is to nurture the faith of the community and those who come close to it *and* to direct those gifts outward—the gifts of God for the people of

God. The leader knows that as a gift of God, faith deepens with attention and flourishes in self-offering.

Pastoral leaders help individuals to grow in their faith in at least two ways: personally and corporately. Pastoral leaders tend the faith of the individuals in their care by identifying and in some cases providing opportunities for them to deepen their lives in God over the course of the events and experiences in their lives. Life provides opportunities for faith to be deepened but often we need help to see the opportunities or to be guided through them. Though this is lifelong work, ministers of children and families are experts in this ministry of faith formation, possessing gifts for using the experiences of children and youth to develop their innate capacity for trust, inquiry, and growth in the Spirit.

Pastoral leaders also help people to grow in their faith by having an eye more broadly focussed on the community of faith as a whole. By upholding the health and vitality of the faith of the community, they tend the communal container for individuals' faith to flourish. This corporate soul-tending is, in fact, the all-encompassing work of strategic leadership exercised in discerning and enacting, or empowering, the collective mission of the faith community. It is indistinguishable from the governing responsibilities we named which include everything from worship to wood rot. Strategic leadership in the context of faith communities is thereby always also pastoral. Board members are pastoral carers, even if they are not commissioned as elders as some uniting traditions continue to do. Through the lens of operative theologies, this means leaders are the readers of the various incarnations of lived faith of the community. They are poised to make decisions that support opportunities for faith to grow and be shared, no matter which expression it takes—evangelical, ecclesial, missional, ecumenical or spiritual, or some unique variant of these!

This means that those seated around a governing table commissioned to make priorities for the budget, ideally will know the strong suit of lived faith most evident in the congregation. They will know this in order to ask themselves whether the budget priorities reflect the way faith is flourishing among them or are based on what the church down the road is doing. If the congregation's lived faith is strongly missional and only weakly spiritual, how best will faith flourish in depth and in self-giving—through refurbishing the shelter beds or through painting a labyrinth on the floor? What about those who are not in the congregation—are they more likely to be drawn to an opportunity to volunteer or by their longing for spiritual journeying or neither of these but by meeting Jesus among you? These are examples of faith-oriented strategically pastoral questions. We are able to imagine how knowledge about the operative theologies in a community of faith, or among those seeking a faith community, is a useful lens to bring to such leadership work.

Leading in the Context of Theological Diversity

Leaders in faith communities are faced with significant interruptions, cataclysmic disruptions, the gravitational pull of patterns from the past, and the incremental emergence of an unknown future. Yet, by far the most pressing situations in which these leaders find themselves are those marked by the demands of everyday ministry. This is a context in which the particular make-up of the faith community's operative theologies interact with each other, with personalities, histories, legacies, and other dynamics in congregational life. We have already acknowledged that points of difference within diverse communities in and of themselves may create places of strength, creativity and flexibility or may unleash unmitigated discord and weakness. Whether theological diversity becomes an asset or liability does not depend on luck; it depends on both skill and wisdom. Skill is needed to find ways for the particular strengths in each expression of lived faith, and compatible relationships between them, to be used for the sake of the whole. This includes finding ways to mitigate their inherent limitations and potential collisions. Wisdom is needed to take seriously the need for each stream to face and wrestle with the potential dangers of its own shadows.

There is sufficient skill and wisdom in the church to create strength and beauty in our life together. We must recognise however, that working with difference is playing with fire; it can warm and it can burn. Developing skills and exercising wisdom serves both to protect the church from harm and to develop and deepen lives of faith for the flourishing of all.

Since the conversations among congregations, faith communities, and their leaders seated around the theological banquet table began several years ago, we have witnessed a variety of ways in which this lens has been carried by skilled and wise leaders into congregational life and into the diversity of lived faith and operative theologies flourishing there. The following case studies illustrate their work.

Artefacts and Antidotes

IT IS SAFE TO ASSUME THAT ALL OR MOST OF THE IDENTIFIED OPERATIVE theologies are alive and well in some proportion in every community. This is not useful information unless these theological worlds are associated with actual lives and with particular programs, specific priorities, tangible influences, and physical manifestations. Lived faith is exactly that—lived. These operative theologies will appear as book studies, guest preachers, liturgical art, and be held in home-based devotions and in the silence of unspoken prayers. All this living is incrementally having the effect of creating, modifying and reimagining legacy theologies which lie beneath the surface of the community of faith. In other words, the community of lived faith is constructing theologies to live by. Nothing could be more creative or exciting for a faith leader than to uncover and witness that process in action. Like catching a glimpse of a communal ultrasound, reading lived faith is like discerning outlines of the Spirit at work within the flesh of the faithful.

When we speak of "reading" in order to "lead," leaders look for "texts." What will tell the story of the congregation's lived faith, or better yet present it in a multi-coloured pie chart? As art, not science, this task is as much interpretation as investigation, but it involves both. It is true that we can collect artefacts, but the interpretation will be subjective to be sure. Still, in every case in which an attempt is made to read the text of a community for its operative theologies, the insights and discoveries are valuable. In some cases, they confirm intuitions. In others, they reveal an untold or misread story. In all cases, to have a "text" to read together provides a focal point—a bit of evidence—which a group might pour over together. In front of them is not first a budget, blueprint, or volunteer roster but a representation of the faith among them, a palette with which to paint their reality or their future. This is the most valuable result of studying a community of faith for its authentic operative theologies.

How is generating such an inventory of lived faith accomplished? Readers of this text are sufficiently familiar with hermeneutics, or interpretation, to know that in an encounter with a text, two things are being read—the text and the reader. The text is always interpreted on a two-way street—through the encounter with what is written and who is reading. This reciprocity of meaning is precisely why the reader of the text must also read themselves, know themselves. In our case, the leader must have taken stock of the contours of their own lived faith and have a good handle on the implicit theologies beneath the surface of their actions and motivations, their worldview and ecclesiology, because this is always the lens through which they read the living text of their community's faith.

Figure 11: Minister's lived faith depicted. Used with permission

A beautiful example of the leaders' responsibility and capacity to read themselves before turning their inevitably coloured lens toward the congregation is that of a newly assembled board in a congregation in Coquitlam, BC. Having learned the streams of lived faith well by character, name, colour, and orientation, the minister led the board in a spiritual exercise in which its members reflected on their spiritual and theological autobiographies. Using the representative colours of the theological banquet's categories of implicit theologies, they made artistic representations of their lived faith and shared them with one another. Beautiful paintings, fabric arts, and woodworking highlighted, sequenced and blended colours in a representation of how faith had been grown in them. Each piece of art brought to the fore the dominant expression of lived faith which now most animated their leadership. The board members reflected on the way in which the exercise brought to light the relationship between their lived faith and the needs of the congregation in this moment. They witnessed this not as an affirmation of themselves but as evidence of the way the Holy Spirit's infinite fabric of faith is judiciously distributed in time and space. It was an exercise in spiritual integration, community building, and preparation for faith-filled leadership. Just like the snapshot we have taken of the communities of faith in this text, each artist communicated only a snapshot, a moment in time, of what is understood to be constantly in motion, under construction. Faith is a living organism, perpetually attuned to the breath of the Spirit who animates our lives in and toward God. We must remind ourselves and our congregations about this fluidity of faith over and over again when we are making these artistic representations or snapshots of ourselves and our communities.

When it comes to reading a living text like a community of faith, the task of interpretation is a thick and demanding one. We have seen as much from the kaleidoscopic nature of the theologies under construction both beneath and above the surface of every community of faith. We trust that any text can be read for the meanings it holds. A key feature in the capacity to read a text, is to have read the reader, as the congregational leaders in Coquitlam did.

The implicit theologies of the living faith of our communities confront us in innumerable ways. Everything a particular community longs to do, chooses to do, opts not to do, and fails to do potentially communicates its implicit theologies. A living faith can be read and interpreted from its actions, communication, appearance and aspirations. These become the artefacts a leadership team, board, council or congregation might collect and analyse for the way they express lived faith. We learn to read congregations by examining everything from their worship style to their websites, their event attendance to their special appeals, the condition of their exterior paint to the retention of their ministry personnel. The skilled interpreter knows that all these actions and inactions express implicit theology.

Category	Sample Activities
Evangelical	house churches, campus ministry, camping ministry, youth & community programmes, bible study, public testimony, international alliances, praise music, prayer groups, church planting, home groups, community outreach & Social Media
Ecclesial	worship focus, building re-developments, partnerships with tenants, capital campaigns, "Messy Church", hospitality (public café's, lunches), senior's ministry, 'discipleship', 'missional', and 'practicing' congregations, thrift shops, faith & the arts
Missional	hands-on community service, food-based ministries - off/on-site café's & food kitchens, employment-based programmes, shelters, street pastors, AA, social entrepreneurship, neighbourhood asset-mapping and partnering, refugee support
Ecumenical	racial injustice, climate action, reconciliation, inter-faith coalitions, international partnerships, individuals and networks working on social justice issues both global (economic) and intra-personal (LGBTQI2S+), anti-poverty advocacy
Spiritual	spiritual direction, spiritual retreats, healing pathways, contemplative practices, pilgrimages, labyrinth, yoga chapel, Celtic Christianlity, evolutionary Christianity, inter-religious, inter-discilplinary, eco-theology, integral Christianity, faith and arts

Table 8: Activities as artefacts

A congregation whose website announces "all are welcome to join us for worship every Sunday at 10:30," is communicating something different about their communally lived faith to what the congregation whose website announces "we are a reconciling community of faith situated on the unceded territory of the Coast Salish people" is communicating about theirs. Even more subtly but equally clearly, the image of the cross on the hill announces something different than does the image of the water spilling over a rock. The congregation who cancels the workshop on gender justice due to low registration but has regular volunteers at the drop-in neighbourhood lunch is expressing something about its lived faith. A church board decision to apply for a grant to start a children's choir expresses a different lived faith from that of the board decision to use the Christmas Eve offering to support a refugee family. In truth, all these micro actions of lived faith may take place under the banner of a single congregation, making the task of interpretation a taxing one. Additionally, many other factors are at play in a congregation, including personalities, generational priorities, power dynamics, histories, legacies, and systems. It is certain, however, that one cannot lead what one has failed to read. We read the faith of our communities in order to lead, to minister, to strengthen, heal, teach, demonstrate, restore, encourage, embolden—the faith of the community.

Leaders who have read the faith of their communities use the lens of the theological banquet in several ways. The following examples illustrate this.

Calling a Minister

Neither the leader nor the congregation wishes to encounter an unforeseen collision based on ignorance of one another's implicit theologies. Though they may less interested in the particular theological home base of a particular candidate than their ability to speak and listen across the whole of the theological spectrum with respect and understanding, a calling committee or personnel minister may make use of their familiarity with the dialects of lived faith operative across the church in a few ways. Congregations who know both their own dominant orientation of lived faith and that of the candidate will be in a position to consider the blend of the two. What will a combination of a strongly ecclesial minister among passionately missional lay leaders create? What about an evangelical leader and a predominantly spiritual congregation? Where are the energizing collaborations and where are the more complicated or incompatible ones? We acknowledged earlier that by virtue of their calls, both pastoral and diaconal ministers may be entrenched in vocationally-formed operative theologies. The calling committee might need to probe a little to uncover the lived faith concealed beneath these ministers' call.

All the more significant is knowledge of the theological home-base of a minister called into a team of a pastoral charge or regional ministry. The possibility for strengths to combine and shadows to be quelled in a team work is great. Bringing the implicit theology of leaders in team to the surface creates the possibility of gifting communities of faith with more than a sum of their parts.

Leadership and Conflict Resolution

"You may need people in your congregation who frustrate you!" When this church leader took to heart the way in which antidotes to our respective shadows are carried in the alchemy of another expression of lived faith, her perspective changed on everything from irritations to conflicts in the context of ministry. She recognized that vitality in the community would not come from a suppression of the collisions between implicit theologies but a more skillful management of them. When an agitated ecclesial came into her office complaining about the barrage of announcements about climate action, this minister was able to smile and say, "that's because you're 'red' (ecclesial) and your love of this community is the way you love God, but Sarah is 'blue' (ecumenical) so she is loving God with her ban on plastic." The complainant's frustration dissipated. In addition to this pastoral approach with respect to the two congregants, the minister went deeper. She drew on her knowledge of the inter-play of shadows and antidotes to build resilience in the eco-system of living faith. The minister gathered two spirituals and called on them to work with her to provide accompaniment for the ecumenicals under attack. The ecumenicals needed allies unthreatened by their priorities, something spirituals are readily able to do. In every respect, this minister joined the Spirit's dance in the community, trusting that what was needed was there and required only a choreographer. Closer to the bone, this minister confessed that she now views a few determined missionals on her Board as much needed antidotes to the dangers of her own shadow, admitting: "I need to be cajoled out of the building into the neighbourhood. When their term is up, I'll make sure they are replaced by more missionals."

At the intra-congregational and regional level, the same dynamic is in play. In supervision, team ministry, interim ministry, amalgamations, calls and conflicts, the spirited kaleidoscope is in motion, creating patterns of strengths and shadows which also need careful choreography. A congregation in crisis over the closure of its twenty-four hour shelter might helpfully be guided by regional staff toward participation in networks and agencies dealing with local social services. A less helpful approach might have been to encourage that same congregation to concentrate on excellence in Sunday worship. This ignores their strong-suit and is a mismatch for their lived faith. The skilled guide can help the congregation lean in the direction of its vitality rather than push its spirit against the grain. Likewise, a congregation who lost its minister over a failed amalgamation needs the reassurance of a highly ecclesial interim, confident in the strength of the church, the faith of the ancestors, and the Spirit's presence in the ties that bind rather than one with dominant commitments in other directions of lived faith. All leaders know context is important. Implicit theology is part of that context; it takes work to read it and skill to take it into account.

Preaching and Worship Leadership

The ecclesial worship leader knows that faith formation happens during the service of worship through everything from the location of the font to the choice of hymns. If there is an occasion to feed the flock across the theological spectrum, it is during worship. This can be done discretely in attention to the details each theological stream would notice and through which each stream would be nourished. Or, it can be done didactically in a sermon series or through a seasonal or even year-long exposure to the way we live together feasting from a theological banquet. For example, Rev. Karen Vervada at St. John's United Church in Sidney, BC spent a full year "under the big tent" of the denomination by hosting a retreat in each liturgical season in which the five theological worlds were introduced and discussed, all the while preaching, praying and designing liturgy both about and from the perspective of each of the five theological streams throughout the year. In addition, she taught bible study and led Christian practices across the theological spectrum, using a sequence of lenses across the five categories of operative theologies to interpret each week's lectionary. At the end of the year, Karen had an intuitive feel for how each theological world animated, inspired or left untouched the people in her congregation. As a skilled interpreter of the living faith of her community, she read their engagement and participation in order to know what fields to sow and which to leave fallow in her long-term vision of nurturing and deepening the faith of her community. She found a way to read in order to lead.

Similarly, but intentionally more didactically, Rev. Cari Copeman-Haynes of Crossroads United in Delta, BC devoted the season of Lent to the five expressions of lived faith:

> This year at Crossroads, we will be tasting worship in the flavours of the Theological Banquet: five streams of operative theology in the United Church of Canada. Each of the five Sundays in Lent before Palm Sunday will be an immersion into one of the five streams, which are five distinct ways in which what we believe shapes the choices we make with our lives, in response to God's grace and call....On each Sunday, our music, the language of prayer, the substance of the sermon, and the "feel" in our worship space will reflect as accurately as possible the five streams of operative theology in the United Church of Canada.

As Cari knows, attention to nurturing the streams of lived faith within a congregation includes attention to the whole of worship life, including the worship space. When Cari walked her congregation through the five theological worlds during the season of Lent, she immersed them weekly not only in the Word as inhabited by a particular stream, but in a worship experience through music, prayer, symbol, and style expressive of each. Nourishing the faith of the community across the theological spectrum may grow to become a perpetual commitment. Placing knowledge of the implicit theologies of those gathered for worship at the heart of worship planning means, for example, that though a spiritual lay worship leader may be drawn to the prayers of John O'Donohue and an evangelical music minister may be deeply connected to Praise Band music, these worship leaders will nonetheless consider how the congregation's lived faith is honoured in words spoken and sung above their own.

Candidacy

> *Essential agreement...means that as the examining committee reflects on a candidate's theological understandings, the committee can conclude that the candidate stands clearly within the Christian tradition...*[2]

Candidates for ordination, commissioning, recognition, admission, and readmission to authorized ministry are examined to determine whether the core of their lived faith (both articulated and animated) sufficiently reflects the Christian tradition to express essential agreement with it. Those committees are suitably immersed in the tradition to make that determination. Their multilingual capacity across the theological spectrum enables them to read the lived faith of the candidate for the theology implicit in their testimony of call.

By accepting the legitimacy and integrity of various expressions of lived faith, we develop a more nuanced eye to the way faith matures and deepens *within* each category of faith rather than looking for some movement *across* them. This counters any prejudice about the various expressions of lived faith. No matter what operative theology is dominant in the candidate's lived faith, what matters is their ability to engage doctrine, to demonstrate maturity of spirit, and congruence of belief and action from that home base.

The skillful committee will hear the language of lived faith in each candidate both implicitly and explicitly expressed in the consonance of the candidates' theological autobiography and their doctrinal interpretations. For example, when a candidate speaks of meeting Jesus as a youth at a Baptist Summer Camp, it will make sense to the committee how central the commitment to teach the power of prayer is to the candidate's call to ministry, and to how personally and intimately they speak about what God is able to do in people's lives. When a candidate speaks about the importance of Eastern religious spiritual practices in deepening their relationship with the Divine, the same committee will not be surprised to hear how the candidate speaks of *kenosis* at the heart of the Trinity. The candidate who stumbled inadvertently into candidacy after attending a World Religions on Climate Conference will speak of the "church" in the broadest global sense, whereas the candidate raised in a thriving congregation will use the word "community" to refer to a congregation. The dialects are subtle but meaningful when candidates have aligned and integrated their lived faith with their explicit theology. While these examples are one-dimensional and make no account of the various ways in which a lived faith is shaped over the course of a lifetime, they are meant to highlight the usefulness of the lens of theological diversity for this critical task of the church.

Chapter Twelve Read to Lead

Pastoral and Strategic Leadership — Case Studies of Interruption and Disruption

We have seen that a leader's ability to cultivate the faith of the community, individually and corporately, relies on their knowledge of the palette of lived faith in the community as well as the members' own theological self-knowledge. With this, the leaders may turn their attention to the question of which opportunities ought to be present in order to deepen and strengthen the faith of the community, and thereby its mission and ministries. Clearly, in terms of opportunities to grow in faith, one size does not fit all! Admittedly, the ability to parse preference and personality from orientation of lived faith is not always possible. Some are drawn to activities unrelated to their life of faith in order to be with friends or to offer needed support to common projects. Nevertheless, we have seen that familiarity with the categories of lived faith and their core orientation—what faith most leads people to want to do—is useful if leaders are hoping to follow the grain of lived faith in pastoral and strategic leadership.

This is best illustrated through case study. Below are two brief accounts—one of interruption and the other of disruption. One describes strategic (deliberate) decisions which were made to attend to the pastoral needs of the faith community in anticipation of a temporary move from a sanctuary to a hotel. The second illustrates how the sudden nature of the disruption of a pandemic prevented opportunity for equally deliberate attention to theological diversity in decision-making, thereby at times thinning the pastoral efficacy of early responses to that disruption.

Pastoral and Strategic Leadership Through Interruption

When congregations are relocated *temporarily* due to renovations or repairs to their buildings, knowledge of the relationship of each stream of lived faith to the church building is important for pastoral care of the members in their time of dislocation and vulnerability. Due to a scheduled seismic up-grade, a congregation had their three Sunday services relocated for two years from a downtown Vancouver heritage sanctuary seating eight hundred with a world class organist, professional choir, teaming nursery, church school and youth group, to a hotel conference room seating one hundred, with adjacent break-out room to accommodate Sunday morning service and children's church, respectively, a carpeted "salon" for Jazz Vespers, and a neighbouring Anglican sanctuary for evening candlelight and music service. A leader using the lens of theological diversity on the dislocated congregation made this observation:

> We were most worried about the spirituals because the experience of worship in the building is literally transcendent. There was no way we could hold their (candlelight and music) service somewhere ugly. Not that they're spiritual snobs! Beauty is the portal to the holy for them. Renting the Anglican chapel for this worship service was critical.
>
> You might imagine that ecclesials would be in a panic about being out of the building but that's a misread. By literally **securing** the building (seismic upgrade), we were feeding a core aspect of their faith—security for future generations. This meant that they could relax in ways very few ecclesials these days can relax. But we also knew what they absolutely couldn't lose: coffee hour! Relationships are more important than stained glass windows for genuine ecclesials. We made sure we had access to space for gathering after church. They actually flourished in the smaller space at the hotel because it was easier to see who was there and who was missing—their faith really does flow through the Body, not the building.
>
> Missionals were okay as long as they had access to the kitchen from which they could serve the needs of those who need them most.
>
> So people had what they needed but they needed different things.

It is not always so straightforward, however. There were inevitably tensions to manage and compromises to make, thereby forcing strategic decisions about what the community's faith needed in order to remain vital under pressure. Moving *back* to the sanctuary will require the same attention to how faith flourished in adaptation and may not have the same conditions for vitality in a return to comforts and familiarity. Leaders' studious attention to how faith is and is not flourishing across its particular landscape of theological diversity, in the context of interruption, offers important information for discerning the shape of its common life. A conversation at various junctures about what is needed to feed the faith and receive the faith across the spectrum of operative theologies is critical. Are missionals still able to help those in need? Are ecclesials able to keep track of one another in a new environment? Faith must be *lived* to survive.

Pastoral and Strategic Leadership During Disruption

Where the example above is an interruption in the patterns of community life which fed the faith of the congregation across its theological diversity, a much greater disruption followed on its heels: the closure of all public gathering places due to a pandemic. Here we have a case study not of managed transition of a worship space, but of an abrupt transition of all congregational activity to virtual space, a disruption that affected every congregation in the country. We learn as much from the quick reads and unintended mismatches in responding to the pastoral needs of the communities of faith across theological difference as we do from the carefully orchestrated matches made by the leaders of the seismic upgrade relocation.

We have already stressed that tending the faith of individuals includes nourishing their faith both in what they receive *and* in what they are enabled to offer; faith needs to be lived. In the case of the sudden disruption due to the pandemic, faith leaders offering pastoral support needed to keep their eye on both of these aspects of living faith across the full spectrum of theological diversity. Here again is the leaders' duty of nurture and beneficence: to support and spend the faith of the community in order to keep it alive. At the two-week and four-month marks after the Health Officer in British Columbia imposed safety measures which banned gatherings, an informal survey of pastoral responses, in particular the on-line pastoral presence communicated through congregational website and Facebook pages, painted this picture of our collective hits and misses from the perspective of theological diversity:

Evangelical

Pastoral attention to evangelicals during the crisis focussed on their need to both hear and offer a message characterized by their particular strengths—intimacy of community, Scripture as touchstone and guide, companionship of Jesus through prayer. The evangelicals' faith would be fed in its own particular dialect of lived faith by words like these from an evangelical church:

> *In the book of Hebrews, we read "And let us consider how we may spur one another on toward love and good deeds, not giving up meeting together, as some are in the habit of doing, but encouraging one another—and all the more as you see the Day approaching." (10:24-25) People are in need; they are fearful, self-obsessed, isolated, and sick. Though we cannot gather physically, we must meet in other ways, pray together with and for one another and for this world in need of Christ's presence.*[3]

Because evangelicals live their faith as messengers, their faith flourishes in sharing assurance of the steadfast love of God. True to form, evangelicals delivered rich scripturally-rooted assurances—sung and spoken—for strength, comfort and hope. For example, the "blessing to the UK"—a choral blessing shared over five million times across Britain—came entirely from evangelical churches from Holy Trinity Brampton to the Servant Church, reassuring Britons that "He will mind you and keep you." This is the evangelical faith at its best, offering a confident, scripturally-based message of assurance and grace. This demographic was also best suited to self-organize small groups for prayer and support, within and beyond denominational lines. The relative youthfulness, and the joy, connectedness (social media), concern for neighbours, and strong faith of this group offered the church as a whole, and the communities it serves, a depth of pastoral care and outreach. In so doing, the faith of the evangelicals who shared those words and actions was also nourished. They served in their dialect of lived faith and they, along with many within and outside the church, benefitted. The number of new people accessing congregations' various on-line pastoral and worship offerings during the pandemic surprised ecclesials and is evidence of the effectiveness of people being faithful in public (Internet) spaces, a central feature of evangelical lived faith.

Not "speak their language" is a significant failing with respect to the messengers' (evangelicals') lived faith. The dominant mode of pastoral communication on congregational and denominational websites, Facebook and improvised worship services featured images of nature accompanied by poetry and meditative music. These very clearly do not speak to the evangelical who is craving scripture, prayer and song. When music, choirs and other forms of public blessing and intimate connection were prohibited and technology not well used to adapt these opportunities for self-offering, the natural out-pouring of evangelical lived faith was interrupted. Singing is not a hobby for evangelicals); it is communion with God. Praying is not only a personal practice; it is a public activity that connects the evangelical with the companionship of Jesus's own life and power. Because choirs are often viewed through an ecclesial lens, attention was paid to alternative sources of music for worship during the pandemic. This missed the interpretation of singing as message-sharing, as evangelical lived faith. These evangelicals robbed of Sunday morning praise, did not need to watch imported music on Sunday morning; they needed to be directed toward other ways to share assurance, praise, hope and love to others. They needed to be given duties for pastoral prayer and one-on-one visits to offer comfort and assurance.

Ecclesial

Faith leaders concentrated their pastoral efforts largely on the ecclesials in their communities of faith. This is one of the expressions of lived faith most severely restricted by the church building closures, protocols for gathering, changes to forms of worship, and the move to virtual children and family ministries.

The servanthood and love for the community at the heart of the ecclesial lived faith needed to be skillfully manipulated around great obstacles when church buildings were closed and worship was cancelled. The pastoral messages appropriately reassured ecclesials of two things: the *temporary* nature of the disruption and the *possibilities for connecting* in the meantime. John Bell's pastoral sensibility speaks directly to what ecclesials most needed to hear: the church community will not be lost.

> *We will meet when the danger is over,*
> *we will meet when the sad days are gone;*
> *we will meet sitting closely together*
> *and be glad our tomorrow has come.*
>
> *We will join to give thanks and sing gladly,*
> *we will join to break bread and share wine;*
> *and the peace that we pass to each other*
> *will more than a casual sign.*[4]
>
> —John Bell and Hans-Olav Moerk

Overall, lay and ordered ecclesial leaders were caring for the particular needs of ecclesials by making sure the community of faith and its sacred space remained healthy and protected. They put things in place to enable the gifts of *servanthood* and *relationship* to continue despite the changes to the way those core features of ecclesial lived faith took place. Ecclesial leaders remained bonded to the beloved community, fostering its faith, caring for its needs, attending to its viability, and above all offered the virtual body of Christ community and communion in worship, prayer and sacrament. They adapted faith formation delivery and engagement for children, youth and adults, continuing in their commitment to nurture the faith of the community. When ecclesials-at-home became unhinged from community, place, and shared life as the most natural fixtures for living a faith of em-Bodied service, the home-based prayer and scripture reading which are strengths of evangelical and spiritual lived faith (the antidotes to ecclesial's shadow) came more into view. Moving faith "home" during the pandemic may or may not have made a lasting mark on an ecclesial lived faith.

While paid accountable ecclesials focussed on adapting first worship, and then programmes and administration to on-line formats, lay ecclesials showed their colours in two ways: connection and protection. Because they *knew* one another, connection-ecclesials were able to share the pastoral responsibilities and care for one another. Throughout the ebbs and flows of the pandemic crisis, the most dedicated of them kept a faithful eye on families and children, singles, and the most vulnerable. Being the most inclined to foster community, connection-ecclesials suffered the prohibition of hosting and gathering people but they were also the most innovative about connecting with the others in the faith community. Congregations have long endured the criticism of being social clubs. As months went by without the possibility of being social, the distinction between *caritas* and cribbage was made increasingly evident. Here, it was possible to see the fine, often blurred, line between social connections and body-of-Christ commitments. For the pastoral leader who had time to notice this, an important story about the heart of the community of faith was being written for the next chapter of the community's life together.

Protection-ecclesials were vigilant about the sustainability of the church at every level. The regional and national church offices maintained their role as protection-ecclesials. They kept in constant communication with ecclesially-minded members and leaders concerning institutional and administrative concerns, chiefly finances, personnel issues, and health protocols for gathering and facilities use. These ecclesials were found engrossed in the business of the church, attending to its viability and mission even in the absence of the possibility to feel the embodiment of the Spirit in the physical presence of the gathered community. Without question, there was a tone and energy in this work focussed on "the return." The ecclesial identity of the church was confirmed by externally in two ways: the way governments dealt with the church largely as a community-who-gathers and as an essential service for sacramental (baptism and communion) and pastoral (funeral) needs. This was surprising to many who experience the church as marginal, even invisible.

Mismatched messages to ecclesials came in two forms: the suggestion that congregations were better off without their buildings (a missional view) and the recommendation that everything be put on hold for a contemplative Sabbath (a spiritual orientation). These recommendations only increased anxiety in both protection-ecclesials and connection-ecclesials, respectively.

Missional

To speak to the missional heart, the pastoral message expressed needs of the social situation, drawing links between this crisis and perpetual local crises suffered by vulnerable sectors and those who help them:

> *We know that this pandemic will hurt people already marginalized the most. Social distancing in response to the pandemic is so hard when you're homeless or in substandard housing. Stocking up on supplies isn't possible when you're already living hand-to-mouth. Our resources—already stretched thin to serve our community—will be truly tested.*[5]
> —First United Church, Vancouver

Many missionals were professionally engaged in responding directly to the crisis (health, emergency response, government, etc.) and those who were normally volunteering in the community kept the church focussed on frontline workers and on the reality of those in most need in the community, often using the occasion to make the connection between the temporary inconveniences of the wealthy and the perpetual deprivation of the marginalized.

Normally obscured in the church by their service *to* the church, congregationally active missionals stood out under COVID-19 conditions as those least content with being hands-off. Missionals may appear to be ecclesials when they are serving coffee every Sunday or driving people to church. However, when the opportunity to serve is removed, it is the *service*, not the *community* missionals miss most. A missional's faith is literally in their hands. Senior missionals were most vulnerable to the abrupt cut-off of their faith-inspired self-offering to a society in significant and obvious practical need. Not to be able to be on the front lines of food and supplies distribution, transporting people in need, *doing* almost anything, became a crisis in faith, if not a crisis of faith, for these senior missionals. Younger missionals—those professionals in the faith community serving society as doctors, nurses, care aids, emergency responders, and medical officers, along with public servants—were held up in prayer and moved to the centre of society's gratitude and attention in the early stages of the pandemic. Whether they remained in the prayers of their communities of faith varied.

Throughout the months of the pandemic, faith leaders needed to be aware of how important it is for missionals to have *access* to ways to help others. Missionals needed the kitchen and the thrift shop, not zoom coffee hour and contemplative prayer. If these were unavailable, a pastoral leader attentive to the core of the missional lived faith would find alternative community agencies or efforts for missional service to be channeled. Missionals need to move; they need something in their hands. Leaders harnessed the compassionate missional lived faith for *concrete* acts of pastoral care needed in the faith community including activities like grocery delivery, assistance with home technology, and the like. A mismatch of the gravest order for missionals was the invitation to embrace the pause in activity for the spiritual discipline of retreat. To stop a missional from reaching out is to clip their wings of faith.

Ecumenical

In the early days of the pandemic, and on the many occasions in which social issues and crises were provoked and exposed, ecumenicals helped the church sustain a wide global view of the pandemic, offering interpretation through their critical socio-political, economic, and ecological lens:

> *When the term is understood as "unveiling," we can then ask the right questions: What does this pandemic unveil? What have we refused to see about ourselves and the precarious world we've built, a world that now stands exposed and tottering in the harsh light of this unasked-for revelation? If we permit this crisis to expose the fissures of our failing world, this pandemic will have served as properly apocalyptic. If instead, despite its devastating toll, we return to an obsolete and unsustainable world, nothing meaningful will have been revealed.*[6]

The lived faith of the ecumenical, so often underfed by congregational life, was nourished when communities of faith turned and sustained their attention to these crises in prayer and conversation. For ecumenicals, the local and global tensions which sparked renewed work in addressing systemic racism and white privilege, women's rights, and the climate crisis, among others, manifest a moment of reckoning for this expression of lived faith. While no one actually said, "We told you so," they could have! Faith leaders supported ecumenicals by affirming the fact that their faithful vigilance when injustice is unnoticed provides them with the expertise to help the church understand and address the issues in moments when issues come to light more widely. Even more than affirmation and giving voice and opportunity for ecumenicals to offer leadership in addressing these issues, faith leaders, including those in the national offices tending these portfolios, supported ecumenicals by joining them—cohosting anti-racism work or writing and preaching about climate justice—thereby offering them the gift of enacted hope.

Though meeting the needs of the ecclesials to keep in touch with one another, the personal and community-focussed nature of conversations in congregational chat-boxes were a mismatch for the serious, global preoccupations of ecumenicals. This fact only served to underline the ecumenicals' need for networks and movements beyond the church with whom to *keep the faith*. As is its inclination, the national body of the denomination kept this expression of lived faith alive through its activities and communications.

Spiritual

The language spoken in words and images by spirituals in our communities of faith, including by many faith leaders, is most often artful, reflective and poetic.

This expression of lived faith appeared to have had the widest appeal and broadest audience during the pandemic crisis. The core message spirituals exchanged conveyed confidence that the Sabbath imposed by the pandemic offered the possibility of reaching a place of compassion and love not easily accessed in the drive of day to day life:

> *"During the dark night there is no choice but to surrender control, give in to unknowing, and stop and listen to whatever signals of wisdom come along.*
> *It's a time of enforced retreat and perhaps unwilling withdrawal. The dark night is more than a learning experience; it's a profound initiation into a realm that nothing in the culture, so preoccupied with eternal concern and material success, prepares you for."*[7] —Thomas Moore

In addition to offering the soul-food of art and beauty on social media, spirituals guided willing people in their faith communities unaccustomed to solitude, slower pace, and reflection toward ways of embracing the moment for spiritual enrichment despite the cause of the Sabbath. They became mentors and guides to both the eager and the curious. This leadership extended beyond the boundaries of faith communities themselves as the church's online presence gained new followers drawn particularly to the spirituals' non-dogmatic language of sacred presence and thoughtful interpretations of the times. Spirituals were unsurprised by this evidence that the ancient wisdom of the church has something to offer a world stopped in its frantic tracks, and plagued with insecurity, increasing violence, and polarization.

These leaders, along with other spirituals who remained connected to faith communities over the months of pandemic, found themselves increasingly at odds with the ecclesials and missionals whose equally valid need to find ways to carry on or to get back to business drove hard and fast against the spiritual energy of contemplation and reflection precipitated by the interruption in patterns of behaviour in church and society.

Languages of faith spoken and heard across the theological spectrum in times of disruption only highlight the perpetual differences which are less pronounced in ordinary circumstances. By ministering across the theological breadth within and beyond our church, faith leaders minister to the way in which, by grace, we are fashioned for one another. The assurance of the gospel, the ties connecting the beloved community, the care of strangers, the hope born of solidarity, and the stillness of a deeply rooted centre: all these combine in both ordinary and critical times to temper and calm our fears, to support and instruct our growing in faith, to inspire and call forth our ministries, and indeed to reveal the very presence of God in whom all life, death, and new life is held. These case studies also reveal the extent to which pressure serves to highlight not only the theological landscape but the very real pastoral needs across it. These pastoral needs provoke strategic choices needed to allow faith to flourish within the context of embodied theological diversity.

Strategically Pastoral Leadership – Thinking about Adaptive Challenges

We have been imagining faith splintering into different expressions the way light refracts through a prism. Here we are acknowledging that events and circumstance might serve as that prism, causing faith to bend and take on a new hue. Living faith morphs and changes, not simply in an individual, but also collectively in a community of faith. Events such as interruptions and disruptions, both immediate and those which happen incrementally over long periods, sometimes create opportunity for the emergence of a new tone of lived faith richer yet than its primary colours. Developing an eye across the operative theological spectrum is useful for minding how each expression of lived faith is faring, as we have seen. This skill also allows leaders to watch those expressions take shape in a particular context. Leaders may even follow the grain of emerging expressions of lived faith to meet the adaptive challenges of their circumstances. We can conceive of adaptation this way: as the mixing of the colours of lived faith in response to changed context.

A beautiful example having the skill to allow faith's encounter with its context to lead is that of Rev. Jenny Carter, minister in Salmon Arm, BC. When Jenny began to serve the congregation made up largely of missionals and ecumenicals, they spoke to her of "getting tired." A pastorally-attuned leader, Jenny knew that the antidote to loss of energy in these streams of lived faith is not rest, but depth of faith (for ecumenical) and more systemic or shared commitment (for missional).

Disheartened activists and carers need evidence of a world transformed by love, community, hope, and beauty. She allowed that lived faith to flow in a life-giving direction by leading the congregation in creating a space in the church building where non-profit organizations, social service agencies and activists could make a home and workspace. By building community for and among those with the same lived faith, or matching lived commitments, as the congregation itself, they infused hope, energy, and joy. The community of faith called this *GreenSpace*[8] because new life was being born there. But the adaptation only began there. Creating the *GreenSpace* led to a reimagining of the congregation and its life of faith in response to the needs of folks beyond the congregation. The community of faith and its building was reimaged as a "*Nexus*," a place to connect and to share music, art, community and conversation. The congregation turned itself inside out: the barriers between who is "in" and who is "out" of the church dissolved entirely. The threshold became the centre. Jenny is minister to whomever gathers, offering spiritual food for the whole community. Faith led. A new "colour" or form followed, emerging from a confluence of streams of living faith leaning in the direction of their own flourishing. Red (ecclesial) became magenta in putting the missionals' purple strength at the centre. There was no cataclysmic event in this situation, only the perennial challenge of a "tired" form of church in a spiritually hungry time, and the sometimes all-too-well-hidden fount of faith that Jenny could see.

Interruption and disruption are two examples of circumstances that forced faith to be lived differently in a changed context. As uncomfortable as it is, pressure forces change or adaptation in order to survive. We know from leadership theory that not all pressure leads to life-giving adaptation. Too much pressure causes stress and retreat; too little pressure creates docility and avoidance. Finding and maintaining the sweet spot for adaptation to changed circumstances is the art of leadership.[9]

The church in the west has been doing an over-the-shoulder check of our capacity for adaptation to our contemporary context for some time.[10] Over the centuries and over the decades, the forms by which the church has spread the gospel, embodied the temporal and mystical body of Christ, and responded to the Great Commission have changed shape, adapted the form to keep the faith. Finding ways to live faith around contextual obstacles or in response to contextual circumstances creates possibilities for new operative theologies to emerge.

As each expression of lived faith faces the adaptive challenges of our time, it brings with it its strengths, its potential shadow, and its particular incarnation of each of the marks of the church. This palette of living faith is surely the multivalent breath of the Holy Spirit, capable of inspiring adaptations in an ever-changing context. Each expression of lived faith is challenged by its circumstances in different ways, giving rise to occasions for operative theologies to be shaped and reshaped accordingly.

For example, as the most racially, culturally and theologically diverse demographic in our denomination, the evangelical stream is no stranger to adaptation. As a stream whose operative theological roots are connected to those in the evangelical world beyond the denomination, this stream faces the question of just how much adaptation or theological reconstruction it is interested in doing with respect to soteriology - the kind of message of salvation it offers and to whom. Evangelical soteriology is under construction in the context of theological diversity both within and beyond united and uniting denominations.

Another example of theologies under construction precipitated by adaptive challenges is located in the ecumenical stream. To protect the vitality of this stream of the denomination's lived faith, an adaptation was attempted some ten years ago in our denomination when the ministries related to justice-seeking were moved from a national to a congregational platform. Ecumenical lived faith is a networked lived faith, a lived faith of organized resistance that depends on relationships to organizations, agencies and networks, worldwide. Congregational ecumenicals are too few and far between to work in the relative isolation this move created. Not as a direct result of this denominational shuffle, but in part aided by it, the ecumenical lived faith has undergone spiritual and theological adaptation, taken on a changed shape that has enabled it to live by becoming what we might call a "sea-green" or teal movement of the spirituality of justice. This combined or integrated movement is part of a larger political, cultural, theological and spiritual shift in consciousness about the relationship of the inner and outer life, a reinterpretation of what it will take to create true and lasting change.

Summary

The post-Christendom church has been under pressure within and without for the better part of a century. For a variety of reasons, this pressure has not consistently or systemically forced strategic decision making about the best form or forms the church might adopt in order for faith to flourish. The church struggles to meet this adaptive challenge. However, when combined with the pressure of a pandemic beginning in the spring of 2020 which radically disrupted congregational activity and both agitated and exposed social and global crises, the question of what matters most and how best to safe-guard, adapt or innovate a future for communities of faith, or the denomination as a whole, presented itself with increased urgency. Whether the sweet spot of urgency might be harnessed for change will take time to see.

With respect to pastoral and strategic leadership, the lens of theological diversity adds complexity and nuance to any question we might pose to a mythically monolithic "church." We discover that splintering that question the way a prism fractures light, provides us with more insight. The question, "what is God calling us to?" can be stultifying in a context of theological diversity unless more than one response is invited.

By no means does this make it the wrong question. It belongs to the critical, perennial work of discernment. The church is polyvocal for a reason. It is in the interplay between its lived theologies, and their responses to the events and circumstances of their time, that any glimpse of the church's futures might be discerned. Strategic decisions provoked by an interruption or disruption to the flow of lived faith within a community, including the ones brought on by the adaptive challenges presented by this chapter in the history of the Christian church, begs to be answered in a chorus, just as the Pentecost cacophony suggested.

Chapter Twelve Read to Lead

Notes

1. Susan Beaumont, How to Lead When You Don't Know Where You're Going: Leading in a Liminal Season (Lanham: Rowan and Littlefield, 2019), 59.
2. Committee on Theology and Inter-church, Interfaith, United Church of Canada, A Background Document on Essential Agreement (Toronto: UCC, 2019), 7.
3. This is an adaptation of the Tenth Avenue Alliance, Vancouver BC, April 2020 website posting. https://www.tenth.ca/ .
4. John Bell and Hans-Olav Moerk, "We Will Meet When the Danger is Over," Wild Goose Resource Group, The Iona Community, Glasgow, Scotland, 2020.
5. First United Church Community Ministry is a downtown mission in Vancouver, B.C. https://firstunited.ca/ . This statement appeared as part of the COVID alert banner on their website in March, 2020.
6. Catherine Keller and John J. Thatamanil, "Is this an Apocalypse? We certainly hope so – you should too," Posted Wed 15 Apr 2020, ABC Religion and Ethics https://www.abc.net.au/religion/.
7. Thomas Moore, Dark Night of the Soul: A Guide to Finding Your Way Through Life's Ordeals, (New York: Gotham, 2004), xiii.
8. The story of GreenSpace and Nexus is found on the First Community website: www.firstcommunity.ca.
9. Adaptive leadership theory has informed the work in Pacific Mountain Region since the early 2000s. See especially Ronald Heifetz The Practice of Adaptive Leadership, (Boston: Harvard Business Review Press, 2009), Sharon Daloz-Parks Leadership Can Be Taught, (Boston: Harvard Business Review Press, 2005) Margaret Wheatley Leadership and the New Science (Oakland: Berrett-Koehler Publishers; Third Edition, 2006).
10. Most notably, Phyllis Tickle, The Great Emergence (Grand Rapids: Baker, 2008) and Diana Butler Bass, A People's History of Christianity: The Other Side of the Story (New York: Harper Collins, 1989).

Chapter Thirteen
The Theological Banquet

The Flesh of our Words

> The vocation of the Body of Christ is…to "become the flesh of our words."[1]
> —Elaine Graham

This project promised nothing more than a group snapshot of "the flesh of our words"—a spontaneous portrait of living faith. We have attempted to read operative theologies by observing how they are embodied. Faith leads; theology follows. It will be obvious by now that there was no attempt made in this project to view each of the theological worlds in light of some ideal Christian faith or doctrine that somehow holds or perfects them all. To return to the image of the statues in the Whispering Gallery, I have attempted to describe the way we are *joining* the early church elders, not merely *echoing* them. The hope is to have heard whispers of a few of the many varied ways people with whom we share Christian life and identity live their faith, and to have been inspired by what we have overheard. Marilynn Legge explains this plainly:

> Theology…is no longer primarily about interpreting "the tradition" as if one transparent trajectory existed; rather theology is about interpreting particular experiences and

practices in specific contexts, engaging others' interpretations, and also being illuminated and transformed into renewed interaction."[2]

In other words, by engaging this work, we not only read the operative theologies at work among us by interpreting our various gestures of love and self-offering, we made sense of those gestures in ways that form and inform the theologies themselves. The community remakes itself by its practice of learning the lived faith of others as the text of the living word.

The project confirmed at least two things about us: our *interest* in theology and our *ability* to use it to serve the faith of the church. Not unlike other occasions on which the church has invited its members into conversation about what they believe,[3] the invitation to the "theological banquet" of lived faith in workshops offered in British Columbia and Alberta over the past several years has reminded us of the enthusiasm and capacity for theological conversation among people of faith. Where faith leads, theologies follow. We should not be surprised then to find that our denomination's commitment to constructive contextual theologies (developing ways of thinking and talking about God for our time and place) has equipped people of faith for this work.

More than this, the conversations themselves demonstrated and confirmed the principle we embraced by gathering at the theological banquet tables: theology may be borne by the church but it is *born* in lives of faith, including those curious about faith. It is true that people are hesitant to debate doctrine but they are eager to reflect on where their lives are most animated by love and longing for God. In that reflection, they both create new and borrow ancient ways of speaking. Like reaching into a common treasure chest of words and images, they use what is there to speak about the ineffable. In that way, the banquet tables across our church are workbenches where our operative theologies are constantly under construction.[4]

Strangely, though people are able and enthusiastic for this task of theological conversation and construction, our communities of faith appear to lack confidence about what they believe. Over and over again, the theological banquet hosted widespread insecurity about the legitimacy of particular experiences or expressions of personal or collective lived faith. The self-perception of many lay people was that their faith was idiosyncratic in some way and that their beliefs sat a little to one side of what they imagined to be a popular orthodoxy of sorts. Many were surprised to learn that what they believe could be considered "legitimate"

Christian theology, given how much it differed from what they hear from the pulpit, read in the book study, or hear in the media. Others were surprised that their beliefs were not out-dated and discarded but had an honourable place at the table. Despite how approximate and clumsy the labels for the five categories of lived faith were, people were pleased and grateful to see mirrored back to them what they believe, under the heading "Christian theologies."

Just why this under-confidence exists is a question for others to pursue. Perhaps our welcome of "whatever you believe or struggle to believe" has left the unintended impression that the faith or curiosity people carry does not belong to a millennia-long conversation which almost certainly echoes in their own experiences of love and longing for God, for one whose holy mystery is wholly love. This doesn't mean that "anything goes," but it does mean that painting a more vivid, fluid picture of what Christian faith is like might shift people's perspective about whether they share it or not. If, as one united denomination coined, "God is still speaking,"[56] the conversation continues. That assertion makes theologians of us all, if we are so inclined. There appears to be more interest in being part of the conversation than we might have imagined.

Even more important than people eagerly taking their place under the name of the operative theology that best represented their lived faith, was what happened at those tables. There they found friends with whom they shared not simply a "set of values" or "way of life" or "perspective," but an implicit kinship in the living Christ. Conversations at those tables were free from derision and defensiveness. From that place of acceptance and humility, hearts were simultaneously strengthened and opened. This open and curious posture is particularly timely. Set as it is against a backdrop of polarisation, entrenchment and arrogance in the church and beyond it, respectful conversation is as much an obligation as it is a gift of being made in the image of God, of love.

In the same way that lay people found their theological voice at the table of their lived faith, leaders also made a discovery at the theological banquet. Rather than being threatened by, or feeling ill-equipped for, traversing the landscape we inhabit as a theologically diverse denomination, leaders recognized their many intrinsic skills for hosting, exploring and constructing diverse theologies in the communities of faith they serve. These skills, in fact, are constantly employed in the tasks of everyday ministry: at the worship committee meeting, planning children's church, writing prayers, making pastoral visits, at the General Council office and in our theological schools. It stands to reason that leaders were enthusiastic and happy to imagine this tacit skill of hosting, navigating and expending the riches of faith-diversely-expressed as the leading edge of their ministry. These leaders are, in every sense, ministers *to the living faith of their congregations*. Despite the many demands of congregational life, ministers are not just *church* leaders; they are *faith* leaders, commissioned to read, interpret and construct operative theologies for the sake of the living faith of the faithful and curious.

It would be unfair to imply that this call and these gifts make the task of ministry amidst theological diversity a simple or harmonious task. Quite the contrary. Diversity is not a passive destination, nor an end in itself. It is a life force, with the power to create and sustain living systems. It is thereby extremely powerful. The liberal notion of merely displaying a buffet of equally valid options is repeatedly challenged by undertaking this work seriously. We have seen that each operative theology has dangerous shadows that can threaten the community of faith. Though by grace, the beauty of the whole is equipped to mend and renew, it is simplistic and negligent to imagine that this happens on its own. Navigating, even piloting, various streams of corporately held theologies is taxing and difficult. It takes skill. The leaders among us are by no means lacking this skill. It is, in fact, a transferable skill. Because they are equipped for the work of adjudication and mediation in the face of the inevitable tensions and collisions inherent in every human community, leaders are also equipped for navigating the theological diversity which has always existed among those whom they serve. Like all leadership tasks, working with theological diversity is a shared endeavour. By teaching the language and lens of theological diversity to the community of faith as a whole, or to the able lay people leading the community of faith, those leaders are able to bring their ample skills to the difficult but critical work of finding ways to live and flourish together without asserting homogeneity as a criteria for vitality.

That which gives life to others, often brings life to us as well. This is true even under the tremendous burden with which church leaders labour today. Many welcome the opportunity to focus on their true vocation—to be caretakers of faith, to build, nurture, foster and celebrate the various incarnations of the living faith in their communities and those curious about them. Focussing their leadership on the multiform "flesh of our words," keeps them consciously and palpably caught-up in the creativity of their call to share in the heart of God. They become midwives of the incarnation of the living faith, front-row witnesses of the on-going outpouring of the divine life among people of faith and curious about faith.

Chapter Thirteen The Theological Banquet

A Word to Leaders

Your faith has made you well. (Luke 17:19b)

As leaders in faith communities, our first responsibility is *faith*. This is a beautiful mandate to have been given, to tend the holy ground on which people encounter God. By discovering the *lived faith* of the community, we allow for the possibility of following the grain of that faith into the future. We begin to imagine the community's on-going life as an expression of its *lived theologies*—its beliefs about who God is and is not, God's relationship to the church and to the world. Because faith is a living thing, this work is never complete. Unlike a building project or a fundraiser, an amalgamation or a burial, we do not move on from the perennial tilling of this share of holy ground.

In my work with congregations and their leaders over many years, reading the lived faith of their community along with them, I witness the Spirit at work among them, inspiring them to take hold of the gift of faith. There is a moment when the awareness of the mantle of *faith leader* dawns on those gathered at a Theological Banquet table or in a fellowship room. The anxiety about having the answers lifts, if temporarily, and leaders glimpse the deeper invitation to *lead the faith* of those they serve. I witnessed a leadership board jump to its feet and rush to the table where five coloured cloths representing five expressions of living faith in their congregation were draped. With the energy of strategic planners, they began to rearrange the cloths to represent their priorities and direction. Feeling the fabric in their hands, something shifted. They became quiet. It was obvious that they were holding more than the cloth, and were responsible for more than plans. Their collective consciousness shifted as they gathered the bright tangle of living faith in their outstretched arms. Another group of board members asked me to repeat myself twice: "You are not leaders of the future of your congregation; you are leaders of the faith of your congregation." They were visibly moved: simultaneously relieved and burdened by the sudden shift in job description. They looked at their minister. "We've got this," she said, and closed the meeting in prayer.

It must be said, and said again, that nothing I have presented in this work leads onto that illusive field called "answers" or "direction" or "future." It is not intended to. Rather, it is intended to provide a lens by which to read what faith looks like when it is lived in and around the little container we call a "community of faith." Should the faith there be strong and vital, curious and central, we trust a "future" will emerge from that fruitful place. Whatever shape that future takes, it will be a meeting place between the divine life and the life of the people, where the Spirit has found the flesh of our lives a hospitable place to dwell.

A very important thing about this work of exploring lived faith is what it won't do: it won't fix anything that is broken. It won't find a path in the thicket. It won't promise success. It won't answer the question we love to ask, "where is God leading us." It may provide a starting place which sets the stage for such work. That is very much the hope. But it will not take us that next step. Theology, we recall, is the church's service industry. It is here to help the church but not to guarantee it anything.

Hosting the Theological Banquet

We bundled this work into an interactive workshop that allows people to explore their living faith in the company of others. A goal was to expose the kaleidoscopic scene that unfolds when we make no assumptions about homogeneity! The material presented here, with or without additional resources, provides all a leader needs to host the kind of conversations those workshops invite. I hope it inspires you to issue an invitation for others to:

Figure 12: BC Conference 2017 (Doug Goodwin photo credit))

Discover that their life expresses their faith, even if they do not have the words for what they believe;

Recognize the deep roots of that faith that connect them to our shared faith;

Distinguish the between branches of living faith in our church;

Identify strengths born from theological diversity;

Uncover the diversity of beliefs within their own faith community;

Discern the ways living faith is at work in your community of faith.

There are four principles on which this conversation was founded which continue to ground the work it inspires: respect, trust, authenticity, and participation.

Respect

The core operating principle of the Theological Banquet is respect:

- Respect for the faith of the people invited to the table;
- Respect for their ability to grapple with the theological work this process invites;
- Respect for the denomination and its endeavours to be faithful in every expression of its mission and ministries;
- Respect for diversity, not as derivation from some undeclared norm, but as constituent of living systems;
- And finally, respect for the voices, faces, activities and congregations portrayed, no matter how well or poorly they represent the implicit lived faith or operative theologies of your particular community.

Trust

Be assured of your congregation's ability to reflect on their faith and to think theologically. After offering the Theological Banquet workshops for a number of years, we have witnessed and are confident in a number of things that you too may trust:

- That there myriad manifestations of living faith in and on the edges of our church which are connected to multiple theologies alive in our congregations and across our church;
- That though leaders *cannot* inhabit every theological worldview, they *can* learn to identify and raise up theological worldviews different from their own in an effort to nurture the faith across the theological spectrum;

That lay people's lives *are* theologically rooted and that the church is a place where they expect to hear that theology expressed and see it practiced;

That congregations are poised to grow in faith across the diversity of the theological spectrum, and that learning and teaching about theological diversity mitigates against liabilities and builds strength.

Authenticity

The value of the Theological Banquet conversations rests on authenticity and testimony as a means to identify and celebrate the ***living faith*** of your community. The extent to which you are able to augment this material with the voices, stories, examples and testimonies of faith that you, as the leader, invite and lift up from among your community of faith, is the extent to which the banquet will come to life and bring life.

Figure 13: BC Conference 2017 (Doug Goodwin photo credit)

Ultimately, **know yourself.** No one is theologically neutral! You will most certainly be limited in your ability to lead these conversations if you have not identified for yourself the dominant operative theology out of which you look out on your community of faith. Moreover, you will be able to help others see themselves by exemplifying what it is to see *yourself.* Perhaps most significantly, this is an opportunity to model what it is not to assume that we are all alike.

Participation

Conversations will be the most valuable part of your process. It is here where participants will experience the *living faith* of their community and feel themselves a vital part of it.

Gather Gladly

> *"Gather gladly. . . Jesus Christ is living bread."*[7]
> —Sylvia Dunstan

In setting the theological banquet table, wherever we do so, we are invited to trust that our capacity for living with and leading amid difference is strengthened through practice—practice in seeing ourselves and in seeing others. We are putting our faith, however it is rooted, in the confounding power of the Holy Spirit—the guardian of both particularity and unity. We are trusting that the same Holy Spirit who gave the first disciples the ability to speak across difference, and gave our denomination's founders the notion of unity amid diversity might grant us the same faith, hope and mutual regard by which to witness and inhabit the incarnate presence of love in our time and place.

These are challenging times not simply for the church but for the world. We need theology – its careful, anchored and open exploration of faith—now, possibly more than ever. We need theology to come to the aid of communities of lived faith against a backdrop of unparalleled global challenges and daily human ones—to give that faith form, expression and understanding. Theology is the imperfect art of articulating the particular shape or dialect of our trust that we are not alone. Being imperfect, when it speaks from its shadows, theology can take on a sureness it does not deserve. Yet this is the last thing theology ever wants to do. Theology wants to help faith, not to seek victory. That is precisely why theology belongs at a table. Theology longs for and belongs to the community. Community is the antidote to theology's shadows. Together, around a table, that millennial-long conversation continues. As if in the circle of conversing statues in the ancient dome, we wrap statements and silences around the love with which our lives are held and offered. There in the circle, by the grace of the embodied Christ, we are able to see one another, to soften the edges of fear, to trust one another and the One God we praise, across the diversity of our faith-in-common.

Notes

1. Elaine Graham, *Words Made Flesh*, (London: SCM 2009), 89.
2. Marilynn J. Legge, "Inside Communities, Outside Conventions: What is at Stake in doing Theology?" *Studies in Religion/Sciences Religieuse* 29 (1), 9.
3. For example, most recently in the *Faith Talk* process initiated by the Theology and Faith Committee in 2002 and Statement of Faith Survey 2005, and in consideration of the remit on subordinate standards through *Our Words of Faith* 2010-2012. See United Church of Canada Archives, Committee on Theology and Inter-Church and Interfaith Relations fonds, Fonds 568, 2018.135C - box 9 - file 8, Faith Talk 2002 and 2019.093C - box 1 - files 6 and 7, Statement of Faith 2005 survey and responses.
4. This approach to doing contextual theology is explained by theologian Natalie Wigg-Stevenson in "What's Really Going on: Ethnographic Theology and the Production of Theological Knowledge." Cultural Studies ↔ Critical Methodologies, vol. 18, no. 6, Dec. 2018, pp. 423–429.
5. Reference to theology of mission associated with Lesslie Newbigen (*The Gospel in a Pluralist Society*, 1989) and David Bosche (*Transforming Mission*, 1991).
6. United Church of Christ, USA. https://www.ucc.org/who-we-are-2/about/god-is-still-speaking.
7. Sylvia Dunstan, "All Who Hunger," *Voices United*, 460.

Postscript

Love in Translation

> They [disciples at Pentecost] believed, rapturously, with no naiveté as to the risk, that they could communicate beyond every boundary. That the community could keep its many selves in tune, while in motion. A global gambit: that love might not get lost in translation.[1] —Catherine Keller

THE CONVERSATION WE HAVE ENGAGED HERE SITS INSIDE CONVERSATIONAL strata many centuries deep. That two-millennia-long conversation keeps the gospel alive, the church animated as Christ's unending servant and disciple, and the quest for life in the Spirit anchored in communities of faith. Imagine that conversation as a multi-volume text. One of those volumes contains the centuries' long chapter belonging to the institutional church in the west and its struggle to live faithfully as the Risen Body of the Life of the World. Among its pages we might picture the one on which we currently find ourselves, the one devoted to our current preoccupation with sorting what the church should preserve and what it should reform simply to keep vital. As if to sound aloud a few words, here we have run our fingers a very short distance across a line on that page. We have made out the contours of one regional and denominational expression of the living church. This particular moment of the church's life is more vibrant, fluid and complex than any set of labels or descriptions is able to capture. In these final reflections, we are deciphering the phonemes in the language love expressed in, through and by communities of faith in this time and place—finding meaning in the short phrase we have run our fingers along together.

Posing for Perspective

We return to the image of a family photo taken in a mirror in order to include the photographer, highlighting the importance of seeing ourselves along-side others. In the interim between presenting that image at the beginning of this text and writing its conclusion, the "Zoom" view of communities of all sizes has become the norm. The zoom-filled screen, like the mirror-aided family photo, includes a self-portrait among the faces. This zoom view is a subtle but important corrective to two more common perspectives: the view which excludes the self and the view which features the self. Both these perspectives raise the self above others. The supposed "objective" or scientific view may have the unhappy consequence of rendering the *viewed* objects as disassociated curiosities. "Selfie" portraits are equally problematic. In those views, the self is captured as the soul subject against which everything else is merely decorative background: the epitome of the subjective worldview.

A third way, the "zoom view," rejects neither of these views outright, but counters the limitations of each. Unlike the view from above or in front, this view is lateral. It gives us a way to see the self and others in a single glance on a flat screen, a family photo caught in a dining room mirror. This lateral view of one-among-many guards against positioning ourselves or considering ourselves the norm (absent) or the exception (predominant). We are simply, one-of-the-many. This perspective is possible only when we situate ourselves along-side others, rather than without them or above them. Love, as Jesus explained it, can be understood in this way as well; it depends on seeing both neighbour and self equally, laterally. To view the world or community laterally is modest and engaging; it requires us to shift physically both to see and to be seen. This is no small thing: that love requires some relocation, shift in posture and vantage point. By learning *from* living together, we incrementally learn *how* to live together. Better, we learn how to live *as one,* not through an imposed or supposed uniformity but as a manifold whole, a genuine *fullness* of life-among-others. Of course, in having taken this snapshot of our shared life in God, we have also depended on things we may have learned by many other means: that we listen best when we are listened to, that respect grows mutually. Without these, mere perspective is insufficient to encounter a neighbour as another self.

We practice our humanity by any and all means, including and maybe especially, through our living faith. Any and every action our faith *most* wants us to do with our lives gives us opportunity to practice life in and with God. Life in God is *always* where we and others flourish because of each other. Surely that is why love of neighbour and love of self are equal gifts, better, *one* gift. Being made in the image of God means our humanity is a collective reverberation of divine love. In other words, we do not *create* unity, or diversity for that matter, we cooperate with the possibility of it when we create communities of conversation laterally, in love. We build collaborations, coalitions, and cooperative ventures with our constitutive parts latterly, across difference, in the hope and expectation that *we* are changed, that we become reflections of a One-made-of-difference. In this divinely beckoned and fashioned at-one-ment, we are never obscured, blurred, or neutralized but collected in a One-made-of-difference in whose image we are made.

A "We" Made-of-difference

> Multicultural education provides tools to play the contradictions of individual and group identities without succumbing to either the illusion of certainty and control or the self-indulgent exercise of unaccountable and uncritical self-affirmation.[2] —Sharon Welch

One of the exercises offered to elementary or nursery school children to enhance their observation and concentration skills is to "spot the difference" between two *nearly* identical pictures with a number of subtle modifications to be discovered on close inspection. An equal and opposite exercise is designed to develop an eye for what is common among distinct objects or living organisms: all multiples of five or all winged creatures. Both of these exercises might be used to illustrate two possible approaches to our life together: one is to follow the sight-line of difference, the other to see what is shared. Social science affirms the place of each in contributing to both identity and cohesion in diverse groups likes ours in the United Church of Canada. It is true that communal connection is achieved through discovering similarities or resemblances (recognized or constructed), but it is also true that it is not necessary for a group to understand itself by way of commonalities alone. Heterogeneity is a creative force which contributes to the vitality as well as the relationships within communities. Indeed, a shared identity does not require even internal contradictions to be overlooked; a "we" can be made-of-difference.[3] One might argue that the United Church of Canada is such a "we."

With respect to the work we have done here in teasing out the distinctions between operative theologies within our faith communities, we have taken on a "spot the difference" exercise. This is intentional. There is a bias here toward what happens when difference is permitted to dominate our read of the community and in this case, its lived theological landscape. By focussing on difference, and approaching difference with genuine curiosity and appreciation, as has been the consistent approach embraced by communities of faith engaging this work, we are learning to trust a collaged reality created by what is seen through multiple lenses. By asking the question, "what is different about your lived faith?" we are loosening our grip on trust in sameness for identity and community cohesion. Looking *past* rather than *through* difference for a path to cohesion is a gesture based on the assumption that what is like is better, stronger, and more reliable than what is unique. It is a left-over legacy of the misguided belief that what is uniform is more trustworthy than what is pluriform.

It must be acknowledged that there are times and circumstances in which difference, particularly difference of opinion, stings. Trusting in difference may be especially difficult in a context with a living memory of differences of opinion, values and theologies having threatened unity and provoked tension, disagreement and pain across the church.[4] It is possible that the legacy of that pain set us back, that thereafter we made a collectively regressive move. Rather than building on what we learned about how to live with our differences, we chose the path of least resistance toward unity, and possibly lost the opportunity to become good at being a "we-made-of-difference." It is also possible that the legacy of that process of discernment and conversation gave us more confidence, not less, that it set us on the path that has allowed for the diversity among us not to intimidate us. Rather than freezing in our tracks, afraid to hurt one another again, we grew increasingly comfortable and capable of being a "we-made-of-difference." Either way, trust in what the spirit is doing among us as a "we-made-of-difference" is not something we acquire once. It is something we choose over and over again: a practice, a discipline, a prayer. It begins by noticing, and by acquiring the ability to look for more than a replica of ourselves.

This practice of being open, self-critical, and interested in the differences we "spot" belongs in and to the world. It is a gift of the Pentecost Spirit, the One who gives life in the form of multiplicity! This way of seeing, this disciplined diversity of views by which we have been shaped by the Spirit and have learned to function as a denomination is a potential self-offering of the church to the world. But it is not *we* who gift the church to the world, but the Spirit. The Spirit's church is undoubtedly infinitely wider than our conception of it. This serves to keep our faith bold and our self-importance in check! *We* are animated by the *Spirit*, not the other way around.

A Yet More Courageous Love

> Poetry is the way we help give name to the nameless so it can be thought.[5]
> —Audre Lorde

Theology is rarely as courageous as poetry but I believe its vocation is the same. As a form of poetry, theology offers words, beautiful and strange, for our ordinary and extraordinary experiences of the holy and ineffable. By doing so, theology provides us with a way of travelling the path of the mundane and already, toward the horizon of the longed-for reality of an unfolding not-yet. This means theology's task is never merely descriptive or imaginative. Theology also serves to help us to invoke and create the very things its words claim and imagine. It "gives name to the nameless so it can be thought," and may even set in motion actions shaped by those thoughts. What might the evidently *multi-lingual* breath of the Spirit be invoking among us or creating through us?

In turning our attention to many forms of faith-shaped love *for* God, we acknowledged that there is more than one way to express *how* we love. But what about *what* we love? Do our multi-formed theologies invoke a more pluriform love, a love *of the many forms*? Is a love-of-many-forms the "nameless love" we are learning to think in our time? The Spirit speaks many languages for a reason, we assume, not least because living things are made of difference. Could the lens we use at the theological banquet help us see not only how our love is diversely *expressed*, but also how love itself is designed for difference? Could love's lens, like a prism, be designed to fracture singularity and reveal the exquisite dimensions of multiplicity? Could this nameless love-of-many-forms be what we learn to do and become, by the grace of the Spirit? Surely, this is a question for our time: is there a way to learn to love the many different forms in which life is variously and intentionally packaged and delivered?

It has become increasingly apparent, though it was far from obscure when this project began, that we are in danger of failing to invoke what theology has helped us to imagine: a multi-form incarnation of love. The divisions among us, in communities and across the globe, are death-dealing to one another and to the planet. If it is true that theology invokes and creates, a critical task is underway in our church. What is being invoked by and created across this spectrum of operative theologies, might be an expression of the polyvocal Spirit for our time—a love greater than the sum of its parts, a love reminiscent of a unity that holds and protects difference and flourishes because of it, a love undivided by difference. Perhaps, as others have observed, we could conceive of this Love as our "longing. . .not to be homogeneous but to be difference-in-equality and be coherent."[6] In other words, to be made, *collectively*, in the image of the One-made-of-difference.

To be clear, theology does not make this so; theology helps us see *that* it is so. Theology, the service industry of faith, helps us to wrap our words and hopes around what we believe or struggle to believe. It helps us to form our actions and relationships around it, helps us to become the flesh of our faith. This means that our constructive theologies—those beliefs our actions *most* show us are real—are by no means inconsequential. They are opportunities for collaboration with what Love itself wants to do in this time, how it wants to sound and to be animated. We have discovered here that for Love not get "lost in translation,"[7] will mean it is *not* translated. Instead, it will be offered in its various distinctive voices. It will be a many-voiced love, a polyvocal love. It will be a *love-made-of-unlike-pieces* in a world at war with little fragments of itself. Understandably, to wrap our lives around this love will take courage and is by no means a given. I am not speaking here of "embracing" or "celebrating" difference, but of an honest look at the death-dealing ways it is despised and resisted. I have witnessed in this work, and over a lifetime in this denomination, a willingness to wrap our flesh, in a variety of ways, around a love that counters death with life. I believe that such love is by nature a love-made-of-difference.

There is no more worthy work for those called to it, than to safeguard, nurture, and grow faith in their time. What has been presented here is for them as much as it is about them. This denomination and its companion united and uniting denominations embody a particular manifestation of Christian faith, one that flourishes in the interplay of its various lived expressions, one that continually tests and challenges itself, that renews and aligns itself, that submits itself to the rigours of God's pluriform calls to choose life in the way of the incarnate Christ, by way of the variegated breath of the living Spirit. This makes the nurture of faith in a constructive theological community like ours an intricate and challenging task. It demands of the faith leader the capacity to listen below where faith is lived, to listen across to how it is spoken, and to listen beyond and through these expressions for its holy call to life. It requires of each of us that we know our beautiful and battered tradition, that we know our capable and culpable selves, and that we know one another and the widest reach of neighbours - the manifold web in which we are brought to life.

I can think of no more urgent task for a "we-made-of-difference" than to loose itself upon the world, in body and in spirit, in words and in silence, in poetry and in praise, in hands and in heads, as presence and as practice. I can think of no more worthy or needful posture than to lean into the dialects of difference that shape our lives in the image of a holy Oneness-made-of-difference. I have no question but that we are by grace made capable of this, capable in a variety of rich and beautiful forms, each tethered to an ancient call to life in the form of Christian faith. Leaders tending communities of faith in this region have only heightened our expectation and anticipation of the flourishing of just this kind of courageous love: a love-made-of-difference.

Notes

1. Catherine Keller, "Love of Postcolonialism: Theology in the Interstices of Empire," in *Postcolonial Theologies: Divinity and Empire*, eds. Catherine Keller, Michael Nausner, Mayra Rivera (St. Louis: Chalice, 2004), 222.
2. Sharon Welch, *Sweet Dreams in America: Making Spirituality and Ethics Work*, (New York: Routledge, 1998), 96.
3. This point is informed by Sharon Welch's reading of Patricia Williams in the chapter "Learning to See Simultaneously Yet Differently" in *Sweet Dreams in America*, pp 53-82 and addressed expansively and contextually in Marilynn J. Legge, "Inside Communities, Outside Conventions: What is at Stake in Doing Theology?" *Studies in Religion/Sciences Religieuse* 29 (1) 3-18.

4. The reference here is to the eight year period before and reaction after the decision of the 32nd General Council in 1988 that all people regardless of sexual orientation be welcome as full members of the United Church, and all members be eligible to be considered for ordered ministry. Subsequent policies to endorse legalization of same-sex marriage (2005) and affirmation of participation of transgender people in ministry (2009) were passed comparatively innocuously.
5. Audre Lorde, "Poetry is not a Luxury," *Sister Outsider*, (Berkeley: Crossing Press 1984), 37.
6. Riet Bons-Storm, "Thinking and Living Diversities in Practical Theology," in *Globalization and Difference: Practical Theology in a World Context,"* Paul Ballard and Pam Couture (eds), (Cardiff: Academic Press, 1999), p 127.
7. Catherine Keller, *Postcolonial Theologies,* 222.

Acknowledgements

THE MCGEACHY FAMILY PROVIDED THE MEANS BY WHICH THE scholarship allowing me to write this manuscript was granted. I am grateful to them and to the committee of the United Church Foundation who chose to support this writing and resource production project in 2018.

I gratefully acknowledge The Pacific Mountain Region (former BC Conference), through its *Leadershift* staff and program, for generously supporting the research, development, and resource production of the Theological Banquet project over the course of several years. This project would not have been possible without their significant on-going investment in the lived faith of this region through this project.

I learned the languages of love this denomination speaks over a lifetime, and am indebted in particular to the congregations and communities by whose lived faith mine own has been shaped, among them: Dunbar Heights United Church in Vancouver, Young Christians for Global Justice (Canadian and World Council of Churches), Project Ploughshares, The Christian Taskforce on Central America, the BC Conference/Pacific Mountain Region of the United Church, committees and working groups of United Church of Canada and its General Council, including the Theology and Faith Committee, and in our sibling denominations, First Congregational Church of Berkeley (UCC) in California, and St. David's Uniting Church (United Reformed Church) in Pontypridd, Wales. The church's theologians serve its councils, congregations, and schools; they are teachers of the living faith in scholarship, example, and friendship and I am indebted to them.

I learned from every group with whom I shared this work from pilot to presentation to publication. I hope you recognize the inspiration of your faith reflected here.

Those I interviewed publicly and privately, in whose words people recognized themselves and their theology, and whose testimonies are among those included in this text and its accompanying resources include: Craig Perry, Murray Groome, Janice Young, Michelle Slater, Jen Cunnings, Gary Paterson, Dan Chambers,

Nancy Talbot, Simon LeSieur, Aaron Miller, Heather Joy James, Sandra Nixon, Steven Chambers, Richard Bott, Trevor Malkinson, Ryan Slifka, David Anderson, Jenny Carter, Cari Copeman-Haynes, Carmen Lansdowne, Gail Miller, Allison Rennie, Kathy Davies, Marc Coulombe, Henri Locke, Eric Hamlyn, Pamela Evans, Rhian Walker, Everest Kao, and Mayon Marcelino.

The Vancouver School of Theology provided a sabbatical leave for me to write, and Westminster College (Cambridge, England) kept me wonderful company while I did so. Highlands United Church in North Vancouver ensured the completion of the project by calling me their writer-in-residence (2020). I am extremely grateful to all three.

Mentors, friends, students, and colleagues play a larger role than they often know. Keith Howard's name belongs at the beginning, middle, and end of these acknowledgements. I am grateful for the support offered to this project's research, writing, and resource development by Brenda Fawkes, Julie Lees, Lydia Ruenzel, Treena Duncan, Rhian Walker, Beth Heyward, Jim Ball, John Pentland, Gary Paterson, and by the 2017 BC Conference Theme and Worship team. I am indebted to Brian Thorpe and especially to Sallie McFague for expertise, guidance, and support, and to my friends for encouragement. Dan Chambers patiently and constructively read every draft. This book would not have been published without the expert and generous support of Gordon Thomas to whom I am most grateful.

What appears to be an individual accomplishment is never that. It is those closest to us who know this most intimately. Thank you to those closest, and above all to these three: Dan, Colleen, and Katherine.

This work is informed by my identity and relationships living on the traditional, ancestral, and unceded territory of the xʷməθkʷəy̓əm (Musqueam), Skwxwú7mesh (Squamish), and Səl̓ílwətaʔ/Selilwitulh (Tsleil-Waututh) Nations.

About the Author

JANET GEAR IS A THEOLOGICAL EDUCATOR AND ORDAINED MINISTER IN the United Church of Canada. She holds Master of Divinity and Master of Arts (Theology) degrees from the Pacific School of Religion (Graduate Theological Union) in Berkeley, California and served as Assistant Professor of Practical Theology and Director of Formation at Vancouver School of Theology for fifteen years. A contributor to many projects and publications of the United Church, she currently serves the denomination in the Office of Vocation, and continues to teach, preach, lead retreats, and consult with leaders navigating theological diversity and spiritual discernment in communities of faith.

Works Cited

Airhart, Phyllis D. *A Church with the Soul of a Nation: Making and Remaking the United Church of Canada* . Montreal and Kingston: McGill-Queen's University Press,, 2014.

Alcorn, Coco Love. "River." *Wonderland*. By Coco Love Alcorn. Prod. Andy Sheppard. 2016. Speak Music.

Anderson, Dave and Richard Bott. *Invitation to Christian Life*. Coquitlam, BC: Becoming: Resources for Jesus People, 2014.

Armstrong, Karen. *The Great Transformation: The Beginning of Our Religious Traditions*. New York: Anchor, 2007.

Bass, Craig Dykstra and Dorothy C. "A theological understanding of Christian practices." M. Volf and D.C. Bass (eds.). *Practicing Theology* . Grand Rapids: Eerdmans, 2002. 13-32.

Bass, Diana Butler. *A People's History of Christianity: The Other Side of the Story*. New York: Harper Collins, 1989.

Bass, Dorothy C. *Practicing Our Faith : A Way of Life for a Searching People*. Minneapolis: Fortress, 1998.

Baum, Gregory. "Goodbye to the Ecumenist." *The Ecumenist* 29.2 (1991).

Bear, Cheryl. "Thoughts from a Mother"(provisional). Prod. St. Andrew's Wesley United Church. Vancouver, 2020. Livestream Worship. www.youtube.com/watch?v=NGkihVymgY&&ab_channel=St. Andrews-WesleyUnitedChurch.

Beardsall, Sandra. ""And Whether Pigs Have Wings": The United Chuch in the 1960s." Don Schweitzer, ed. *The United Church of Canada: A History*. Waterloo: Wilfred Laurier Press, 2011. 97-118.

Bell, John and Graham Maule. *Inspired by Love and Anger*. Iona Community, Glasgow.

Bell, John and Hans-Olav Moerk. *We Will Meet When the Danger is Over.* Wild Goose Resource Group, Glasgow.

Bell, Rob. *Love Wins.* San Francisco: Harper One, 2011.

Bellah, Robert. *Habits of the Heart: Individualism and Commitment in American Life.* Berkeley, CA: University of California Press, 1985.

Betcher, Sharon. "Monstrosities, Miracles, and Mission: Religion and the Politics of Disablement." Catherine Keller, Michael Nauusner, Mayra Rivera (eds). *Postcolonial Theologies: Divinity and Empire.* St. Louis: Chalice, 2004. 79-99.

Bokma, Anne. *My Year of Living Spiritually: From Woo-Woo to Wonderful – One Woman's Secular Quest for a More Soulful Life*. Madiera Park, BC: Douglas and McIntyre, 2019.

Bolz-Weber, Nadia. *Pastrix: The Cranky, Beautiful Faith of a Sinner and Saint.* New York: Jericho Books, 2014.

Bons-Storm, Riet. "Thinking and Living Diversities in Practical Theology." Ballard, Paul and Pamela Couture (eds). *Globalisation and Difference: Practical Theology in a World Context.* Cardiff: Cardiff Academic Press, 1999. 123-127.

Bourgeois, Michael. "Awash in Theology: Issues in Theology and The United Church of Canada." Schweitzer, Donald. *The United Church of Canada: A History.* Waterloo: Wilfred Laurier Press, 2012. 259-78.

Bowman, Donna. *The Divine Decision: A Process Doctrine of Election.* Louisville: Westminster John Knox, 2002.

Brotsky, Tressa. *Theological Banquet symbols.* United Church of Canada Pacific Mountain Region, Victoria.

Caron, Charlotte. *Eager for worship : theologies, practices, and perspectives on worship in the United Church of Canada.* Toronto: United Church of Canada, 2000. McGeachy Papers.

Chittister, Joan. "Daily Meditation: Consumed with Love." 05 July 2019. *Centre for Contemplation and Action.* <https://cac.org/consumed-with-love-2019-07-05.>.

Clayton, Phillip. *The Predicament of Belief: Science, Philosophy, and Christian Minimalism.* Oxford: Oxford University Press, 2011.

Cockburn, Bruce. "Rumours of Glory." *Humans.* By Bruce Cockburn. Prod. Eugene Martynec. True North Records, 1980.

Committee on Theology and Inter-church, Interfaith, UCC. *A Background Document on Essential Agreement.* Toronto: United Church of Canada, 2019.

Works Cited

Daloz-Parks, Sharon. *Leadership Can Be Taught: A Bold Approach for a Complex World*. Boston: Harvard Business Review Press, 2006.

Dare to Be/Oser être. United Church of Canada. Creative Commons. 2010.

Dempsey, Carol. "The Wilderness: Sacred Space, Endangered Homeland, Hope for Our Planet." (eds), Julia Brumaugh and Natalia Imperatori-Lee. *Turning to the Heavens and the Earth*. Collegeville: Liturgical Press, 2016. 69-82.

Evans, Don. "Comment: When I Walk to work at Our Place, I Feel Empathy, Not Fear." 29 March 2019. *Times Colonist*. <www.timescolonist.com/>.

Fredrick Buechner. *Wishful Thinking: A Seekers ABC, expanded ed*. San Francisco: Harper Collins, 1993.

Fresh Expressions. 2017. Space to Breathe. 09 2019. <https://freshexpressions.org.uk/>.

Friesen, Dwight J., Paul Sparks, and Tim Soerens. *The New Parish: How Neighborhood Churches Are Transforming Mission, Discipleship and Community*. Downers Grove, IL: Intervarsity, 2014.

Frye, Northrop. *The Double Vision: Language and Meaning in Religion*. Toronto: University of Toronto Press, 1991.

Graham, Elaine. *Words Made Flesh*. London: SCM, 2009.

Greene, Mark. *Fruitfulness on the Frontline: Making a Difference Where You Are*. Downers Grove, IL: Intervarsity, 2017.

Guite, Malcolm. "Easter 2020." 12 April 2020. *Wordpress*. <https://malcolmguite.wordpress.com/>.

Hall, Douglas John. *The Cross in Our Context: Jesus and the Suffering World*. Minneapolis: Fortress, 2003.

Halliday, Adelle. "What I Need From White People." 3 June 2020. *Broadview*.

Haught, John. "Theology, Cosmos and Hope." (eds), Julia Brumaugh and Natalia Imperatori-Lee. *Turning to the Heavens and the Earth*. Collegeville: Liturgical Press, 2016.

Heiftez, Ronald, Alexander Grashow, and Marty Linsky. *The Practice of Adaptive Leadership: Tools and Tactics for Changing your Organization and the World*. Boston: Harvard Business Review Press, 2009.

Huey-Heck, Lois and Jim Kalnin. *The Spirituality of Art*. Kelowna: Northstone, 2006.

Huntly, Alyson. *Daring to Be United: Including Lesbians and Gays in the United Church of Canada*. Toronto: United Church Publishing House, 1998.

Hyk Cho. " Practicing God's Mission beyond Canada." Don Schweitzer, Robert Fennel, Michael Bourgeois. *Theology of the United Church of Canada*. Waterloo: Wilfred Laurier Press, 2019. 251- 278 .

Inter–church and Inter–faith Committee United Church of Canada. "Mending the World: An Ecumenical Vision for Healing and Reconciliation." Record of Proceedings of the 36th General Council. 1997.

Keller, Catherine. "Love of Postcolonialism: Theology in the Interstices of Empire." Catherine Keller, Michael Nausner, Mayra Rivera (eds). *Postcolonial Theologies: Divinity and Empire*. St. Louis: Chalice Press, 2004. 221-242.

Kendrick, Graham. *Shine, Jesus, Shine*. Make Way Music, Tunbridge Wells, England.

Kervin, William. " in "Sacraments and Sacramentality in the United Church of Canada," in , 223-250." S, Don. *The Theology of the United Church of Canada*. n.d.

Kim Craig, Hye-Ran. *Interdependence: A Postcolonial Feminist Practical Theology*. Eugene: Wipf and Stock, 2018.

Kim-Cragg, HyeRan. *Interdependence: A Postcolonial Feminist Practical Theology*. Eugene: Pickwick, 2018.

Klein, Naomi. *On Fire: The Burning Case for a Green New Deal* . New York: Knopf, 2019.

Korten, David. *The Great Turning: From Empire to Earth Community* . San Francisco: Barrett-Koehler, 2006.

Lansdowne, Carmen Rae. "Bearing Witness: Wearing a Broken Indigene Heart on the Sleeve of the Missio Dei." Source: *DAI-A 77/09(E), Dissertation Abstracts International*. Berkeley, CA: Graduate Theological Union, Februrary 2016. dissertation. <https://pqdtopen.proquest.com/>.

Leddy, Mary Jo. *The Other Face of God: When the Stranger Calls Us Home*. Maryknoll, NY: Orbis, 2011.

Legge, Marilynn J. "Inside Communities, Outside Conventions: What is at Stake in Doing Theology?" *Studies in Religion/Sciences Religieuse* 29.1 (2000): 3-18.

Lorde, Audre. *Sister Outsider*. Berkeley: Crossing Press, 1984.

Loyola Press. "About Arts and Faith ." n.d. *Loyola Press*. 2020. <https://www.loyolapress.com/catholic-resources/prayer/arts-and-faith/about-arts-and-faith/>.

Works Cited

MacIntyre, Alasdair. *After Virtue*. Notre Dame: University of Notre Dame Press, 1981.

MacKenzie Shepherd, Loraine. "United Church's Mission work within Canada and Its Impact on Indigenous and Ethnic Minority Communities." Don Schweitzer, Robert Fennell, Michael Bourgeois (eds). *The Theology of the United Church of Canada*. Waterloo: Wilfred Laurier Press, n.d. 279-312,.

MacLean, Catherine. "The Triune God." Don Schweitzer, Robert C. Fennell, Michael Bourgeois, eds. *TheTheology of the United Church of Canada*. Waterloo: Wilfred Laurier Press, n.d. 21-50.

Macy, Joanna. *A Wild Love for the World*. Ed. Stephanie Kaza. Boulder, CO: Shambhala, 2020.

McFague, Sallie. *Blessed are the Consumers: Climate Change and the Practice of Restraint*. Minneapolis: Fortress, 2013.

McIntire, C. T. "Unity Among Many." *The United Church of Canada: A History*. Ed. Don Schweitzer. Waterloo, ON: Wilfred Laurier Press, 2011. 22.

McLaren, Brian. *Faith After Doubt*. London: St. Martin's Essentials, 2021.

Michael Bourgeios, Connie denBok, Catherine Faith McLean, John Young. *Our Words of Faith - Cherished, Honoured, and Living*. Toronto: United Church of Canada, 2010.

Moore, Thomas. *Dark Nights of the Soul: A Guide to Finding Your Way Through Life's Ordeals*. New York: Gotham Books, 2004.

Morisy, Ann. *Journeying Out: A New Approach to Christian Mission*. London: Continuum, 2004.

Morris, Barry K. *A Faithful Public-Prophetic Witness*. Eugene: WipfStock, 2019.

Morrison, Brad. *Already Missional: Congregations and Community Partners*. Eugene: Wipfandstock, 2016.

Moschella, Mary Clark. " Practice Matters: New Directions in Ethnography and Qualitative Research." (ed), Nancy Ramsay. *Pastoral Theology and Care: Critical Trajectories in Theory and Practice*. Oxford: Blackwell, 2018.

Newell, John Phillip. *Christianity's Struggle for New Beginnings: The Rebirthing of God, Christian Journeys*. Woodstock VT: Skylight Paths, 2014.

Oord, Thomas J. *God Can't: How to Believe in God and Love after Tragedy, Abuse, and Other Evils*. Grasmere, ID: Sacrasage Press, 2018.

Paynter, Neil. *Blessed Be Our Table: Graces for Mealtimes and Reflections on Food*. Glasgow: Wild Goose, 2006.

Pentland, John. *Fishing on the Other Side: How Curiosity Transformed a Community of Faith*. Toronto: The Edge, 2015.

Phipps, Bill. *Cause for Hope: Humanity at the Crossroads*. Kelowna: Copperhouse Woodlake, 2007.

Pope Francis. *Laudato Si': O Care for Our Common Home,*. Italy: Libreria Editrice, 2015.

Richards, Jan. *Circles of Grace*. Orlando: Wanton Gospeller, 2015.

Roxburgh, Alan. *Joining God, Remaking Church, Changing the World: The New Shape of the Church in Our Time*. New York: Morehouse, 2015.

—. *Missional: Joining God in the Neighbourhood*. Ada, MI: Baker, 2011.

Sanguin, Bruce. *Darwin, Divinity and the Dance of the Cosmos: An Ecological Christianity*. Kelowna: Copperhouse , 2007.

Schwartzentruber, Michael (ed). *The Emerging Christian Way: Thoughts, Stories and Wisdom for*. Kelowna, BC: Copperhouse, 2006.

Schweitzer, Don, Robert Fennell, Michael Bourgeois (eds). "The Theology of the United Church of Canada." Waterloo: Wilfred Laurier Press, 2019.

Sung, Andrew Park. *Triune Atonement: Christ's Healing for Sinners, Victims, and the Whole Creation*. Louisville: Westminster John Knox, 2009.

Swimme, Brian, and Thomas Berry. *The Universe Story: From the Primordial Flaring Forth to the Ecozoic Era-a Celebration of the Unfolding of the Cosmos*. San Francisco: HarperSanFrancisco, 1994.

Taylor, Barbara Brown. *An Altar in the World: A Geography of Faith*. New York: Harper Collins, 2009.

Teilhard de Chardin, Pierre. *The Prayer of the Universe,*. Trans. R. Hague. London: Collins, 1977.

Ter Kuile, Casper and Angie Thurston. "Something More." 2016. < https://sacred.design/insights>.

Ter Kuile, Casper. "How We Gather." 04 2015. *caspertk.files*. PDF. <https://caspertk.files.wordpress.com/2015/04/how-we-gather.pdf>.

Thatamanil, Catherine Keller and John J. *Is this an Apocalypse? We certainly hope so – you should too*. 15 April 2020. <https://www.abc.net.au/>.

The United Church of Canada. *The Manual*. Toronto: United Church Publishing House, 1925-2019.

Thomas Berry, The Great Work: Our Way into the Future, (New York: Bell Tower, 1999). *The Great Work: Our Way into the Future.* New York: Bell Tower, 1999.

Thornton, Sharon G. *Broken Yet Beloved: A Pastoral Theology of the Cross.* St. Louis: Chalice Press, 2002.

Tickle, Phyllis. *The Great Emergence: How Christianity is Changing annd Why.* Grand Rapids: Baker Books, 2008.

United Church of Canada Archives. *United Church of Canada Committee on Theology and Inter-Church and Interfaith Relations.* Fonds 568. n.d.

United Church of Canada. *More Voices.* Toronto and Kelowna: United Church Publishing House & Woodlake Books, 2007.

—. *Voices United: The Hymn and Worship Book of the United Church of Canada.* Toronto: United Church of Canada Publishing House, 1996.

United Reformed Church. "Walking the Way Resources." 2017. *United Reformed Church.* 2019. <https://urc.org.uk/images/WalkingtheWay/documents/A5-WtW-leaflet-2017.pdf >.

Wagamese, Richard. *Embers: One Ojibway's Meditations.* Madeira Park, BC: Douglas and McIntyre, 2016.

Wall, Phillip. "Salvation and the School of Christ: A Theological-Ethnographic Exploration of the Relationship Between Soteriology, Missiology and Pedagogy in the Fresh Expressions of Church." *Research Portal Kings College London.* London, 2014. <https://kclpure.kcl.ac.uk/>.

Weil, Simone. "Gravity and Grace." London: Routledge, 1963 (French 1947).

Welch, Sharon. *Sweet Dreams in America: Making Spirituality and Ethics Work.* New York: Routledge, 1998.

Wheatley, Margaret J. *Leadership and the New Science: Discovering Order in a Chaotic World.* Oakland: Berrett-Koehler Publishers, 2006.

—. *Turning to One Another: Simple Conversations to Restore Hope to the Future.* New York: Berrett-Koehler Publishers, 2002.

Wigg-Stevenson, Natalie. "What's Really Going on: Ethnographic Theology and the Production of Theological Knowledge." *Cultural Studies ↔ Critical Methodologies* 18.6 (2018): 423-429.

Wilson, Lois. *Turning the World Upside Down: A Memoir .* Toronto: Doubleday, 1989.

Wyschogrod, Edith. *Saints and Postmodernism: Revisioning Moral Philosophy*. Chicago: The University of Chicago, 1990.

Young, John H. "A Golden Age: The United Church of Canada, 1946–1960." Don Schweitzer, ed. *The United Church of Canada: A History*. Waterloo: Wilfrid Laurier University Press (Nov. 1 2011), 2011. 77-96.

—. "Evangelism in the United Church of Canada: Templeton to Emerging Spirit." *Touchstone* January 2009: 26-35.

Printed in the USA
CPSIA information can be obtained
at www.ICGtesting.com
LVHW071504300823
756639LV00010B/80